DAY HIKING
Columbia
River Gorge

*Previous page: Profuse wildflowers grace
Grassy Knob. (Hike 39)*

Looking north to Mount Adams from Mount Defiance (Hike 88)

Silver Star adds a nice backdrop to slopes of showy wildflowers. (Hike 15)

Replica canoe at Cottonwood Beach (Hike 11)

Remains of an old narrow-gauge railway (Hike 25)

Soda Peaks Lake is nestled in a basin high above Trapper Creek. (Hike 31)

Maples add plenty of autumn foliage along the PCT near Dry Creek Falls. (Hike 83)

Benson Bridge and Multnomah Falls (Hike 68)

Bear grass growing on Larch Mountain's Sherrard Point (Hike 70)

The Kiwa Trail traverses sprawling wetlands that teem with birds. (Hike 4)

Warrior Rock Lighthouse on Sauvie Island (Hike 51)

DAY HIKING
Columbia
River Gorge

national scenic area/silver star scenic area/
portland–vancouver to the dalles

Craig Romano

THE MOUNTAINEERS BOOKS

THE MOUNTAINEERS BOOKS
*is the nonprofit publishing arm of The Mountaineers, an organization
founded in 1906 and dedicated to the exploration, preservation, and
enjoyment of outdoor and wilderness areas.*

1001 SW Klickitat Way, Suite 201, Seattle, WA 98134

First edition, 2011

Manufactured in the United States of America

Copy Editor: Julie Van Pelt
Cover and Book Design: The Mountaineers Books
Layout: Laura Lind Design
Cartographer: Pease Press Cartography
All photographs by author unless otherwise noted.

Cover photograph: *Sunrise overlooking the Columbia River surrounded by wildflowers at Tom
McCall Nature Preserve near Hood River, Oregon* © Alan Bauer
Frontispiece: Wahclella Falls (Hike 77)

Maps shown in this book were produced using National Geographic's *TOPO!*
software. For more information, go to *www.nationalgeographic.com/topo*.

Library of Congress Cataloging-in-Publication Data
Romano, Craig.
  Day hiking Columbia River Gorge : National scenic area/Silver Star scenic
area/Portland–Vancouver to the Dalles / by Craig Romano.
    p. cm.
  ISBN 978-1-59485-368-5 (pbk.) —
  ISBN 978-1-59485-369-2 (ebook)
 1. Hiking—Columbia River Gorge (Or. and
Wash.)—Guidebooks. 2. Columbia River Gorge
(Or. and Wash.)—Guidebooks. I. Title.
  GV199.42.C64R66 2011
  796.5109797—dc22
                    2010046310

Table of Contents

Portland Metro 165

Columbia River Gorge, Oregon: West 191

Columbia River Gorge, Oregon: East 243

LEGEND

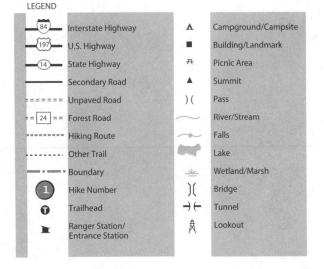

84	Interstate Highway	▲	Campground/Campsite
197	U.S. Highway	■	Building/Landmark
14	State Highway	⊼	Picnic Area
	Secondary Road	▲	Summit
= = = = = =	Unpaved Road	) (	Pass
= = 24 = =	Forest Road		River/Stream
▪▪▪▪▪▪▪▪	Hiking Route		Falls
▪ ▪ ▪ ▪ ▪ ▪	Other Trail		Lake
	Boundary		Wetland/Marsh
1	Hike Number	)(	Bridge
T	Trailhead	→ ←	Tunnel
▪	Ranger Station/Entrance Station	木	Lookout

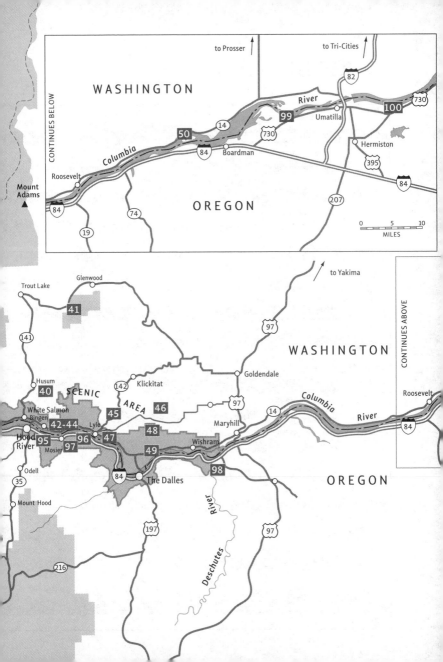

Hikes at a Glance

HIKE	DISTANCE (round-trip)	DIFFI-CULTY	HIKEABLE ALL YEAR	KID-FRIENDLY	DOG-FRIENDL
VANCOUVER AND CLARK COUNTY					
1. Paradise Point State Park	2.2 mi.	1	x	x	x
2. La Center Bottoms	2.2 mi.	1	x	x	x
3. Ridgefield NWR: Oaks to Wetlands Trail	2 mi.	1	x	x	
4. Ridgefield NWR: Kiwa Trail	1.5 mi.	1		x	
5. Battle Ground Lake State Park	2.1 mi.	2	x	x	x
6. Lewisville Regional Park	2.5 mi.	1	x	x	x
7. Moulton Falls	6 mi.	1	x	x	x
8. Bells Mountain	6.5 mi.	3	x	x	x
9. Lacamas Heritage Trail	7 mi.	1	x	x	x
10. Lacamas Park	4.5 mi.	2	x	x	x
11. Cottonwood Beach–East Dike Trail	7 mi.	1	x	x	x
SILVER STAR SCENIC AREA					
12. Larch Mountain	5.6 mi.	3	x	x	x
13. Silver Star via Pyramid/Sturgeon Rocks	8.3 mi.	3		x	x
14. Silver Star via North Ridge	5 mi.	3			
15. Little Baldy	8.4 mi.	3			
COLUMBIA RIVER GORGE, WASHINGTON: WEST					
16. Steigerwald Lake NWR	2.8 mi.	1	x	x	
17. Cape Horn	7 mi.	3	x		
18. Sams-Walker Nature Trail	1.2 mi.	1	x	x	x
19. Beacon Rock	1.8 mi.	2	x	x	
20. Hamilton Mountain	8.2 mi.	4	x		
21. Hardy Ridge	7.6 mi.	3	x		x
22. Aldrich Butte	3.6 mi.	3	x	x	x
23. Table Mountain	9 mi.	5			
24. Strawberry Island	2.8 mi.	1	x	x	x
25. Fort Cascades	1.2 mi.	1	x	x	x
26. Gillette Lake/Greenleaf Overlook	6/8.6 mi.	2/3	x	x	x
27. Bunker Hill	4.4 mi.	3		x	x
28. Whistle Punk Trail	1.5 mi.	1		x	
29. Sedum Point	10 mi.	3			x
TRAPPER CREEK WILDERNESS					
30. Trapper Creek	9 mi.	3		x	x

BIRD-WATCHING	WILD-FLOWERS	WATER-FALLS	OLD GROWTH	HISTOR-ICAL	WILDER-NESS	WHEELCHAIR ACCESSIBLE	BIKES OK	CAR CAMP NEARBY	BACK-PACKING
		X						X	
X	X					X		X	
X			X	X					
X	X					X			
				X				X	
			X	X		X			
		X		X		X	X	X	
							X	X	
						X	X		
	X	X	X			partial	partial		
X				X		X	X		
	X						X		
	X			X			X		
	X			X			partial	X	
	X			X			X	X	
X	X			X		X			
	X	X		X					
X	X			X		X		X	
				X				X	
	X	X		X				X	
	X						partial	X	
	X			X				X	
	X							X	
X	X			X			X	X	
X				X		X		X	
								X	
			X	X					
			X	X		X			
	X		X						X
			X	X	X			X	X

HIKE	DISTANCE (round-trip)	DIFFI-CULTY	HIKEABLE ALL YEAR	KID-FRIENDLY	DOG-FRIENDL
31. Soda Peaks Lake	7 mi.	5			x
32. Observation Peak via Howe Ridge	13 mi.	5			x
33. Dry Creek	8.4 mi.	2	x	x	x
34. Big Hollow	9.2 mi.	4			x
35. Sister Rocks/Observation Peak	7 mi.	3		x	x
COLUMBIA RIVER GORGE, WASHINGTON: EAST					
36. Wind Mountain	2.8 mi.	3			
37. Dog Mountain	7.3 mi.	4		x	x
38. Augspurger Mountain	13.8 mi.	5			x
39. Grassy Knoll/Big Huckleberry Mountain	4.4/11.2 mi.	3/4		x	x
40. Weldon Wagon Road	5.4 mi.	3	x	x	x
41. Conboy Lake NWR	3 mi.	1		x	x
42. Coyote Wall	6 mi.	3	x		
43. Catherine Creek: The Labyrinth	4.3 mi.	3	x	x	x
44. Catherine Creek: Natural Arch	2.3 mi.	2	x	x	x
45. Klickitat Trail: Klickitat River	21 mi.	2	x	x	x
46. Klickitat Trail: Swale Canyon	11.4 mi.	3		x	x
47. Lyle Cherry Orchard	5 mi.	3	x	x	x
48. Stacker Butte	5 mi.	3		x	
49. Horsethief Butte	1.2 mi.	2	x		
50. Crow Butte	2 mi.	2	x		
PORTLAND METRO					
51. Sauvie Island: Warrior Rock Lighthouse	6.5 mi.	1	x	x	x
52. Sauvie Island: Oak Island Loop	2.9 mi.	1		x	x
53. Sauvie Island: Wapato Access Greenway	2.4 mi.	1	x	x	x
54. Forest Park North	8.1 mi.	2	x	x	x
55. Forest Park South: Balch Creek Canyon	2.4 mi.	1	x	x	x
56. Macleay Park: Pittock Mansion	2.3 mi.	2	x	x	x
57. Tryon Creek State Natural Area	2.1 mi.	2	x	x	x
58. Oaks Bottom Wildlife Refuge	2.8 mi.	1	x	x	
59. Powell Butte Nature Park	2.1 mi.	1	x	x	x
60. Mount Talbert	2.8 mi.	2	x	x	
61. Oxbow Regional Park	4.5 mi.	2	x	x	
COLUMBIA RIVER GORGE, OREGON: WEST					
62. Sandy River Delta	6.7 mi.	1	x	x	x
63. Rooster Rock State Park	3.3 mi.	2	x	x	x
64. Latourell Falls	2.3 mi.	2	x	x	

BIRD-WATCHING	WILD-FLOWERS	WATER-FALLS	OLD GROWTH	HISTOR-ICAL	WILDER-NESS	WHEELCHAIR ACCESSIBLE	BIKES OK	CAR CAMP NEARBY	BACK-PACKING
			X	X	X			X	X
	X		X	X	X			X	X
			X	X				X	X
			X					X	X
	X		X	X	X				X
				X					
	X								
	X								
	X		X						X
	X			X					
X	X			X					
	X						X		
	X	X		X					
X	X								
X	X			X		partial	X		
X	X			X			X		
	X			X					
	X							X	
X	X			X				X	
X	X			X				X	
X				X					
X	X								
X	X					partial			
							partial		
		X	X	X		partial			
			X	X					
	X					partial			
X				X		partial	partial		
	X			X		partial			
	X								
			X				partial	X	
X				X		partial	partial		
				X					
		X		X					

HIKE	DISTANCE (round-trip)	DIFFI-CULTY	HIKEABLE ALL YEAR	KID-FRIENDLY	DOG-FRIENDL
65. Bridal Veil Falls	1.2 mi.	1	X	X	
66. Angels Rest	4.6 mi.	3	X	X	
67. Devils Rest	8.3 mi.	3	X	X	X
68. Multnomah Falls–Wahkeena Falls	5.4 mi.	3	X	X	
69. Larch Mountain	14.4 mi.	4			X
70. Larch Mountain Crater	6.6 mi.	3		X	X
71. Franklin Ridge	12.2 mi.	4			X
72. Oneonta Gorge	2.7 mi.	2	X	X	
73. Rock of Ages Ridge	10.9 mi.	5			
74. Bell Creek	15.3 mi.	4			X
75. Nesmith Point	10 mi.	5			
76. Elowah/Upper McCord Creek Falls	3.4 mi.	2	X	X	
77. Wahclella Falls	1.8 mi.	2	X	X	
78. Tooth Rock	2.1 mi.	1	X	X	X
79. Dublin Lake	13 mi.	5			X
80. Wauna Viewpoint	3.8 mi.	3	X	X	
81. Eagle Creek	12 mi.	3			
82. Benson Plateau via Ruckel Creek	11.2 mi.	5			X
83. Dry Creek Falls	5.2 mi.	3	X	X	X
84. Benson Plateau via Pacific Crest Trail	16 mi.	5			X
COLUMBIA RIVER GORGE, OREGON: EAST					
85. Herman Creek Ancient Cedars	15 mi.	4			X
86. Nick Eaton Ridge	8.8 mi.	4		X	X
87. North Lake	13.6 mi.	5			X
88. Mount Defiance	12.9 mi.	5			
89. Wygant Peak	9.2 mi.	4			X
90. Mitchell Point	2.2 mi.	3	X		
91. Wahtum Lake/Chinidere Mountain	4.2 mi.	3		X	X
92. Tomlike Mountain	6 mi.	3			
93. Indian Mountain	9.4 mi.	4			X
94. Bear Lake	2.4 mi.	2		X	X
95. Mosier Twin Tunnels	9.4 mi.	2	X	X	X
96. Rowena Plateau	2.2 mi.	2	X	X	
97. Tom McCall Point	3.2 mi.	3		X	
98. Deschutes River	4.6 mi.	3	X	X	X
99. Columbia River Heritage Trail	4 mi.	2	X		
100. Hat Rock	0.75 mi.	1	X	X	X

BIRD-WATCHING	WILD-FLOWERS	WATER-FALLS	OLD GROWTH	HISTOR-ICAL	WILDER-NESS	WHEELCHAIR ACCESSIBLE	BIKES OK	CAR CAMP NEARBY	BACK-PACKING
	X	X		X		partial			
	X	X						X	
		X	X					X	
		X		X				X	
	X	X	X	X	X			X	X
	X		X	X			partial		X
	X	X	X	X	X			X	X
		X		X				X	
	X	X	X		X			X	
		X	X		X			X	X
	X		X	X	X			X	
		X						X	
		X						X	
				X		X	X	X	
		X	X		X		partial	X	X
	X							X	
		X	X	X	X			X	X
	X	X	X	X	X			X	X
		X						X	X
		X	X		X			X	X
	X		X		X			X	X
			X	X	X			X	X
	X	X	X		X			X	X
	X							X	
	X			X				X	
	X		X		X			X	X
	X				X			X	X
	X		X		X			X	X
	X				X				X
	X			X		X	X		
	X							X	
X	X							X	
X	X			X			partial	X	
X	X			X					
X	X			X		X			

Acknowledgments

Like the powerful forces of nature that created the Columbia River Gorge, many a force assisted me in creating this book.

First, I want to thank God, the greatest force—for watching over me on the trail and providing me with so many things to be thankful for—my health, family, friends, and beautiful natural creations, the Columbia River Gorge being one, of course. Also, a huge *grazie* to my in-laws Virginia and Vince Scott for letting me set up shop at their Clark County home for many a week at a time. And thanks, too, to Virginia for the salmon and pizza waiting for me after all those long days hiking.

Mille grazie once again to all of the great people at Mountaineers Books, especially Helen Cherullo, publisher, and Kate Rogers, editor in chief, for supporting me and believing in me. *Mille grazie* to my project manager, Mary Metz, for her encouragement, support, and sympathetic ear. I want to especially acknowledge my editor, Julie Van Pelt, whose professionalism and attention to detail greatly contributed to making this book a finer volume. I look forward to working with her on future hiking books—that is, if she can handle any more of my bad puns and tendency to alliterate.

Grazie to Ryan Ojerio of the Washington Trails Association for his research and help on trail issues in southwest Washington. Ryan does an excellent job, and I am proud to support the WTA! Thanks as well to all the great folks who accompanied me on the trail. *Grazie* to John Osaki, Patrick and Suzanne Feeney, Jennie Holland, Stephanie Reed, Kim Brown, Susan Elderkin, Douglas Romano, Alex and Galvin Lockard, Crystal Barnhart, Paul DiRusso, and Janet Kolen.

And lastly, but most importantly, I want to thank my loving wife, Heather, for believing in me while I worked hard on yet another guidebook and for accompanying me to some of the special places in this book. I am grateful for her patience, understanding, and support while I spent so many days away from her working on this book. Her absence only made me long to get back home and finish this book so that we could once again spend time together on the trail. *Mille grazie mia amore—ti voglio bene!*

Preface

It was the mountains that lured me to the Pacific Northwest in the summer of 1989, and the mountains have kept me firmly planted here ever since. While there's no shortage of excellent hiking in this region, the Columbia River Gorge is a standout, ranking among the most spectacular places to hike in the nation. I first visited the Gorge in 1992, hiking Hamilton and Dog Mountains. In 1996 I met a young woman (who would later become my wife) from Vancouver, Washington. How fortunate—there would be a lot of Columbia River Gorge hikes in my life!

The Gorge is a one-of-a-kind natural landmark. Nowhere else in America does one of her mightiest and longest rivers slice through one of her longest and most dramatic mountain chains—and practically at sea level. And nowhere else in the country are there so many waterfalls, nor is there such a dramatic shift from wet, saturated coastal mountains to arid, sun-kissed flowered bluffs.

Long a major transportation route for First Peoples, explorers, traders, and emigrants, the Gorge played a vital role in the development of the Northwest and the nation. Yet, despite its proximity to a major metropolitan area and its continual use as a busy transportation corridor, it remains remarkably wild and natural. The Gorge would most certainly have become one of America's cherished national parks were it not for the people- and energy-moving infrastructure there. But in 1986, through the insight and hard work of dedicated citizens and maneuvering by enlightened politicians, the bulk of the Columbia River Gorge became a national scenic area, the only one of its kind in the country—and a fitting designation for such an important ecological, cultural, and spectacularly beautiful place.

This book celebrates the natural beauty and the natural and human history of the Gorge and its excellent hiking opportunities. It highlights fifty hikes on each side of the river, and it goes beyond the national scenic area boundaries to include special places and trails within the Portland–Vancouver metropolitan area, the Silver Star Scenic Area, the Trapper Creek Wilderness, and on isolated buttes and in wildlife areas in the river's far-eastern hinterlands. I'm excited to share these great hikes with you!

And with that, it's time once again for my battle cry from previous titles in the Day Hiking series. As our world continues to urbanize, as we grow more sedentary, materialistic, and disconnected from the natural world, life for many has lost its real meaning. Nature may need us to protect it from becoming paved over, but we need nature to protect us from the encroaching world of consumption and shallow pursuits. Henry David Thoreau proclaimed, "In wildness is the preservation of the world." And I would like to add, "In wildness is also the salvation of our souls, the meaning of life, and the preservation of our humanness." You don't need to go looking for it in the mountains of Nepal or Peru—it's right here in our backyards. So, shun the mall, turn off the TV, ditch the smart phone, and hit the trail! I've lined up 100 magnificent hikes that will help you celebrate nature, life, the incredible landscapes of the Columbia River Gorge, and you. Yes, you! Go take a hike! Celebrate life and return from the natural world a more content person. You don't need a lot of money or fancy equipment—just a little energy, direction, and wanderlust.

If I'm preaching to the choir, then help me introduce new disciples to the sacred world of nature. While we sometimes relish our solitude on the trail, we need more like-minded souls to help us keep what little wildlands remain. Help nature by introducing family members, coworkers, your neighbors, children, and politicians to our wonderful trails. I'm convinced that a society that hikes is not only good for our wild and natural places (people will be willing to protect them) but is also good for us (it helps us live healthy and connected lives).

Enjoy this book. I've enjoyed writing it. I'm convinced that we can change our world for the better, one hike at a time. I hope to see you on the trail.

Introduction

Why day hike? It's great exercise for one thing. And God knows we Americans don't get enough of that. But day hiking also offers us exercise for our souls: a chance to get out of the city and reflect on what's truly important—like the natural world and our role in it, even the meaning of life! Day hiking is a great excuse to leave the television, computer, BlackBerry, and all those other life-cluttering electronic devices behind. As the United States grows ever more urban, day hiking may very well be one of our last portals to a simpler yet more fulfilling life. When was the last time you were stuck in traffic on a mountaintop? Forced to give a presentation at an alpine lake? Had to pay bills in a meadow of wildflowers? Felt inadequate watching a field full of elk? Seek rejuvenation and give day hiking a try if you haven't before. And if you're already well-versed on the trail, help introduce your fellow members of the human family to this wonderful pastime.

Why day hiking instead of backpacking? Day hiking is egalitarian. It can be done by just about anyone at almost any time. Backpacking involves more skill, planning, and is often more regulated. Now, don't get me wrong, I love to backpack too. And you can find plenty of choice destinations in my *Backpacking Washington*. But this day hiking guidebook focuses on what you can do in a day, often on a whim and with minimal planning. Of course plenty of the hikes in this book can be turned into overnighters, and I encourage you to do so if you're inclined and the area permits it.

The book you are now holding focuses on the best day hikes within the Columbia River Gorge, with a little spillover into adjoining areas: basically, the best day hikes from the Portland–Vancouver metropolitan area east for as long as the mighty Columbia forms the border between Washington and Oregon. You'll find hikes on both sides of the river, Oregon and Washington treated equally, with fifty of each state's finest Gorge hikes. You'll find excellent hikes right in Portland and throughout Washington's Clark County; fantastic trails within the Columbia River Gorge National

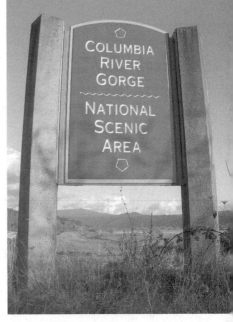

Columbia River Gorge National Scenic Area entrance sign at Washougal

Scenic Area, from the saturated west to the sun-kissed east; and trails to waterfalls, lakeshores, mountaintops, old-growth forests, islands, desert-steppe hills and fire lookouts. Dedicated sections describe hikes in the Silver Star Scenic Area and in the Trapper Creek Wilderness, and plenty of hikes take you into the newly expanded Mark O. Hatfield Wilderness. You'll explore national forests, state forests, state parks, county parks, city parks, and national wildlife refuges.

Choose from hikes that are perfect for children, friendly to dogs, and that are accessible year-round. Explore trails of historical relevance, those of interest to wildflower and waterfall connoisseurs, and great places for observing wildlife. They're all included in this packed-with-adventure, 100-hike volume. And nearly all of these hikes are only a 30-minute to 2-hour drive from the Portland–Vancouver metropolitan region. So what are you waiting for? Let's hit the trail!

USING THIS BOOK

The Day Hiking guidebooks strike a fine balance. They were developed to be as easy to use as possible while still providing enough detail to help you explore a region. As a result, *Day Hiking: Columbia River Gorge* includes all the information you need to find and enjoy the hikes but leaves enough room for you to make your own discoveries. I have hiked every mile of trail described in this book so that you can follow my directions and advice with confidence. Conditions do, however, change. So read on for tips on choosing your hike and staying up-to-date.

What the Ratings Mean

Each hike in this book starts with two subjective ratings: a *rating* of 1 to 5 stars for overall appeal, and numerical score of 1

to 5 for each route's *difficulty*. This is purely subjective, based on my impressions of each hike. But these assessments do follow a formula of sorts.

The overall **rating** is based on scenic beauty, natural wonder, and other unique qualities, such as solitude potential and wildlife-viewing opportunities.

***** Unmatched hiking adventure, great scenic beauty, and wonderful trail experience

**** Excellent experience, sure to please all

*** A great hike, with one or more fabulous features to enjoy

** May lack the "killer view" features, but offers lots of little moments to enjoy

* Worth doing as a refreshing wild-country walk, especially if you're in the neighborhood

The **difficulty** score is based on trail length, overall elevation gain, steepness, and trail conditions. Generally, trails that are rated more difficult (4 or 5) are longer and steeper than average. But it's not a simple equation. A short, steep trail over talus slopes may be rated 5, while a long, smooth trail with little elevation gain may be rated 2.

5 Extremely difficult: Excessive elevation gain and/or more than 6 miles one-way, and/or bushwhacking required

4 Difficult: Some steep sections, possibly rough trail or poorly maintained trail

3 Moderate: A good workout, but no real problems

2 Moderately easy: Relatively flat or short route with good trail

1 Easy: A relaxing stroll in the woods

The Columbia River Gorge is also renowned for its wide array of wildflowers.

To help explain the difficulty score, you'll also find the **round-trip mileage** (unless otherwise noted as one-way), total **elevation gain**, and **high point**. While I have measured most of the trails using GPS and maps, and I have consulted the governing land agencies for all hikes in this book, a trip's distance may not be exact but it'll be pretty close. The elevation gain measures the *cumulative* amount that you'll go up on a hike—not only the difference between the high and low points, but also all other significant changes in elevation along the way. As for a hike's high point, it's worth noting that not all high points are at the end of a trail—a route may run over a high ridge before dropping to a lake basin, for instance.

The recommended **season** is another tool meant to help you choose a hike. Many trails can be enjoyed from the time they lose their winter snowpack right up until they are buried in fresh snow the following fall. But the snowpack varies from year to year, so a trail that is open in May one year may be snow covered until mid-July the next. The hiking season for each trail is an estimate. Contact land managers for current conditions.

The **maps** noted for each hike are either USGS maps or Green Trails maps, the latter based on the standard 7.5-minute USGS topographical maps. Green Trails maps are available at most outdoor retailers in the Portland metro area as well as at many National Park Service and U.S. Forest Service visitor centers. I also mention if there's a useful nontopographic trail map available from an on-site kiosk or agency website. Each hike then lists the land-management agency to **contact** for current information; **notes** about permits, road conditions, and seasonal closures; and trailhead **GPS coordinates** to help you get back to your car if you wander off-trail.

Finally, **icons** at the start of each hike description give a quick overview of what each trail has to offer. Kid-friendly hikes are generally easier, pose few if any obstacles, and often consist of natural features that should intrigue and engage youngsters. A dog-friendly hike is one where dogs are not only allowed but that is easy on the paws, with adequate shade and water. A bird-watching hike affords up close and personal time with the avian world of the Columbia. Hikes with especially abundant seasonal wildflowers are also highlighted, as are hikes

with abundant waterfalls and exceptional old-growth forests. Historical hikes take you through the region's human story of First Peoples and early European settlement. Endangered Trails are threatened due to lack of maintenance, motorized encroachment, or other actions detrimental to their existence. Saved Trails, on the other hand, are reasons to rejoice—these hikes have been revived and restored, often by passionate hikers just like you.

Kid-friendly

Dog-friendly

Bird-watching

Wildflowers

Waterfalls

Historical

Endangered Trail

Saved Trail

The route descriptions themselves provide detailed descriptions of what you might find on your hike, including geographic features, scenic views, flora and fauna potential, and more. Thorough driving directions from the nearest large town or geographic feature will get you to the trailhead, and options for extending your trip round out each hike so that, if you want, you can add more miles or even days to your outing.

Of course, you'll need some information long before you leave home. So, as you plan your trips consider the following issues.

PERMITS, REGULATIONS, AND FEES

As our public lands have become increasingly popular, and as both state and federal funding have continued to decline, regulations and permits have become necessary components in managing our natural heritage. It's important that you know, understand, and abide by them. To help keep our wilderness areas wild and our trails safe and well-maintained, land managers—especially the National Park Service and U.S. Forest Service—have implemented a sometimes complex set of rules and regulations governing use of these lands.

Generally, most developed trailheads in Washington and Oregon national forests fall under the Region 6 forest pass program. Simply stated, in order to park legally at these designated trailheads, you must display a Northwest Forest Pass on your windshield. These sell for $5 per day or $30 for an annual pass good throughout Region 6.

In Washington and Oregon national parks, popular access points usually require a park entrance fee. Your best bet if you hike a lot in both national parks and forests is to buy an America the Beautiful Pass (store.usgs .gov/pass) for $80. This pass grants you and three other adults in your vehicle access to all federal recreation sites that charge a day-use fee (children under sixteen are admitted free). These include national parks, national forests, national wildlife refuges, and Bureau of Land Management areas not only in the Northwest but throughout the country.

There is no day-use charge in Washington's state parks (though that is expected to change in 2012), but several of Oregon's more popular state parks require a daily parking pass, currently $5 and available at the park in question. Annual and two-year passes are available for $30 and $50 respectively and can be purchased from most state

Named in honor of Senator Mark O. Hatfield, this wilderness area protects over 60,000 acres within the Columbia River Gorge.

park offices. Oregon's Sauvie Island Wildlife Area requires a parking pass that costs $7 per day or $22 annually, which can be purchased from vendors on the island; Portland's Oxbow Park requires a $5 day-use fee (payable at the park entrance). Some Clark County parks, in Washington, charge a $3 day-use fee (payable at each park); the Ridgefield National Wildlife Refuge, also in Washington, charges a $3 day-use fee, but you can use your America the Beautiful Pass there.

Finally, hikes in the Columbia River Gorge National Scenic Area (see "Acting to Save the Gorge" in the Western Washington section)

WHOSE LAND IS THIS?

Almost all of the hikes in this book are on public land. That is, they belong to you and me and the rest of the citizenry. What's confusing, however, is just who exactly is in charge of this public trust. More than half a dozen governing agencies manage lands described in this guide.

The agency that oversees the Columbia River Gorge National Scenic Area, where many of the hikes in this guidebook are, is the U.S. Forest Service. A division of the Department of Agriculture, the Forest Service strives to "sustain the health, diversity, and productivity of the Nation's forests and grasslands to meet the needs of present and future genera- tions." The agency purports to do this under the doctrine of "multiple-use," in which lands are managed for wildlife preservation and timber harvest, foot traffic and motorbikes. However, supplying timber products, managing wildlife habitat, and developing motorized and nonmotorized recreation options have a tendency to conflict with each other. Some of these uses may not exactly sustain the health of the land either. Several areas administered by the Forest Service have been afforded stringent protections as federal wilderness (see "Untrammeled Columbia River Gorge" in the western Oregon section), barring develop- ment, roads, and motorized recreation.

The National Park Service, a division of the Department of the Interior, manages hun- dreds of thousands of acres of land within the Northwest but very little within the Colum- bia River Gorge region (Fort Vancouver being an exception). The Park Service's primary objective is quite different from that of the Forest Service. The agency mandate is "to con- serve the scenery and natural and historic objects and the wildlife therein and to provide for the enjoyment of the same in such a manner and by such means as will leave them unimpaired for the enjoyment of future generations." In other words, the primary focus of the Park Service is preservation.

Other public lands you'll encounter in this book are Washington and Oregon state parks, managed primarily for recreation and preservation. Washington Department of Natural Resources land, managed mainly for timber harvesting, has pockets of natural-area pre- serves. National wildlife refuges and state wildlife preserves are managed for wildlife habitat protection and for hunting and fishing. And county parks are often like state parks but are managed at a more local level.

It's important that you know what agency manages the land you'll be hiking on, for each has its own fees and rules (like for dogs: generally no in national parks and national wildlife refuges, yes in national forests, and yes but on-leash in state parks). Confusing, yes? But it's our land and we should understand how it's managed for us. And remember that we have a say in how our lands are managed, too, and can let the agencies know whether we like what they're doing or not.

are administered by a number of different land-management agencies that may or may not require a fee. All required fees and permits are clearly listed for each hike.

WEATHER

Mountain weather is famously unpredictable, and in the Gorge, with the Columbia River's near sea-level passage through the Cascades, you can expect all kinds of interesting weather events, from high winds and thunderstorms to ice storms. Weather patterns are radically different in the west and east ends of the Gorge. The west side is influenced by Pacific Ocean currents, creating a more temperate climate with a copious amount of rainfall, heavy from November to April. Summers are generally mild, with extended periods of no or low rainfall. July through early October is usually a delightful time to hike the western region. In the Gorge's east, weather patterns are representative of a continental climate, with cold winters and hot, dry summers. Snowfall is usually light due to the Cascades' rainshadow effect. But higher elevations see ample snowfall, as storm clouds move eastward and are pushed up over the mountains, cooling and releasing their moisture. Heaviest snows usually occur at or near the Cascade crest.

Plan your hike according to your weather preference. But no matter where you hike in the region, always pack raingear. Being caught in a sudden rain and wind storm without adequate clothing can lead to hypothermia (loss of body temperature), which is deadly if not immediately treated. Most hikers who die of such exposure do so, not in winter, but during the milder months when a sudden change of temperature accompanied by winds and rain sneaks up on them. Always carry extra clothing layers, including rain and wind protection.

While snow blankets the high country primarily from November through May, it can occur anytime of year. Be prepared. Lightning is rare along the west slopes but quite common during the summer months in the eastern half of the Gorge. If you hear thunder, waste no time getting off of summits and away from water. Take shelter, but not under big trees or rock ledges. If caught in an electrical storm, crouch down making minimal contact with the ground and wait for the boomer to pass. Remove your metal-framed pack and ditch the trekking poles! For more detailed information and fascinating reading on this subject, refer to Jeff Renner's excellent book, *Lightning Strikes: Staying Safe Under Stormy Skies.*

Other weather-induced hazards you should be aware of result from past episodes of rain and snow. River and creek crossings can be extremely dangerous after periods of heavy rain or snowmelt. Always use caution and sound judgment when fording. Also be aware of snowfields left over from the previous winter. Depending on the severity of the past winter, and the weather conditions of the spring and early summer, some trails may not melt out until well into summer. In addition to treacherous footing and difficulties in routefinding, lingering snowfields can be prone to avalanches or slides. Use caution crossing them. Finally, strong winds are another concern in the Gorge. Avoid hiking during extreme windy periods, which can fell trees and branches.

ROAD AND TRAIL CONDITIONS

In general, trails change little year to year. But change can and does occur, sometimes very quickly. A heavy storm can cause a river to jump its channel, washing out sections of trail or access road in moments. Windstorms can blow down trees by the hundreds across trails, making paths unhikeable. And snow can bury trails well into the summer. Avalanches, landslides, and forest fires can also bring serious damage and obliteration to our trails. Fires (and subsequent slides) were responsible for the loss of the Perdition Trail near Multnomah Falls and the deterioration of the Eagle-Benson Trail. Lack of funding plays a role in trail neglect and degradation as well.

With this in mind, each hike in this book lists the land manager's contact information so you can phone the agency prior to your trip and ensure that your chosen road and trail are open and safe to travel.

On the topic of trail conditions, it is vital that we thank the countless volunteers who donate tens of thousands of hours to trail maintenance each year. The Washington Trails Association (WTA) and the Trailkeepers of Oregon alone coordinate upward of 100,000 hours of volunteer trail maintenance annually.

As enormous as the volunteer efforts have become, there is always a need for more. Our trail system faces ever-increasing threats, including (but by no means limited to) ever-shrinking trail funding, inappropriate trail uses, and conflicting land-management policies and practices. Decades ago, the biggest threat to our trails was the overharvesting of timber and the wanton building of roads to access it. Ironically, as timber harvesting has all but ceased in much of our federal forests, one of the biggest threats to our trails now is access. Many roads once used for hauling timber (and by hikers to get to trailheads) are no longer maintained. Many of these roads are slumping and growing over and are becoming downright dangerous to drive. Many, too, are washing out, severing access. While this author supports the decommis-

sioning of many of the trunk roads that go "nowhere" as both economically and environmentally prudent, I am deeply disturbed by the number of main roads that are falling into disrepair. Once a road has been closed for several years, the trails radiating from it often receive no maintenance, which often leads them to becoming unhikeable.

On the other end of the threat scale is the increased motorized use of many of our trails. Despite also being open to hiking, motorized vehicles on trails tend to discourage hikers—the noise, speed, and negative impact on the natural environment are not compatible with quiet, muscle-powered modes of backcountry travel. Even when motorized users obey rules and regulations—and most do—wheels tear up tread far greater than boots. This is especially true in the high country, where fragile soils and lush meadows are easily damaged. While the majority of motorcyclists are decent people and I have shared trails with them, hiking with them is simply not a wilderness experience. And while I support the rights of motorized recreation users to have access to public lands, many of the trails currently open to them should never have allowed them. Only one trail in this book is open to motorcycles.

This guide includes several trails that are threatened and in danger of becoming unhikeable due to motorized use, access problems, and other issues. These Endangered Trails are marked with a special icon. On the other side of the coin, we've had some great trail successes in recent years, thanks in large part to a massive volunteer movement spearheaded by WTA and other organizations. These Saved Trails are also marked, to help show you that individual efforts do make a difference. As you enjoy these Saved Trails, stop to consider the contributions made by your fellow hikers that helped protect our trail resources. And consider getting involved so that you too can make a difference.

WILDERNESS ETHICS

As wonderful as volunteer trail maintenance programs are, they aren't the only way to help save our trails. Indeed, these on-the-ground efforts provide quality trails today, but to ensure the long-term survival of our trails—and more specifically, to preserve the wildlands they cross—we must embrace and practice a sound wilderness ethic.

A strong, positive wilderness ethic includes making sure you leave the wilderness as good (or even better) than you found it. But a sound wilderness ethic goes deeper than simply picking up after ourselves (and others) when we go for a hike. It must carry over into our daily lives. We need to ensure that our elected officials and public land managers recognize and respond to our wilderness needs and desires. Get involved with groups and organizations that safeguard, watchdog, and advocate for land protection. And get on the phone and keyboard and let land managers and public officials know how important protecting lands and trails is to you.

TRAIL GIANTS

I grew up in rural New Hampshire and was introduced to hiking and respect for our wildlands at a young age. I grew to admire the men and women responsible for saving and protecting many of our trails and wilderness areas as I became more aware of the often tumultuous history behind the preservation efforts.

When I moved to Washington in 1989, I immediately gained a respect for Harvey Manning and Ira Spring. Through their pioneering 100 Hikes guidebooks, I was introduced to and fell in love with the Washington backcountry. I joined The Mountaineers, the Washington Trails Association, Friends of the Columbia Gorge, and other local trail and conservation organizations so that I could help protect these places and carry on this legacy to future generations.

WANT TO PROTECT LAND AROUND THE COLUMBIA? BUY IT!

What's the fastest, most sure-fired, and often least controversial way to protect land? Buy it yourself! That's exactly what land trusts across the country do. A concept that began in Massachusetts in the late 1800s, land trusts today exist in the thousands, from coast to coast, nearly all of them nonprofit organizations whose primary purpose is to buy land and secure development rights in order to protect natural areas, farmland, shorelines, wildlife habitat, and recreational lands. Once the land is secured, trusts usually then transfer it with legally bound stipulations to government agencies to be managed for the public. Many trusts, however, also maintain their own preserves, and most of these are open to the public. There are several land trusts operating in the Columbia River Gorge region, including the Columbia Land Trust (www.columbialandtrust.org). Based in Vancouver, Washington, the 2500-member Columbia Land Trust began in 1990 and has been responsible for protecting over 10,000 acres. Consider joining them!

Showy flowers like bitterroot can be found in the Gorge's eastern reaches.

I believe 100 percent in what Ira Spring termed "green bonding." We must, in Ira's words, "get people onto trails. They need to bond with the wilderness." This is essential in building public support for trails and trail funding. When hikers get complacent, trails suffer. And while Harvey Manning's legendary tirades and diatribes lambasting public officials' short-sighted and misguided land practices could often be off-putting, I almost always tacitly agreed with him. Harvey may have been a bit combative, a tad too polarizing at times, but sometimes you have to raise a little hell to get results.

As you get out and hike the trails described here, consider that many of these trails would have long ago ceased to exist without the phenomenal efforts of people like Ira Spring, Harvey Manning, Louise Marshall, and Nancy Russell, not to mention the scores of unnamed hikers who joined them in their push for wildland protection, trail funding, and strong environmental stewardship programs.

When you get home, take a page from their playbook and write a letter to your congressperson or state representative, asking for better trail and public lands funding. Call your local Forest Service office and let them know how you feel about converting wilderness trails into motorized trails.

If you're not already a member, consider joining an organization devoted to wilderness, backcountry trails, or other wild-country issues. Organizations like the Friends of the Columbia Gorge, Columbia Land Trust, The Mountaineers, the Mazamas mountaineering club, Washington Trails Association, Trailkeepers of Oregon, and countless others help leverage individual contributions and efforts to ensure the future of our trails and the wonderful wilderness legacy we've inherited. Buy a specialty license plate for Washington's state parks or an Oregon salmon plate (benefiting Oregon's state parks), and let everybody on the way to the trailhead see what you value and support.

TRAIL ETIQUETTE

We need to not only be sensitive to the environment surrounding our trails but to other trail users as well. Many of the trails in this book are open to an array of trail users. Some are hiker-only, but others allow equestrians and mountain bikers too.

When you encounter other trail users—whether they are hikers, climbers, runners, bicyclists, or horse riders—the only hard-and-fast rule is to follow common sense and exercise simple courtesy. It's hard to over-state just how vital these two things—common sense and courtesy—are to maintaining an enjoyable, safe, and friendly situation when different types of trail users meet.

With this Golden Rule of Trail Etiquette firmly in mind, here are other things you can do during trail encounters to make every-one's trip more enjoyable:

- **Right-of-way.** When meeting other hik-ers, the uphill group has the right-of-way. There are two general reasons for this. First, on steep ascents, hikers may be watching the trail and might not notice the approach of descending hikers until they're face-to-face. More importantly, it's easier for descending hikers to break stride and step off-trail than it is for those who have gotten into a good climbing rhythm. But by all means, if you're the up-hill trekker and you wish to grant passage to oncoming hikers, go right ahead with this act of trail kindness.
- **Moving off-trail.** When meeting other user groups (like bicyclists and horseback riders), the hiker should move off the trail. This is because hikers are more mobile and flexible than other users, making it easier for them to step off the trail.
- **Encountering horses.** When meeting horseback riders, the hiker should step off the downhill side of the trail unless the terrain makes this difficult or dangerous. In that case, move to the uphill side of the trail, but crouch down a bit so you don't tower over the horses' heads. Also, make yourself visible so as not to spook the big beastie, and talk in a normal voice to the riders. This calms the horses. If hiking with a dog, keep your buddy under control.

- **Stay on trails,** and practice minimum impact. Don't cut switchbacks, take short-cuts, or make new trails. If your destina-tion is off-trail, stick to snow and rock when possible so as not to damage fragile alpine meadows. Spread out when travel-ing off-trail; don't hike in line if in a group, as this greatly increases the chance of compacting thin soils and crushing deli-cate plant environments.
- **Obey the rules** specific to the trail you're visiting. Many trails are closed to certain types of use, including hiking with dogs and travel by mountain bike.
- **Hiking with dogs.** Hikers who take dogs on the trails should have their dog on a leash or under very strict voice command at all times. And if leashes are required (such as in all state parks and on many of the Columbia River Gorge National Scenic Area trails), then this *does* apply to you. Too many dog owners flagrantly disregard this regulation, setting them-selves up for tickets, hostile words from fellow hikers, and the possibility of losing the right to bring Fido out on that trail in the future. One of the most contentious issues in hiking circles is whether dogs should be allowed on trails. Far too many hikers (this author included, who happens to love dogs) have had very negative trail encounters with dogs (actually, the dog owners). Remember that many hikers are not fond of dogs on the trail (and some are actually afraid of your pet). Respect their right not to be approached by your love-able Lab. A well-behaved leashed dog, however, can certainly help warm up these hikers to your buddy.
- **Avoid disturbing wildlife.** Observe from a distance, resisting the urge to move closer to wildlife (use your telephoto lens).

This not only keeps you safer, but it prevents the animal from having to exert itself unnecessarily fleeing from you.

- **Take only photographs.** Leave all natural things, features, and historical artifacts as you found them for others to enjoy.
- **Never roll rocks off trails or cliffs.** You risk endangering lives below you.

These are just a few of the things you can do to maintain a safe and harmonious trail environment. And while not every situation is addressed by these rules, you can avoid problems by always remembering that *common sense and courtesy are in order*.

Remember, too, that anything you pack in must be packed out, even biodegradable items like orange peels and pistachio shells. "Leave only footprints, take only pictures" is a worthy slogan to live by when visiting the wilderness.

Another important Leave No Trace principle focuses on the business of taking care of business. The first rule of backcountry bathroom etiquette says that if an outhouse exists, use it. They help keep backcountry water supplies free from contamination and the surrounding countryside from turning into a minefield of human waste decorated with toilet-paper flowers. Composting privies can actually improve the environment. I once spent a summer as a backcountry ranger in which one of my duties was composting the duty. Once the "stew" was sterile, we spread it on damaged alpine meadows, helping to restore the turf.

When privies aren't provided however, the key factor to consider is location. Choose a site at least 200 feet from water, campsites, and the trail. Dig a cat hole. Once you're done, bury your waste with organic duff and a Microbes at Work sign (just kidding about the sign—but making an **X** marks the spot with a couple of sticks is a fine idea).

Water

As a general rule you should assume that all backcountry water sources are contaminated with *Giardia* (a waterborne parasite) or other aquatic nasties. Treating water can be as simple as boiling it, chemically purifying it (adding tiny iodine tablets), or pumping it through a water filter and purifier. (Note: Pump units labeled as filters generally remove everything but viruses, which are too small to be filtered out. Pumps labeled as purifiers use a chemical element, usually iodine, to render viruses inactive after filtering all the other bugs out.)

Hunting

Hikers should be aware that many of our public lands are seasonally open to hunting. The dates vary, but generally big game hunting begins in early August and ends in late November. While hiking in areas frequented by hunters, it's best to make yourself visible by donning an orange cap and vest. If hiking with a dog, your buddy should wear an orange vest too. The vast majority of hunters are responsible, decent folks (and are conservationists who also support our public lands), so you should have little concern when encountering them in the backcountry. Still, if being around outdoors people schlepping rifles is unnerving to you, then stick to hiking in national and state parks where hunting is prohibited.

WILDLIFE
The Bear Essentials

The Columbia Gorge and, in particular, places like the Trapper Creek Wilderness and Silver Star Scenic Area harbor healthy populations

The Silver Star Scenic Area is important habitat for area wildlife.

of black bears, and your chance of eventually seeing one is pretty good. Your encounter will most likely involve just catching a glimpse of his bear behind. But occasionally the bruin may actually want to get a look at *you.* In very rare cases (and I repeat, rare) a bear may act aggressively. To avoid an un-*bear*-able encounter, heed the following advice, compliments of fellow guidebook writer and man of many bear encounters, Dan Nelson:

- **Respect a bear's need for personal space.** If you see a bear in the distance, make a wide detour around it. If that's not possible, leave the area.
- **Remain calm** if you do encounter a bear at close range. Do not run, as this may trigger a predator-prey reaction from the bear.

- **Talk in a low-voiced, calm manner** to the bear to help identify yourself as a human.
- **Hold your arms out from your body,** and if wearing a jacket hold open the front so you appear as big as possible.
- **Don't stare directly at the bear**—the bear may interpret this as a direct threat or challenge. Watch the animal without making direct eye-to-eye contact.
- **Slowly move upwind** of the bear if you can do so without crowding the bear. The bear's strongest sense is its sense of smell, and if it can sniff you and identify you as human, it may retreat.
- **Know how to interpret bear actions.** A nervous bear will often rumble in its chest, clack its teeth, and "pop" its jaw. It may paw the ground and swing its head

violently side to side. If the bear does this, watch it closely (without staring directly at it). Continue to speak low and calmly.

- **A bear may bluff-charge**—run at you but stop well before reaching you—to try and intimidate you. Resist the urge to run, as that would turn the bluff into a real charge and you will *not* be able to outrun the bear (black bears can run at speeds up to 35 miles per hour through log-strewn forests).
- If you surprise a bear and it does charge from close range, **lie down and play dead.** A surprised bear will leave you once the perceived threat is neutralized. However, if the bear wasn't attacking because it was surprised—if it charges from a long distance, or if it has had a chance to identify you and still attacks—you should fight back. A bear in this situation is behaving in a predatory manner (as opposed to the defensive attack of a surprised bear) and is looking at you as food. Kick, stab, punch at the bear. If it knows you will fight back, it may leave you and search for easier prey.
- **Carry a 12-ounce (or larger) can of pepper spray bear deterrent.** The spray—a high concentration of oils from hot peppers—should fire out at least 20 or 30 feet in a broad mist. Don't use the spray unless a bear is actually charging and is in range of the spray.

This Is Cougar Country

Very few hikers ever see cougars in the wild. I've been tracked by them, but in all of my hiking throughout North and South America I have only seen one of these elusive kitties, and it was in Washington's Blue Mountains. Both Washington and Oregon support healthy pop-ulations of the shy and solitary *Felix concolor*. While cougar encounters are extremely rare in the Columbia Gorge, they do occur. To make sure the encounter is a positive one (at least for you), you need to understand these wildcats.

Cougars are curious (after all, they're cats). They will follow hikers simply to see what kind of beasts we are, but they rarely (almost never) attack adult humans. If you do encounter one, remember that cougars rely on prey that can't, or won't fight back. Fellow guidebook writer Dan Nelson, a Washington State University Cougar who grew up in cougar country (the Blue Mountains of southeast Washington), offers the following advice should you run into one of these cats:

- **Do not run!** Running may trigger a cougar's attack instinct.
- **Stand up and face it.** Virtually every recorded cougar attack of humans has been a predator-prey attack. If you appear as another aggressive predator rather than as prey, the cougar will back down.
- **Try to appear large.** Wave your arms or a jacket over your head.
- **Pick up children and small dogs.**
- **Maintain eye contact** with the animal. The cougar will interpret this as a show of dominance on your part.
- **Back away slowly** if you can safely do so.
- **Do not turn your back** or take your eyes off the cougar. Remain standing.
- **Throw things,** provided you don't have to bend over to pick them up. If you have a water bottle on your belt, chuck it at the cat. Wave your trekking pole, and if the cat gets close enough, whack it *hard* with your pole.
- **Shout loudly.**
- **Fight back** aggressively.

Opposite: The Columbia River Gorge is renowned for its waterfalls.

And you can minimize the already slim chances of having a negative cougar encounter by doing the following:

- **Do not hike or run alone** (runners look like fleeing prey to a predator).
- **Keep children within sight** and close at all times.
- **Avoid dead animals.**
- **Keep dogs on-leash and under control.** A cougar may attack a loose, solitary dog, but a leashed dog next to you makes two foes for the cougar to deal with—and cougars are too smart to take on two aggressive animals at once.

Poison oak is profuse in the Gorge—leaves of three, let it be.

Poison Oak, Ticks, and Rattlesnakes: The Gorge's Triple Nuisance

Compared with other parts of the world that I have hiked in, natural nuisances in the Columbia River Gorge are minimal. But poison oak is pretty ubiquitous, ticks are numerous in early season, and rattlesnakes are fairly common in the Gorge's eastern reaches. Don't be alarmed—just be aware!

Poison oak: Not a member of the elegant *Quercus* (oak) genus but of the sumac family, this shrub thrives in the dry, open (nonpoisonous) oak forests of the eastern Gorge. The leaves and twigs of this plant contain urushiol—a surface oil that causes an allergic reaction in most people who come in contact with it. Symptoms range from mild itching to blistering, and the reaction can last up to two weeks, inflicting some discomfort. In areas rife with poison oak, wear long pants and be sure to wash them after your hike to rid them of any lingering oils. Learn to recognize poison oak by its toothed, lobed, somewhat glossy leaves that grow in compounds of three. Remember, leaves of three, let them be!

Ticks: This nuisance you should be far more concerned with. Other than the fact that most people (this author included) find these hard-shelled arachnids disgusting (and fascinating too, I admit), it's ticks' role as a disease vector that raises alarm. Ticks are parasites that live off the blood of their host. Hikers make great hosts, and ticks will cling to them if given the opportunity. Generally active in the spring (and mainly on the lower slopes of the eastern side of the Gorge, especially in the oak forests), ticks inhabit shrubs and tall grasses. When you brush up against these plants, the tick gets an opportunity to hitch a ride. During tick season wear long sleeves and tuck pant legs into socks. Be sure to check yourself after hiking, particularly at waist and sock lines. And if one of the little buggers has fastened itself to you, get out your tweezers. Gently squeeze its head until it lets go (try not to break the head off, or it may become lodged and infected). Wash and disinfect the bite area. Most ticks in the Northwest do not carry Lyme disease. Still, it's best to monitor the bite. If a rash develops, immediately seek medical help.

Rattlesnakes: There's no need for concern on the wet west side of the Gorge, but in the sunnier eastern reaches, and in particular in lower elevation dry canyon areas, northern Pacific rattlesnakes may be found. A viper that is as intent on avoiding you as you are it, rattlesnakes generally keep to themselves. But if you get too close, they'll set off an alarm by rattling their tails. Should this happen, walk away, allowing the snake to retreat. Never, ever try to catch, provoke, or pursue one. Rattlesnake bites in Washington and Oregon are extremely rare; deaths by rattlesnake bites even rarer. If bit, however, remain calm. Wash the bite. Immobilize the limb. Apply a wet wrap. Seek medical attention immediately.

GEAR

While a full description of all available gear is beyond the scope of this book (which is about where to hike, not how to hike), it's worth noting a few pointers here. No hiker should venture far up a trail without being properly equipped. Starting with your feet, a good pair of boots can make all the difference between a wonderful hike and a blistering affair. Keep your feet happy and you'll be happy.

You can't talk boots without talking socks. Synthetic socks work best. Liners worn with wool socks are also good choices. For clothing, wear whatever is most comfortable, unless it's cotton. Cotton is a wonderful fabric but not the best to hike in. When it gets wet, it stays wet and lacks any insulation value. In fact, wet cotton sucks away body heat, leaving you susceptible to hypothermia. Think synthetics and layering.

While the list of what you pack will vary from what another hiker on the same trail is carrying, there are a few items everyone should have in their packs. Every hiker who ventures deep into the woods should be prepared to spend the night out with emergency food and shelter. Mountain storms can whip up in a hurry, catching fair-weather hikers by surprise. What was an easy to follow trail during a calm, clear day can disappear into a confusing world of fog and rain—or snow. Therefore, every hiker should pack the Ten Essentials as well as a few other items that aren't necessarily essential but that would be good to have on hand in an emergency.

The Ten Essentials

1. **Navigation (map and compass):** Carry a topographic map of the area you plan to be in and knowledge of how to read it. Likewise a compass—again, make sure you know how to use it.

2. **Sun protection (sunglasses and sunscreen):** Even on wet days, carry sunscreen and sunglasses; you never know when the clouds will lift. At higher elevations your exposure to UV rays is much more intense than at sea level. You can easily burn on snow and near water.

3. **Insulation (extra clothing):** It may be 70 degrees Fahrenheit at the trailhead, but at the summit it can be 45 and windy. Storms can and do blow in rapidly. In the high country it can snow anytime of year. Be sure to carry rain gear, wind gear, and extra layers.

4. **Illumination (flashlight/headlamp):** If caught after dark, you'll need a headlamp or flashlight to be able to follow the trail. If forced to spend the night, you'll need it to set up emergency camp, gather wood, and so on. Carry extra batteries too.

5. **First-aid supplies:** At the very least your kit should include bandages, gauze, scissors, tape, tweezers, pain relievers, antiseptics, and perhaps a small manual. Consider first-aid training through a program such as MOFA (Mountaineering Oriented First Aid).

6. **Fire (firestarter and matches):** If you're forced to spend the night out, an emergency campfire will provide warmth. Be sure you keep your matches dry. Resealable plastic bags do the trick. A candle can come in handy too.

7. **Repair kit and tools (including a knife):** A knife is helpful; a multitool is better. You never know when you might need a small pair of pliers or scissors, both of which are commonly found on compact multitools. A basic repair kit should include such things as nylon cord, a small roll of duct tape, some 1-inch webbing and extra webbing buckles (to fix broken pack straps), and a small tube of superglue. A handful of safety pins can do wonders too.

8. **Nutrition (extra food):** Always pack more food than what you need for your hike. If you're forced to spend the night, you'll be prepared. Better to have extra and not need it than the other way around. Pack energy bars for emergency pick-me-ups.

9. **Hydration (extra water):** Carry two full 32-ounce water bottles, unless you're hiking entirely along a water source.

You'll need to carry iodine tablets or a filter too, so as not to catch any waterborne nasties like *Giardia*.

10. **Emergency shelter:** This can be as simple as a garbage bag or something more efficient like a reflective space blanket. A poncho can double as an emergency tarp.

TRAILHEAD CONCERNS

Sadly, the topic of trailhead and trail crime must be addressed. As urban areas encroach upon our green spaces, societal ills follow along. While violent crime is extremely rare (practically absent on most of our public lands, thankfully), it is a grim reminder that we are never truly free from the worst elements of society.

By and large our hiking trails are safe places—far safer than most city streets. Common sense and vigilance, however, are still in order. This is true for all hikers, but particularly so for solo hikers. Be aware of your surroundings at all times. Leave your itinerary with someone back home. If something doesn't feel right, it probably isn't. Take action by leaving the place or situation immediately. But remember, most hikers are friendly, decent people. Some may be a little introverted, but that's no cause for worry.

By far your biggest concern should be with trailhead theft. Car break-ins are far too common at some of our trailheads, especially at trails on the popular western Oregon side of the Gorge. Do not—absolutely under no circumstances—leave anything of value in your vehicle while out hiking. Take your wallet, cell phone, and listening devices with you—or better yet, don't bring them along in the first place. Don't leave anything in your car that may appear valuable. A duffle bag on the back seat may contain dirty T-shirts, but a thief may think there's a laptop in it. Save yourself the hassle of returning to a busted window by not giving criminals a reason to clout your car.

If you arrive at a trailhead and someone looks suspicious, don't discount your intuition. Take notes on the person and his or her vehicle. Record the license plate and report the behavior to the authorities. Do not confront the person. Leave and go to another trail.

While most car break-ins are crimes of opportunity by drug addicts looking for loot to support their fix, organized gangs intent on stealing IDs have also been known to target parked cars at trailheads. While some trailheads are regularly targeted, and others rarely if at all, there's no sure way of preventing this from happening to you other than being dropped off at the trailhead or taking the bus (rarely an option, either way). But you can make your car less of a target by not leaving anything of value in it. And contact your government officials and demand that law enforcement be a priority on our public lands. We taxpayers have a right to recreate safely.

ENJOY THE TRAILS

Most importantly, though, be safe and enjoy the trails in this book. They exist for our enjoyment and for the enjoyment of future generations of hikers. We can use them and protect them at the same time if we're careful with our actions and forthright in demanding that our state and federal representatives continue and further the protection of our wildlands.

Throughout the last century, wilderness lovers helped secure protection for many of the lands we enjoy today. President Theodore Roosevelt was visionary in establishing the national forest system and in greatly

Volunteer-built trail at Portland's Forest Park

expanding our public lands (by over 40 million acres). President Franklin Roosevelt was ingenious in stimulating infrastructure on our public lands and also in expanding our parks and preserves.

Republicans, Democrats, city dwellers, country folks, Americans of all walks of life have helped establish and protect our open spaces and wilderness areas. As we cruise into the twenty-first century, we must see to it that those protections continue and that the last bits of wildlands are also preserved for the enjoyment of future generations.

If you enjoy these trails, get involved! Trails may wind through trees, but they don't grow on them. Your involvement can be as simple as picking up trash, attending a work party, joining a trail advocacy group, educating fellow citizens, or writing Congress or your state representatives a letter. All of these seemingly small acts can make a big difference. Introduce children to our trails.

We need to continue a legacy of good trail stewards. At the end of this book you'll find a list of organizations working on behalf of our trails and wildlands in the Columbia River Gorge region. Consider getting involved with a few of them.

Happy Hiking!

A NOTE ABOUT SAFETY

Safety is an important concern in all outdoor activities. No guidebook can alert you to every hazard or anticipate the limitations of every reader. Therefore, the descriptions of roads, trails, routes, and natural features in this book are not representations that a particular place or excursion will be safe for your party. When you follow any of the routes described in this book, you assume responsibility for your own safety. Under normal conditions, such excursions require the usual attention to traffic, road and trail conditions, weather, terrain, the capabilities of your party, and other factors. Because many of the lands in this book are subject to development and/or change of ownership, conditions may have changed since this book was written that make your use of some of these routes unwise. Always check for current conditions, obey posted private property signs, and avoid confrontations with property owners or managers. Keeping informed on current conditions and exercising common sense are the keys to a safe, enjoyable outing.

—*The Mountaineers Books*

Opposite: East Fork Lewis River, Paradise Point State Park

vancouver and
clark county

Much has changed in Washington's first county since its creation by the Oregon Territory provisional government in 1845. Named in honor of William Clark (of Lewis and Clark fame) and home to Washington's oldest permanent non-Native settlement, Vancouver (started as Fort Vancouver in 1824), is now the state's fourth-largest city; Vancouver and Clark County have seen explosive growth in the last twenty-five years. Fortunately, civic leaders backed by concerned citizens have made it a priority to protect natural areas and expand parks and trails. Washington's second most densely populated county has a surprisingly wide array of natural areas to explore and an excellent and growing trail system.

The East Fork of the Lewis River is the highlight at Paradise Point State Park.

1 Paradise Point State Park

RATING/ DIFFICULTY	ROUND-TRIP	ELEV GAIN/ HIGH POINT	SEASON
★★/1	2.2 miles	250 feet/ 180 feet	Year-round

Map: USGS Ridgefield; **Contact:** Paradise Point State Park, (360) 263-2350, www.parks.wa.gov; **Notes:** Dogs permitted on-leash; **GPS:** N 45 52.355 W 122 42.631

  While I-5 unfortunately cuts through this pretty 88-acre state park on the East Fork Lewis River, paradise is not entirely lost. Follow the park's riverside trail upstream, and the songs of wrens and thrushes eventually replace the buzz of whizzing motor vehicles. Amble over bluff and across grassy shoreline alongside this ecologically important southwest Washington river; then hike up a small forested ravine to a hidden little cascade. It's quite a contrast from the madness of the freeway.

GETTING THERE
From Vancouver, head north on I-5 to exit 16. Turn right onto La Center Road and then immediately turn left onto Paradise Park Road. Continue north, entering the state park in 0.8 mile and coming to a junction 0.2 mile farther. Turn left, and after 0.6 mile come to a day-use parking and picnic area (elev. 30 ft). Privy available.

ON THE TRAIL
From the east end of the picnic area, find the trail heading upriver. The way quickly climbs a forested bluff (elev. 80 ft) and then hastily returns to river level. Then once again it's up, winding alongside showy boughs of ferns, through patches of invasive and nuisance

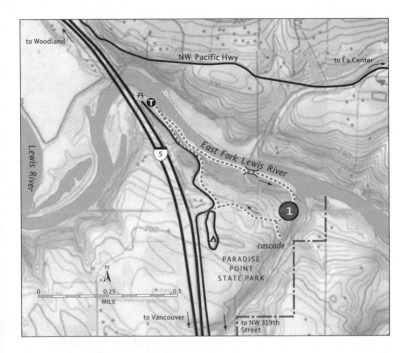

ivy, and beneath mature oak, cedar, and fir. After rounding another 80-foot bluff, the trail steeply descends, passing a wonderful viewpoint over the river before once again reaching river level. Here, just before reaching a wide grassy riverbank, is a tight spot that might be tricky to negotiate when the river is running high.

Beyond this spot, however, it's pure paradise with the trail following a grassy bank alongside the lazy river. Named not for Meriwether of Lewis and Clark fame but for Adolphus Lee Lewis, an early settler, the East Fork Lewis drains much of Clark County and is the center of a large greenbelt extending from Paradise Point State Park to Moulton Falls (Hike 7). The

land directly across the river was recently purchased with Clark County Conservation Futures funded through real estate taxes. Since its inception in 1985, nearly 4000 acres of prime recreation, agricultural, and ecological lands have been protected through this program.

Saunter along the sluggish waterway searching for kingfishers, herons, eagles, waterfowl, beaver, and otters. Cast a friendly wave to passing boaters and kayakers. Cross a tributary on a handsome bridge and continue upriver, now alongside grassy wetlands.

At 0.9 mile, just past a section of trail prone to flooding, the way turns right, away from the river, to follow a small stream up a ravine. At 1 mile, in a grove of cedars, a short spur continues left to an overlook (elev. 80 ft) of a small cascade. Enjoy the soothing tumble uninterrupted by the commotion of the hurried world you left behind at the freeway.

Return the way you came, or take the trail left from the junction, climbing through inviting walk-in campsites and terminating at the main campground (elev. 180 ft) in 0.4 mile. Then walk the road 0.7 mile back to your vehicle.

② La Center Bottoms

RATING/ DIFFICULTY	ROUND-TRIP	ELEV GAIN/ HIGH POINT	SEASON
★★/1	2.2 miles	None/ 30 feet	Year-round

Maps: USGS Ridgefield, trail map from Vancouver–Clark County Parks website; **Contact:** Vancouver–Clark County Parks, (360) 619-1111, www.cityofvancouver.us /parks-recreation; **Notes:** Wheelchair accessible, in part. Dogs permitted on-leash; **GPS:** N 45 51.631 W 122 40.309

A National Watchable Wildlife site, La Center Bottoms is the crown jewel of the 1000-plus-acre, 10-mile-long East Fork Lewis River Greenway. Here, hikers of all ages and abilities (much of the site is wheelchair accessible) can explore a sprawling wetland saturated with wildlife—especially birds. And if the myriad species of resident and migratory waterfowl don't entrance you, the adjacent river and Mount Hood in the background most certainly will.

GETTING THERE
From Vancouver, head north on I-5 to exit 16. Turn right onto La Center Road and proceed

for 1.6 miles to the bridge over the East Fork Lewis River. Immediately upon crossing the bridge and entering the town of La Center, turn right on Aspen Avenue, and then immediately turn right again. Find trailhead parking (elev. 30 ft) near the water reclamation plant.

ON THE TRAIL
Starting on a paved path, the way swings to the south of a new water treatment plant. The utility company along with the city of La Center, TDS Telecom, and private individuals were instrumental in preserving the 300-plus-acre La Center Bottoms. Rounding the treatment plant, the path skirts Sternwheeler Park, a gorgeous manicured city park with sculptures,

La Center Bottoms' grassy marshes provide excellent habitat for area birds.

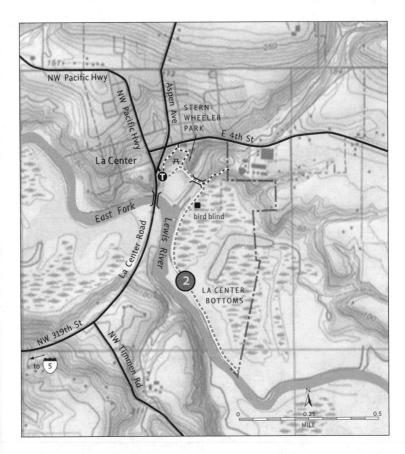

picnic tables, historical displays, and an outdoor amphitheater. Feel free to roam Sternwheeler's grounds, especially its stairways leading to nice views overlooking the bottoms.

Continue on the main path, crossing Brezee Creek on a little bridge at 0.2 mile. Now on gravel, reach a T-junction shortly afterward. The path left climbs 70 feet or so up a wooded bluff to terminate at a school. Head right instead, passing some majestic

oaks before coming to a bird blind and great view of the sprawling wetland bottoms. In winter the area becomes a shallow lake, harboring hundreds of geese and ducks and a few tundra swans thrown in for good measure. Eagles frequently survey the grounds from surrounding trees.

Now, walk past the blind and cross a channel on a sturdy bridge. The path proceeds south, with the bottoms to the east and the

East Fork Lewis River to the west. At about 0.6 mile you'll reach the end of gravel accessible trail. The way, however, continues for another 0.5 mile on a grassy path, ending at a fence line on the preserve's southern boundary.

3 Ridgefield National Wildlife Refuge: Oaks to Wetlands Trail

RATING/ DIFFICULTY	ROUND-TRIP	ELEV GAIN/ HIGH POINT	SEASON
***/1	2 miles	75 feet/ 75 feet	Year-round

Maps: USGS Saint Helens, USGS Ridgefield, trail map from refuge website; **Contact:** Ridgefield National Wildlife Refuge, (360) 887-4106, www.fws.gov/ridgefieldrefuges; **Notes:** $3 per vehicle entry fee (America the Beautiful Pass accepted). Dogs prohibited; **GPS:** N 45 49.872 W 122 44.918

The 5248-acre Ridgefield National Wildlife Refuge is not only a sanctuary for scores of wintering and resident birds in rapidly developing Clark County but is also a haven for local nature lovers. The refuge's Oaks to Wetlands Trail introduces visitors to a fascinating and diverse riparian world of sprawling floodplains, wildlife-rich sloughs, and majestic groves of old-growth Garry oaks, plus a replica of a longhouse and exceptional bird-watching opportunities.

GETTING THERE

From exit 14 on I-5, north of Vancouver, head west 3 miles on State Route 501 (Pioneer Avenue) to its end at a junction in downtown Ridgefield. Turn right onto N Main Avenue and proceed 1 mile to the Carty Unit of the Ridgefield National Wildlife Refuge. The trailhead (elev. 75 ft) is located just west of refuge office. Privy available.

Old growth Oregon White Oaks line the way along the Oaks to Wetlands Trail.

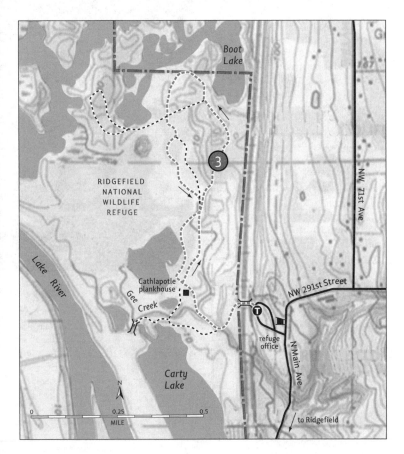

ON THE TRAIL

The hike starts by heading over a set of railroad tracks on an arched bridge. Soon afterward, reach a junction in a field sloping toward the Columbia River. That trail heads straight for a bridge over Gee Creek to extensive river flats ripe for further exploring. Head right instead, reaching the former site of Cathlapotle, a large Chinook village and now occupied by a beautifully crafted replica cedar plankhouse.

Just north of the plankhouse, reach a junction. Bear right. You'll be returning on the Service Road Trail that comes in from the left. Now amble among stately oaks and Oregon ash, some of the finest specimens in Washington of these western hardwoods. Merge with the Service Road Trail and cross a small creek, reaching a three-way junction.

Bear right, heading through thick timber. At 0.7 mile reach a junction with a shortcut to the Service Road Trail. Head right once more, coming to Boot Lake, its shallow waters wallowing with wapato, an arrow-leafed aquatic plant that produced a tuber important to the area's First Peoples. Continue along the lake, reaching the refuge's northern boundary, and begin looping back to the trailhead.

Skirting pools and sloughs bursting with birdlife, pass a side trail (or take it right) to a small peninsula. At about 1.5 miles, come to a familiar three-way junction. Head right on the Service Road Trail, returning to the plankhouse. Then follow the main trail back to the trailhead.

EXTENDING YOUR TRIP
From the first junction, follow the path to Gee Creek, crossing it and continuing 0.3 mile or so to a service road. You can continue north on this road for nearly a mile along Lake River (a channel of the Columbia). In spring and fall watch for sandhill cranes. In winter watch for mud and be aware of possible flooding.

4 Ridgefield National Wildlife Refuge: Kiwa Trail

RATING/ DIFFICULTY	LOOP	ELEV GAIN/ HIGH POINT	SEASON
***/1	1.5 miles	None/ 10 feet	May 1– Sept 30

Maps: USGS Saint Helens, USGS Ridgefield, trail map from refuge website; **Contact:** Ridgefield National Wildlife Refuge, (360) 887-4106, www.fws.gov/ridgefieldrefuges; **Notes:** $3 per vehicle entry fee (America the Beautiful Pass accepted). Wheelchair accessible. Dogs prohibited. Entrance gate closes at 9:00 pm, trail closed for wildlife protection Oct 1–Apr 30; **GPS:** N 45 47.948 W 122 45.382

Keep your voice low for better wildlife observing.

You're in for a slough of surprises (and a couple of shallow lakes) on this delightful loop that probably packs more species per square acre than any other trail in this book. On this level trail through Columbia River bottomlands, look for sun-basking turtles, playful otters, trotting coyotes, grazing deer—and birds. Lots of birds! From teals to rails, yellowthroats to bitterns.

GETTING THERE
From exit 14 on I-5, north of Vancouver, head west 2.7 miles on State Route 501 (Pioneer Street), turning left just before town onto 9th Avenue (which quickly becomes Hillhurst Road). After 0.7 mile, turn right into the River "S" Unit of the Ridgefield National Wildlife Refuge, continuing 0.6 mile to the entrance station. Bear right on the dirt 4.2-Mile Auto

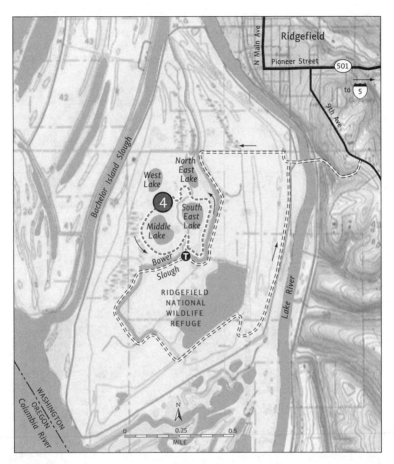

Tour Route, and after 1.4 miles come to the trailhead (elev. 10 ft). Privy available.

ON THE TRAIL

In 1964 a huge earthquake rocked Alaska, damaging prime nesting areas for the dusky subspecies of the Canada goose. The Ridgefield National Wildlife Refuge was established one year later to provide winter habitat for this bird. The refuge has since grown to 5248 acres, protecting quality Columbia River habitat not only for Canada geese but for a myriad of other birds as well—guaranteeing these species a place to breed and winter in rapidly developing Clark County.

The Kiwa Trail offers an excellent opportunity to look for many of the refuge's avian residents. And to hear them—especially in spring when the sloughs, lakes, and ash groves come alive, giving even the London Philharmonic some serious competition.

Start by passing the Bower Slough, a good place to look for turtles. Come to a big trail sign and the start of the loop. Go either direction. To the right takes you through Oregon ashes and then across sprawling marshy grasslands between Middle Lake and South East Lake. Enjoy, too, moseying across a boardwalk over North East Lake.

Birds are the big draw and there are lots to look for—including cinnamon teals, yellowthroats, American bitterns, Virginia rails, and soras. But also check out the lush vegetation—wapato, red osier dogwood, cattails, and bog buttercups. And occasionally glance upward across the floodplain to the scrappy green hills in Oregon. Return often, bird book and binoculars in hand.

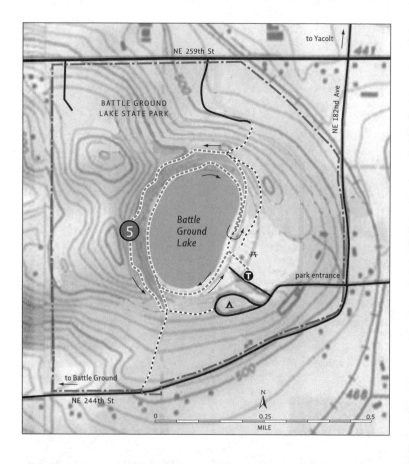

EXTENDING YOUR TRIP

Need more walking? Nearby Whipple Creek County Park off of 179th Street (exit 9 on I-5) contains 4 miles of nice wooded trails on its 300-plus acres. Popular with equestrians, the trails can get muddy at times.

5 Battle Ground Lake State Park

RATING/ DIFFICULTY	LOOP	ELEV GAIN/ HIGH POINT	SEASON
**/2	2.1 miles	210 feet/ 720 feet	Year-round

Maps: USGS Yacolt, trail map from Washington State Parks website; **Contact:** Battle Ground Lake State Park, (360) 687-4621, www.parks.wa.gov; **Notes:** Dogs permitted on-leash; **GPS:** N 45 48.175 W 122 29.463

The battle never occurred, but the name stuck after residents of nearby Fort Vancouver were sure a skirmish would break out between several Indians who escaped from the compound and the army soldiers. This little lake was nevertheless born during an upheaval: a collapsed volcanic cone, Battle Ground Lake is in essence a miniature Crater Lake. The spring-fed caldera is a popular place for local anglers, but hikers will find much to their liking in the forested trails that ring the lake.

GETTING THERE

From Vancouver, head north on I-5 to exit 11 and then follow State Route 502 east for 6 miles to Battle Ground (alternatively, take exit 30 on I-205 and follow SR 500 east for 1.4 miles; then take SR 503 north 7.7 miles to the junction with SR 502). From the junction of SR 502 and SR 503 continue east on

Battle Ground Lake sits in a small caldera surrounded by big trees.

Main Street for 0.9 mile. Turn left (north) onto NE Grace Avenue, which becomes NE 142nd Avenue in 0.4 mile. In another 0.1 mile, turn right onto NE 10th, which becomes NE Heisson Road in 0.6 mile. Continue for 0.8 mile, bearing right onto NE 244th Street, and after another mile turn left into Battle Ground Lake State Park. Proceed for 0.3 mile to large day-use parking area (elev. 590 ft). Privy available.

ON THE TRAIL

Battle Ground Lake has been attracting local visitors for decades. Once a private resort, today over 280 acres surrounding and encompassing the lake are public property compliments of Washington State Parks. While the lake is by far the most popular attraction in the park, there are miles of trails to satisfy hikers, runners, and equestrians. The 0.8-mile trail that encircles the lake and the 1-mile trail that circles the caldera rim are hiker-only. This hike combines them.

From the parking area, walk a paved path 0.1 mile through picnic grounds, dropping down to the lake near a beach and boat launch (elev. 550). Head left (but it doesn't matter which direction you choose) on a well-used, at times muddy trail that hugs the lakeshore. Do your part to help this well-loved park by packing out a piece of litter left behind from less-than-enlightened visitors.

At 0.35 mile come to a junction with a trail leading to the campground and the Upper Lake Trail—your return route. Continue rounding the lake, passing impressive old cedars and firs and a few rocky and ledgy areas sure to entice younger hikers to jump and climb (and hopefully avoid twisting an ankle or bruising a knee). Watch and listen for eagles—and if it's a calm day, savor soothing images of tall timber reflecting upon the spring-fed lake's placid waters.

At 0.8 mile come to a junction with the Upper Lake Trail. If content for the day, head right to return to your car, reaching it in 0.2 mile. Otherwise, head left and gently climb above the lake along the rim of the small caldera. At 1 mile, a trail approaches from the right from the walk-in campground. Continue left, ignoring numerous side trails. Enjoy big trees but not much viewing of the lake below. Scenic viewpoints marked on park maps may have provided views years ago, but the vegetative understory has since claimed the vistas. Come in October,

however, and enjoy the vine maples adding a little color to the heavily forested landscape.

The trail tops out at about 720 feet before steadily dropping back to lake level. Be sure to veer left at a T-intersection (right goes to the campground), soon coming back to the Lower Lake Trail. Return right for 0.35 mile to your vehicle.

EXTENDING YOUR TRIP

Spend a night in the park's car campground, walk-in campground, or cabins. Feel free to hike the park's equestrian trails, but be sure your dog is under strict control and yield right-of-way to any horse riders you encounter.

6 Lewisville Regional Park

RATING/ DIFFICULTY	LOOP	ELEV GAIN/ HIGH POINT	SEASON
**/1	2.5 miles	200 feet/ 310 feet	Year-round

Maps: USGS Battle Ground, trail map from Vancouver–Clark County Parks website; **Contact:** Vancouver–Clark County Parks, (360) 619-1111, www.cityofvancouver.us /parks-recreation; **Notes:** $3 day-use fee. Wheelchair accessible. Dogs permitted on-leash; **GPS:** N 45 49.065 W 122 32.487

Developed in 1936 by the Works Progress Administration (WPA), Lewisville is Clark County's oldest park. Graced with sprawling lawns, manicured grounds, and log picnic pavilions, it's also one of the county's more delightful and well-liked parks, especially popular with families and folks hosting get-togethers, reunions, and celebrations. But the park has natural elements too—old-growth conifer

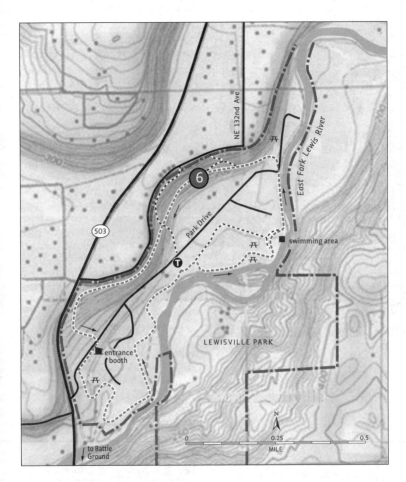

groves and more than a mile of frontage on the free-flowing East Fork Lewis River. A lovely loop trail helps you enjoy them.

GETTING THERE

From Vancouver, head north on I-5 to exit 11 and then follow State Route 502 east for 6 miles to Battle Ground (alternatively, take exit 30 on I-205 and follow SR 500 east for 1.4 miles; then take SR 503 north 7.7 miles to the junction with SR 502). From the junction of SR 502 and SR 503, continue north on SR 503 for 2.1 miles, turning right into the park just after the bridge over the East Fork Lewis River. Follow the main park road past the entrance booth for 0.5 mile to a large parking

Old-growth firs line the way.

lot near a small covered bridge (elev. 165 ft). Privy available.

ON THE TRAIL

While you can access the loop trail from numerous areas in the park, this parking lot is a good place to start, allowing you to shorten the loop if desired by using the nature trail. Pick up the loop trail just to the south and head left (east), following alongside the rippling East Fork Lewis River. Skirt a swimming area—or feel free to soak if passing by on a warm summer's day. Then, skirt some ball fields and come to the park road at 0.5 mile.

The trail resumes on the other side of the road. Here, beneath a canopy of big Douglas-firs, the trail makes a short climb to a bench (elev. 310 ft) above the river floodplain. Ignore a side trail on the right and continue on a rolling course through majestic forest. At 1 mile come to a junction. The nature trail on the left heads back to your vehicle. The right-hand trail heads to a road. Go straight to continue the loop.

After more short climbs and dips, at 1.4 miles the trail reaches the main park road near the caretaker's home. Turn right (west) and walk the road for a few hundred feet, picking up the trail near the park entrance sign. The way then drops back to the floodplain, passing a couple of picnic pavilions. Make a sharp right, crossing a channel that may or may not be flowing, to an area that may or may not be an island. The trail meets up once more with the river, following the beautiful waterway upstream. Look for eagles in the tall timber lining the riverbank.

After once again crossing a channel, make a sharp right and soon reach your vehicle, completing the 2.5-mile loop. You can now see why area walkers and runners return to this park day after day.

7 Moulton Falls

RATING/ DIFFICULTY	ROUND-TRIP	ELEV GAIN/ HIGH POINT	SEASON
**/1	6 miles	200 feet/ 660 feet	Year-round

Maps: USGS Dole, USGS Yacolt, trail map from Vancouver–Clark County Parks website; **Contact:** Vancouver–Clark County Parks, (360) 619-1111, www.cityofvancouver.us/parks-recreation; **Notes:** Wheelchair accessible. Dogs permitted on-leash; **GPS:** N 45 50.265 W 122 26.081

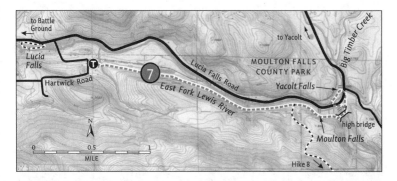

The showy centerpiece of a sprawling green-belt along the East Fork Lewis River, *Moulton Falls County Park contains big rapids, big trees, and a big bridge over an impressive chasm. While these charming features can easily be reached by a series of short trails, this hike allows you to get a good workout and build up anticipation. Following a nearly level trail through deep timber along the East Fork Lewis River, this hike is a delight any time of year but especially in winter, when the river runs high.*

GETTING THERE

From Vancouver, head north on I-5 to exit 11 and then follow State Route 502 east for 6 miles to Battle Ground. Turn left onto SR 503 and drive north for 5.6 miles, turning right onto Rock Creek Road (which eventually becomes Lucia Falls Road). Continue east for 5.3 miles, turning right onto Hartwick Road (the turnoff is 0.3 mile past Lucia Falls County Park). Follow Hartwick Road for 0.5 mile to the trailhead (elev. 550 ft). Privy available.

ON THE TRAIL

Starting in the Cascades east of Silver Star Mountain, the East Fork Lewis River flows westward through the heart of Clark County on its way to the Lewis River at Woodland. An important salmon river, the East Fork is also coveted by recreationists. Most of its western watershed is within the Gifford Pinchot National Forest. Its eastern reaches have been the focus of a county-driven greenbelt, and a good portion of the 3-mile stretch between Lucia and Moulton falls is contained within this greenway. This hike takes you along that stretch.

From the Hartwick Road trailhead, the way starts out paved, descending slightly into a forest of mature evergreens and mossy maples and crossing over a nice little creek. At 0.8 mile, the pavement ends at a picnic area on a small alder-lined pond (elev. 550 ft). Continue hiking, and in another 0.5 mile the paralleling railroad tracks, used by the Chelatchie Prairie Railroad, cross the river on a trestle.

The trail now parallels the lovely river. While the opposite riverbank sports numerous cabins, the surroundings on this side are still fairly wild, the trail marching through thick forest beneath ledges and steep hillside. Pass numerous rapids and cross several side creeks, which cascade in winter rains. Admire big cedars, too, and watch for dippers below and kingfishers above.

Moulton Falls' high arched bridge

At 2.3 miles, come to the junction with the Bells Mountain Trail (Hike 8). Just beyond are Moulton Falls, a low-lying series of rapids that plunge over a rocky shelf. While hardly qualifying as a waterfall, they are pretty nonetheless and pretty popular in the summer months for lounging around.

The trail continues upstream, passing a picnic spot before approaching a high arched bridge (elev. 630 ft) over the East Fork at 2.7 miles. On the far side of the bridge, a trail loops right, providing nice glimpses into the chasm that cradles the rocky river below.

The main trail continues, dropping to a junction. Left goes to river level, past a popular swimming hole and to the park's main parking area (and alternative start). The trail right climbs to the park's upper parking lot (elev. 660 ft) and then continues, crossing Lucia

Falls Road to a beautiful waterfall (locally known as Yacolt Falls) on Big Timber Creek.

Cross the creek on a metal swinging bridge (closed in winter) and loop around 0.3 mile to the main parking area (elev. 570 ft). Return to the main trail and retrace your steps back to the start.

EXTENDING YOUR TRIP

Visit Lucia Falls (county park) downstream and Sunset Falls (U.S. Forest Service) upstream while in the area. Both areas have small nature trails, and Sunset Falls offers nice car camping.

8 Bells Mountain

RATING/ DIFFICULTY	ROUND-TRIP	ELEV GAIN/ HIGH POINT	SEASON
**/3	6.5 miles	1140 feet/ 1600 feet	Year-round

Maps: USGS Dole, USGS Yacolt., trail map from Vancouver–Clark County Parks website; **Contact:** Washington DNR, Pacific Cascade Region (Castle Rock), (360) 577-2025, www.dnr.wa.gov, and Vancouver–Clark County Parks, www.cityofvancouver.us/parks-recreation; **GPS:** N 45 49.901 W 122 23.354

  Not many hikers chime in on the virtues of Bells Mountain, namely because they've yet to strike out for it. But after taking this well-built trail through pretty forest to a series of excellent viewpoints, they'll soon be ringing in the virtues of this trail, one of the best kept secrets in Clark County.

GETTING THERE

From Vancouver, head north on I-5 to exit 11 and then follow State Route 502 east for 6 miles to Battle Ground (alternatively, take exit 30 on I-205 and follow SR 500 east for 1.4 miles; then take SR 503 north 7.7 miles to the junction with SR 502). Turn left onto SR 503 and drive north 5.6 miles, turning right onto Rock Creek Road (which eventually becomes Lucia Falls Road). Continue east for 8.1 miles to Moulton Falls County Park (elev. 570 ft). If the parking area is full, proceed to the upper parking lot 0.3 mile farther. Privy available.

ON THE TRAIL

Starting at popular Moulton Falls County Park, follow the trail taking off east and paralleling the road. Cross Big Timber Creek and pass through a picnic area. At 0.2 mile, bear right at a junction with a trail that accesses the upper parking area. Just a little bit farther, come to the high arched bridge (elev. 630 ft) spanning the East Fork Lewis River at a dramatic chasm. Continue right at a junction past the bridge on a wide trail, heading

downriver and passing another picnic area. Catch some good views of Moulton Falls before coming to the junction (elev. 580 ft) with the Bells Mountain Trail at 0.7 mile.

The main trail continues along the East Fork Lewis River for 2.3 miles (Hike 7) and makes for a great rainy-day leg stretcher. Your objective is the Bells Mountain Trail to the left, announced with a fancy granite signpost stating its national recreation trail status. Part of the Chinook Trail (see "Circling the Gorge" on page 63), this work in progress will eventually tie together more than 300 miles of trail on a circuitous route within and near the Columbia River Gorge National Scenic Area.

Dense forest covers Bells Mountain's lower slopes.

Leaving the river valley, the Bells Mountain Trail steadily climbs through a luxuriant forest of maturing conifers swaddled in mosses and ferns. At 0.9 mile, cross a cascading creek. At about 1.2 miles the grade eases somewhat. Soon after that, come to the first trail-distance signpost. These mark half-mile increments, and this first one seems a tad bit off.

At 1.7 miles, ignore a side trail that leads right. Continue climbing. Crossing several creeks (all nicely bridged), let the sound of cascading water coupled with the song of the winter wren help soften your grind.

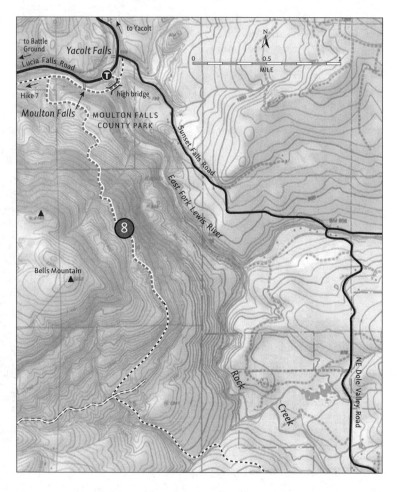

CIRCLING THE GORGE

At the start of the Bells Mountain Trail, an inscribed stone celebrates the designation of 29 miles of the Chinook Trail between Lucia Falls and Bluff Mountain as a national recreation trail. It's a designation that recognizes exemplary trails of local and regional significance. The trail was the brainchild of the Vancouver-based Chinook Trail Association, founded in the 1990s to advocate for the development of a 300-mile two-state rim-top loop trail around the Columbia River Gorge. To make this trail a reality, the volunteer association works closely with the federal, state, and local governments that manage the public lands the trail crosses. While only a small portion of the trail has been developed, the dream has not faded. Many of the original members of the association are getting up there in miles and need fresh blood to help make what would become a spectacular long-distance trail a reality. Countless day-hiking opportunities would also be created by following portions of the Chinook Trail and its feeder trails. The association recently reopened a historic trail in Beacon Rock State Park and developed a new one in the park, helping to move the envisioned 300-mile Chinook Trail a little closer to reality.

At 2.5 miles, come to the first viewpoint (elev. 1600 ft). Okay, it's an old clear-cut, but what a view! Mount Saint Helens hovers above a sea of scrappy green peaks, while directly below is the Dole Valley, a part of Clark County that time (and developers) have forgotten.

Continue farther along the trail, returning to forest and then once again clear-cut—this one provides even better views, with Silver Star and Larch Mountain stealing the show. Feel free to continue to yet another clear-cut (elev. 1540 ft) and more excellent views, at 3.25 miles. This is a good place to turn around—beyond, the trail descends into thick forest.

The immediate landscape that you are staring at, including Bells Mountain (the 2223-foot summit is to your west), is all part of the Yacolt Burn State Forest. In 1902, nearly a quarter million acres of this forest went up in flames, the worst forest fire in Washington's history (see "Burning Down the Forest" in the Silver Star Scenic Area sec-

tion). In 1929 the Dole Valley Fire consumed another 150,000 acres. Today, even with the clear-cuts, this area looks remarkably different (and better!).

EXTENDING YOUR TRIP

If you can arrange for a car shuttle, continue on the Bells Mountain Trail for another 5 miles, dropping into a deep gorge before skirting Spotted Deer Mountain and dropping (once more) to follow Cold Creek. The trail ends at the Tarbell Trail, from which it's just under a mile to your awaiting second vehicle at either DNR Road L1200 or DNR Road L1000N.

9 Lacamas Heritage Trail

RATING/ DIFFICULTY	ROUND-TRIP	ELEV GAIN/ HIGH POINT	SEASON
**/1	7 miles	Minimal/ 180 feet	Year-round

Maps: USGS Camas, USGS Lacamas Creek, trail map from Vancouver–Clark County

Trail hugs the shoreline of pretty Lacamas Lake.

Parks website; **Contact:** Vancouver–Clark County Parks, (360) 619-1111, www.cityof vancouver.us/parks-recreation; **Notes:** Wheelchair accessible. Dogs permitted on-leash; **GPS:** N 45 36.325 W 122 24.663

Teeming with walkers, runners, and hikers, rain or shine year-round, this wonderful trail runs along the full length of slender Lacamas Lake and beside the creek of the same name feeding into it. While the surrounding hills have exploded with subdivisions over the past two decades, surprisingly much of Lacamas Lake's shoreline remains undeveloped. This trail captures Clark County's fading rural heritage, giving cause to celebrate recent conservation victories within the Lacamas Creek watershed and to lament the otherwise continuing suburbanization.

GETTING THERE

From Vancouver, head east on State Route 14 for 12 miles, taking exit 12 into Camas. Follow signs for Business SR 14, coming to a junction with SR 500 South (NE Dallas Street) in 1.6 miles. Continue straight for 0.2 mile to a junction with SR 500 North (NE Garfield Street). Turn left and follow SR 500 for 1.3 miles, turning left onto NW Lake Road. Come to the Lacamas Heritage trailhead (elev. 180 ft) in 0.3 mile. Privy available.

ON THE TRAIL

From the manicured picnic grounds, pick up the Lacamas Heritage Trail heading northwest. Paved for its first 0.25 mile, the trail winds around some trailers before becoming soft surface at Lacamas Lake's eastern end. Prepare now for a visual treat. While the trail parallels Lake Road, it's positioned below the embankment in an attractive forest of oak, fir, and maple, giving you the feeling of being far removed from suburbia.

Winding through attractive forested groves, the trail hugs the lakeshore. Nearly the entire way is shaded, but there are plenty of good viewpoints of and over the lake. And while nearly zero elevation is gained from the trail's start to its end, the route is full of lots of little bumps and dips, making it especially fun for running.

At 0.6 mile a spur climbs left to a housing development. At 1.3 miles reach a boat launch and play area. Turn left on pavement and immediately find the trail's continuation, heading right. Avoid a spur that leads left to a subdivision of megahomes, and after skirting a few showy residences the way returns to a more natural and attractive setting.

Now travel beneath big firs, across wetlands of dogwood, and along the snaking and duck-dabbling Lacamas Creek. The woodlands across the attractive and easily paddled waterway belong to Camp Currie.

The 249-acre youth camp was founded in the 1940s and recently protected from development thanks to Clark County's Conservation Futures Open Space Program.

After crossing a third bridge at about 2.7 miles, the trail once again leaves a natural setting to skirt a golf course, road, and church camp. Call it quits here, or continue another 0.8 mile to the NE Goodwin Road trailhead. The walking is still good, if the scenery is somewhat less than pastoral.

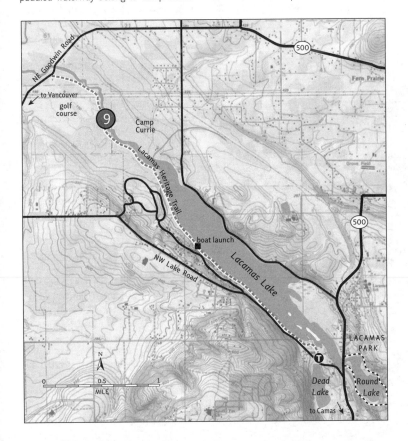

10 Lacamas Park

RATING/ DIFFICULTY	LOOP	ELEV GAIN/ HIGH POINT	SEASON
***/2	4.5 miles	350 feet/ 400 feet	Year-round

Maps: USGS Camas, trail map from Vancouver–Clark County Parks website; **Contact:** Vancouver–Clark County Parks, (360) 619-1111, www.cityofvancouver.us/parks-recreation; **Notes:** Partially wheelchair accessible. Dogs permitted on-leash; **GPS:** N 45 35.357 W 122 23.506

Lacamas Creek cascades through Lacamas Park.

 *An incredibly wild and diverse 312-acre preserve within the city limits of Camas, Lacamas Park contains more than 6 miles of excellent trails. A gift to the people of Clark County from the Crown Zellerbach Company in 1964, the park contains a lake, several waterfalls, and gorgeous old-growth forest—and a bluff that blossoms with the park's namesake, la camas. That's what the French Canadians of the Hudson's Bay Company called these violet blue flowers of the Camassia genus. The area's First Peoples called them quamash. Most call them camas. I call them simply beautiful.*

GETTING THERE

From Vancouver, head east on State Route 14 for 12 miles, taking exit 12 into Camas. Follow signs for Business SR 14, coming to a junction with SR 500 South (NE Dallas Street) in 1.6 miles. Continue straight for 0.2 mile to a junction with SR 500 North (NE Garfield Street). Proceed on Business SR 14 straight for 0.4 mile, turning left (just before the bridge over Lacamas Creek) to the trailhead (elev. 50 ft). Privy available.

ON THE TRAIL

This recommended lollipop loop captures the park's finest features while making for a good half-day hike. Feel free to shorten or lengthen your adventure. Follow a good trail away and above Lacamas Creek, passing through nice stands of mature maple and fir. At 0.3 mile ignore a side trail taking off left for a neighborhood. At 0.6 mile arrive at a picnic area beside a beautiful cascade (Lower Falls) on Lacamas Creek (elev. 100 ft). Cross above the frothing plunging water by way of a long and sturdy bridge, coming to a junction.

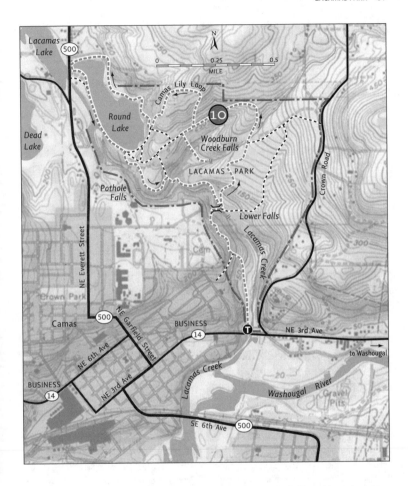

The trail on the left will be your return. The trail to the right is a primitive path along the creek. Head up the trail (actually an old road) straight, and after 0.1 mile come to a junction with the Lower Falls Shortcut. Head left here on real trail, climbing through patches of old growth and coming back to the old road after 0.5 mile.

Continue left on the old road, dipping slightly to cross Woodburn Creek on a wide bridge. After about 0.3 mile on this road, come to a junction with the Camas Lily Loop (elev. 325 ft). You'll be following it right—but before tiptoeing through the camas fields, consider a side trip to pretty little Woodburn Creek Falls. Continue on the road for a short distance, taking an unmarked but obvious side trail left. Follow this good path for about 0.3 mile, losing 75 feet or so to the small fanned falls in a hidden ravine. Retreat back to the Camas Lily Loop.

Now follow this hiker-only trail (snarl at any mountain bikers who ignore this rule and threaten this rare and delicate ecosystem) for 0.5 mile, climbing onto a rocky bluff (elev. 400 ft) adorned with stunted oaks and fields of camas. This once-abundant flower in the Northwest usually displays its showy blossoms in April and May. At the west end of the bluff, the trail splits. Veer right, rapidly losing elevation and coming to a junction with another road trail. Now head right, continuing to lose elevation to Round Lake.

The road trail reaches the lake (elev. 190 ft) and continues north along its murky waters. Ringed by tall timber, the placid waters often reflect the trees quite nicely. The road trail ends at Leonard Road. Turn left, taking the sidewalk a short distance to Everett Street (SR 500). Turn left again and follow the sidewalk across Lacamas Creek, coming to the busy main entrance to Lacamas Park (alternative starting point).

Now follow a paved path through picnic grounds along Round Lake's western shore, coming to a dam in about 0.25 mile. Cross the dam, admiring the silvery string of cascading water spilling over it. The road trail continues left, circling the lake. Take a side trail right instead, to follow along Lacamas Creek high above on a bluff. Reach a good overlook of small but impressive Pothole Falls.

Continue right (ignoring side trails that lead left) on the Lower Falls Trail, traveling across a ledgy area blossoming with camas in midspring before dropping into a dank mossy ravine that sports impressive old-growth cedars, yews, and Doug-firs. Con-

tinue losing elevation, following tumbling Lacamas Creek. Look for dippers prodding the frothing water. Continue along, crossing Woodburn Creek before returning to the familiar long bridge at the Lower Falls. Turn right, retracing the stem of the lollipop loop. Your vehicle is 0.6 mile away.

EXTENDING YOUR TRIP
Check out the nearby Washougal River Greenway Trail (access is off of NE 3rd Avenue). Currently, about a mile of trail is in place. Eventually this trail will tie in to the Lacamas Heritage Trail.

11 Cottonwood Beach– East Dike Trail

RATING/ DIFFICULTY	ROUND-TRIP	ELEV GAIN/ HIGH POINT	SEASON
**/1	7 miles	10 feet/ 20 feet	Year-round

Maps: USGS Washougal, trail map from Vancouver–Clark County Parks website; **Contact:** Vancouver–Clark County Parks, (360) 619-1111, www.cityofvancouver.us /parks-recreation; **Notes:** Wheelchair accessible. Dogs permitted on-leash; **GPS:** N 45 34.081 W 122 20.365

Follow this nearly flat trail for more than 3 miles along the Columbia River from the old river town of Washougal to the wildlife saturated sloughs of Steigerwald Lake National Wildlife Refuge. Transition from the eastern edge of Clark County's urban sprawl to the emerald gates of the Columbia River Gorge National Scenic Area. En route pass historical relics and sites and through pastures granting spectacular vistas of snowy Mount Hood hovering over verdant Reed Island.

GETTING THERE

From Vancouver, head east on State Route 14 for 16 miles, turning right at milepost 16 onto 15th Street into Steamboat Landing Park (elev. 10 ft). Privy available. Alternative trailheads and parking can be accessed from Front and Index Streets.

ON THE TRAIL

On an extensive dike, the trail immediately heads east along the Columbia River. But before heading upriver, check out the floating dock for an excellent view up and down the river. Here, too, see well-weathered pilings, the remains of an old dock that once serviced steam paddle-wheel boats from the 1880s until 1916.

You can follow the dock back to the main trail for a small loop. Just beyond is a new trail leading left under SR 14, connecting the East Dike Trail to Washougal's historical downtown. Continue straight,

Enjoy easy, level hiking on the East Dike Trail.

passing observation decks and interpretive displays. At 1 mile come to Recognition Plaza in the Captain William Clark Park, complete with its replica dug-out canoes and plaques recognizing donors who helped make this wonderful park a reality.

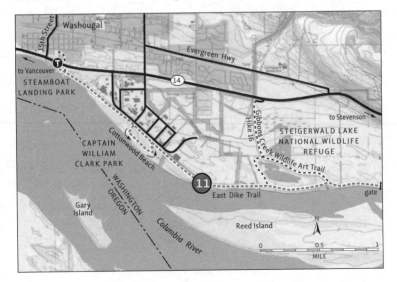

Continue straight on the East Dike Trail, or head right for a slightly longer loop option delivering you to lovely Cottonwood Beach. Lewis and Clark camped at the beach for six days from March 31 to April 6, 1806, on their return trip east. From this campsite, Captain Clark, led by a Native guide, "discovered" the Multnomah (later to be named Willamette) River. Earlier, the Corps of Discovery had missed the river as they traveled up and down the Columbia.

Cottonwood's sandy beaches can be walked for over a mile. And while it's located 125 miles inland from the Pacific Ocean, the Columbia here is still tidal, its water levels fluctuating throughout the day.

The Cottonwood Beach Loop Trail rejoins the East Dike Trail 0.25 mile east of the Recognition Plaza. Continue hiking upriver, entering the Steigerwald Lake National Wildlife Refuge after another 0.15 mile. The trail now traverses a more pastoral landscape across farmland and along rows of giant cottonwoods. After another 1.1 miles (2.5 miles from trailhead), come to the west junction with the Gibbons Creek Wildlife Art Trail (Hike 16).

Continue east on the main trail, passing the east junction of the Gibbons Creek Wildlife Art Trail after another half mile. The East Dike Trail continues for another 0.5 mile, ending at a gate marking the refuge's eastern boundary. Soak up excellent views of Crown Point and Mount Hood across the river and Reed Island in the river. Five-hundred-acre Reed Island is protected as a Washington State Park and offers excellent camping and wildlife observing. You'll need your own watercraft to get there. So best now to turn around and retreat back to the trailhead.

GETTING TO THE "CORPS" OF DISCOVERY

Any hiker taking to the trails and parks along the shores of the Columbia River will not only be bombarded with beautiful scenery but also with memorials, interpretive displays, and artifacts commemorating the Lewis and Clark expedition, called the Corps of Discovery. Departing Saint Louis in the spring of 1804, Meriwether Lewis and William Clark, accompanied by a black slave named York, the fur trapper Toussaint Charbonneau, and his young Shoshone wife Sacagawea and their infant son, led the party of thirty-three across the continent to the Pacific and back. Commissioned by President Thomas Jefferson, the expedition's mission was to explore the newly acquired Louisiana Purchase. They first entered what would become Washington State in the autumn of 1805, following the Snake River to the Columbia and then to that huge river's mouth on the Pacific, where they wintered at Fort Clatsop in what would later become Oregon. They returned along the Columbia in the spring of 1806, further exploring the river, its tributaries, and its environs. Their findings would later help encourage American settlement, enabling the Oregon Country to become U.S. soil in 1846. As you hike the shores of the Columbia, take time to learn more about these fascinating explorers and their most amazing journey.

Opposite: Ed's Trail with Mount St. Helens in background

silver star scenic area

Named for its starlike radiating ridges, 4390-foot Silver Star Mountain straddles the Clark–Skamania county line less than 25 miles from Vancouver. Centerpiece of a 10,000-plus-acre roadless area managed by the Gifford National Forest and Washington Department of Natural Resources, the mountain and its environs were heavily forested until 1902, when the nearly 250,000-acre Yacolt Burn consumed most of its timber. With the fire having radically altered the region's environment, the lofty peak and its satellites now harbor some of the finest wildflower meadows in the Cascades. Crisscrossed with old jeep tracks, since closed and converted to trails, the area once the domain of four-wheelers is now welcoming to families and nature enthusiasts who admire outstanding vistas and spectacular floral shows. Home to the threatened Larch Mountain salamander and historical Native American vision quest sites, Silver Star shines with surprises and excellent hiking opportunities.

12 Larch Mountain

RATING/ DIFFICULTY	ROUND-TRIP	ELEV GAIN/ HIGH POINT	SEASON
***/3	5.6 miles	1150 feet/ 3496 feet	Year-round

Maps: USGS Larch Mountain, trail map from Washington DNR website; **Contact:** Washington DNR, Pacific Cascade Region (Castle Rock), (360) 577-2025, www.dnr.wa.gov; **GPS:** N 45 43.302 W 122 16.168

Larch Mountain provides excellent views of nearby Silver Star Mountain.

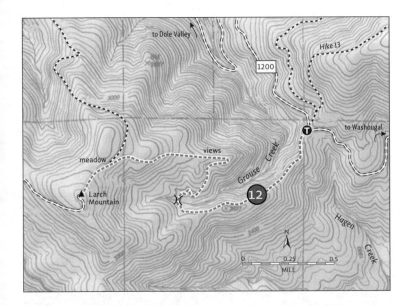

Though this is the highest peak that sits entirely within Clark County, not many hikers find their way to its summit. Shadowed by adjacent Silver Star Mountain, Larch lacks that well-loved mountain's sprawling flower arrangements—but also its crowds. And while Larch's summit is marred by towers, the way up is pleasant enough with attractive forests, fields of bear grass, and some pretty good views of Silver Star too.

GETTING THERE

From Vancouver, head east on State Route 14, turning left (at milepost 16) onto the Washougal River Road. Follow this winding road for just shy of 7 miles, turning left onto NE Hughes Road (signed for Bear Prairie). Continue on this main arterial for 3.2 miles and turn left onto the Skamania Mines Road (just before the county line). The pavement ends at 1.3 miles. After another 1.4 miles, bear left. And 0.1 mile beyond that, bear left again onto DNR Road 1200. Follow this narrow and bumpy road (passable for cars, but the last 2 miles are a little rough) for 5.7 miles to the trailhead at a small pass (elev. 2400 ft). While the trailhead can be reached from the north via Dole Valley, it is unadvisable due to the rugged nature of that road.

ON THE TRAIL

While everyone heads east to Silver Star (Hikes 13 and 14), head west on the Tarbell Trail, which at first follows an old jeep track. Nature and man have not been kind to this area over the past 100 years. In 1902, Larch went up in flames. And while the forest has returned (and is periodically harvested), much of the state forest housing Larch Mountain has been ravaged by both legal and illegal off-road-vehicle use. The Tarbell Trail is now officially closed to motor vehicles, but a handful of scofflaws continue to do what they please. And to make things worse, the governor and legislature has left DNR no money to patrol and manage this trail. Report all offenders to DNR and write a letter to your legislator demanding that critical funding for trails be reinstated.

The way steadily climbs along a ridge crest. Sounds of industry can be heard on the left, while the soothing sound of nature—particularly babbling Grouse Creek—drifts in on the right. At 0.4 mile, bear left. While most of the way follows old roads, the tread is smooth and mostly free of rocks, unlike Silver Star's old roads.

After a short, steep climb and then a drop, the way skirts a clear-cut where good views of Mount Hood and Oregon's Larch Mountain can be seen. Just like on that other Larch Mountain, there are no larches on this peak either—early loggers referred to noble firs as larches.

At about 1 mile, ignore a side trail that heads right. Shortly afterward, bear right. The way should be signed—stay on the Tarbell Trail. At 1.2 miles, in an attractive grove of mature timber, cross Grouse Creek (elev. 2800 ft) on a big bridge. Then, after passing by shrubby vine maple patches (pretty in fall), emerge at 1.7 miles on a bear-grass-rimmed ridge (elev. 2975 ft) above a big talus slope and find excellent views of Silver Star Mountain, the Dole Valley, and Mount Saint Helens in the distance. This is the highlight of this hike. Feel free to call it quits here.

But if you're summit bound, continue another 0.7 mile along pleasant trail lined with ferns and bear grass to a signed junction (elev. 3300 ft). Head left on a rocky path for 0.4 mile, passing a spur on the right to a sprawling bear grass meadow. Arrive at the 3496-foot summit, where towers and a road greet you. Some good views to Portland and Vancouver can be had by walking a short way west down a jeep track—then make your way back to that bear grass meadow for lunch.

EXTENDING YOUR TRIP

If you can arrange a car shuttle, for a variation on the return continue on the Tarbell Trail northwest for 5 miles, following alongside Cold Creek to DNR Road L1000 near the Larch Corrections Center. DNR-supervised work crews from this minimum-security facility provide such services as trail construction and park maintenance.

13 Silver Star via Pyramid and Sturgeon Rocks

RATING/ DIFFICULTY	ROUND-TRIP	ELEV GAIN/ HIGH POINT	SEASON
****/3	8.3 miles	2200 feet/ 4390 feet	May–Nov

Maps: Green Trails Bridal Veil No. 428, trail map from Washington DNR website, www.dnr.wa.gov; **Contact:** Gifford Pinchot National Forest, Mount Adams Ranger District, Trout Lake, (509) 395-3400, www.fs.fed.us/gpnf; **GPS:** N 45 43.304 W 122 16.165

Follow an old road on a gentle odyssey to southwestern Washington's supreme floral gardens. Traverse slope upon slope of mountainside that was scorched clean of greenery a century ago, leaving in the flames' wake an alpine wonderland of brilliant blossoms and bountiful berries. Now sustaining habitat for a bevy of foraging beasties, Silver Star's open slopes also provide some of the best viewing anywhere. From Hood to Rainier, Adams to downtown Portland—and everything in between.

GETTING THERE

From Vancouver, head east on State Route 14, turning left (at milepost 16) onto the Washougal River Road. Follow this winding road for just shy of 7 miles, turning left onto NE Hughes Road (signed for Bear Prairie). Continue on this main arterial for 3.2 miles and turn left onto the Skamania Mines Road (just before the county line). The pavement ends at 1.3 miles. After another 1.4 miles, bear left. And 0.1 mile beyond that, bear left again onto DNR Road 1200. Follow this narrow and bumpy road (passable for cars, but the last 2 miles are a little rough) for 5.7 miles to the trailhead at a small pass (elev. 2400 ft). While the trailhead can be reached from the north via Dole Valley, it is unadvisable due to the rugged nature of that road.

ON THE TRAIL

The way starts on the Tarbell Trail, a 24-mile, multiuse, nonmotorized loop trail. Head east on it, coming to a junction in 0.1 mile. The Tarbell Trail continues left (north). You'll be returning on it. Continue right, following the Grouse Vista Trail, which like many of Silver Star's trails was once an old 4x4 road. The Forest Service began closing the mountain to motorized use in the 1960s, completely phasing it out by the 1980s. Unfortunately, some illegal off-roading still exists, and the mountain is marred with many roads and tracks from this less-than-environmentally sound policy of the past. While the roads generally now make good

Good views of Little Baldy from the Indian Pits

wide trails with mostly decent grades, they are often plagued with loose rocks, so take care not to twist an ankle.

After climbing steeply for about 0.5 mile, the grade eases—and soon forest cover yields to shrubs, then yielding to rocky flowery open slopes. Bear grass, penstemon, sunflower, paintbrush, lupine, parsley, phlox—the list goes on!

At 1.4 miles, bear left at a junction (elev. 3300 ft). The old road right leads around the back end of clearly visible 3442-foot Pyramid Rock. Descend slightly about 50 feet to skirt beneath the impressive landmark, crossing a talus slope in the process. The climb steepens again, and you soon encounter a cool pocket of silver firs. At 2.3 miles reach a junction (elev. 3830 ft) with the Silver Star Trail. Right heads down the south ridge, a lonely and lovely alternative approach. You want to veer left, coming to a four-way junction (elev. 4050 ft) at 2.8 miles.

Departing left is the old Silver Road, your return route after reaching the summit. Branching right is the Indian Pits Trail, an intriguing and worthwhile side trip (see Extending Your Trip). For now, continue straight, reaching yet another junction in 0.1 mile. The Silver Star Trail continues north (see Hike 14). You want to proceed right for 0.3 mile to the 4390-foot summit, once topped by a fire tower. The view is superb! North to Rainier and Saint Helens. East to Lookout, the Trapper Creek Wilderness, and Indian Heaven peaks. South to majestic Mount Hood and the Gorge landmarks Tanner, Larch, Nesmith, and more. And west to the Portland–Vancouver metropolitan area sitting so close to the wilderness fringe.

Venture on over to the south summit too, and then return to the four-way junction. Now follow the old Silver Road through forest on a rutted, eroded track at first, then reaching much better tread. Pass a side trail on the right and skirt beneath the 4100-foot basalt outcropping, Sturgeon Rock (Clark County's high point).

After following this trail for 1.4 miles, intersect the Tarbell Trail (elev. 3100 ft). Head left (south) on this pleasant, generally forested path, crossing several side creeks before crossing Rock Creek near a small cascade on a solid bridge (elev. 2600 ft) in 1.4 miles. The way then dips and climbs, several times crossing openings granting views to Pyramid and Sturgeon rocks and reaching the Grouse Vista Trail after 1.8 miles. Turn right to reach the trailhead.

EXTENDING YOUR TRIP

One option is to follow the Tarbell Trail north from Silver Road for 2 miles to pretty

BURNING DOWN THE FOREST

On September 11, 1902, the Yacolt Burn, the largest forest fire in Washington's history, broke out. The cause of the conflagration was never determined, but loggers burning slash in the Wind River valley may have contributed to it. Fanned by unusually dry winds, the fire quickly spread, darkening the skies and dropping more than half an inch of ash on Portland. Smoke reached Seattle, and many thought that Mount Saint Helens or Mount Rainier had erupted. In three days the fire scorched more than 238,000 acres and killed thirty-eight people in Clark, Cowlitz, and Skamania Counties. A forest ranger who had recently been reprimanded for employing a fire crew took no action, fearing he would be disciplined again. Rains eventually put out the blaze. Consequently, the following year, the Washington State legislature established a state fire warden. In 1910, after the Great Fire scorched more than 3 million acres of Inland Northwest and northern Rockies forest (see Timothy Egan's *The Big Burn*), the U.S. Forest Service under President Taft was transformed into a much larger and organized agency and actively began fire-suppression programs. Almost all of the Silver Star Scenic Area and lands east toward the Wind River valley were touched by the Yacolt Burn of 1902 and still show signs of that epic fire.

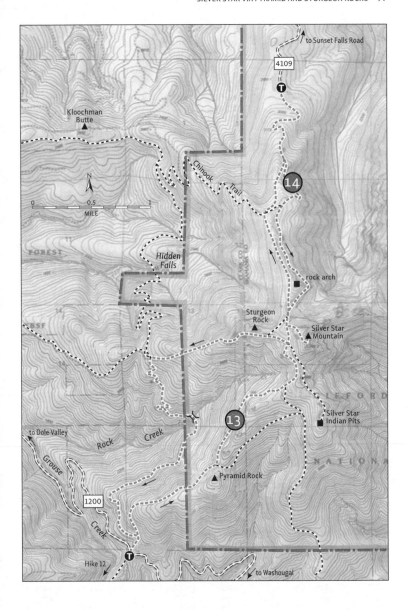

Hidden Falls. Another is to take the Indian Pits Trail 0.8 mile on an up-and-down course (gaining and losing 500 cumulative feet) to an outstanding arrangement of rock pits once used by young Native Americans for vision quests. When clouds are swirling, the place is ethereal. Enjoy but don't disturb this important archeological site.

14 Silver Star via North Ridge

RATING/ DIFFICULTY	ROUND-TRIP	ELEV GAIN/ HIGH POINT	SEASON
*****/3	5 miles	1440 feet/ 4390 feet	June–Nov

Maps: Green Trails Lookout Mtn No. 396, Bridal Veil No. 428, trail map from Washington DNR website, www.dnr.wa.gov; **Contact:** Gifford Pinchot National Forest, Mount Adams Ranger District, Trout Lake, (509) 395-3400, www.fs.fed.us/gpnf; **Notes:** FR 4109 is extremely rough, high-clearance vehicles only. Ed's Trail has two short sections requiring use of hands, best to avoid trail in wet conditions.; **GPS:** N 45 46.346 W 122 14.675

The shortest and most popular route to Silver Star's stellar summit, this loop uses one of the mountain's old jeep roads (since converted to trail) and its newest trail (part of the long-distance Chinook Trail). Starting high, almost immediately saunter across sprawling flower gardens set against a backdrop of snowy showy volcanoes. En route, pass through a rock arch and a landscape that looks straight out of the Southwest—except for all of the greenery!

GETTING THERE

From Vancouver, head north on I-5 to exit 11 and then follow State Route 502 east for 6 miles to Battle Ground. Turn left onto SR 503 and drive north 5.6 miles, turning right onto Rock Creek Road (which eventually becomes Lucia Falls Road). Continue east for 8.4 miles and turn right onto Sunset Falls Road. Follow this paved road for 7.3 miles to the Sunset Campground. Turn right onto Forest Road 41, proceeding through the campground to a bridge over the East Fork Lewis River. Turn left and follow the potholed and very rough FR 41 for 3.5 miles. Turn sharply right onto (unmarked) FR 4109, and after 1.5 miles bear left. Continue on this terribly rough road for 2.7 miles to the trailhead at road's end (elev. 3100 ft). It is also possible (and a little less bumpy) to follow DNR Road L1100 from the Dole Valley Road (2.4 miles from Sunset Falls Road) past the Tarbell Campground to FR 4109, turning right to reach the trailhead.

ON THE TRAIL

Thankfully, Silver Star's trails are in better shape than the roads leading to them. From the trailhead kiosk, take the route right (the old road left is rocky and eroded), barreling through a tunnel of shrubby vine maple. At 0.4 mile meet up with the old road, and 500 feet farther come to a junction (elev. 3450 ft). You'll be returning on the old road (Silver Star Trail No. 180) from the right—so veer left onto Ed's Trail, named for Edward Robertson, who passed away in 1994, one of the pioneers of the Chinook Trail Association (see "Circling the Gorge" in the Vancouver and Clark County section).

Traveling along the rim of a small canyon and across meadows of flowers and swaying grasses, parallel the old road, occasionally passing a shortcut spur connecting to it. At 1 mile (elev. 3800 ft), come to an old jeep track (evidence of past off-road abuses allowed on

Rock arch on Ed's Trail

this special mountain) and the Chinook Trail, coming in from the west. Continue straight on Ed's Trail, now part of the Chinook route. Continue climbing across a landscape that re-markably resembles Arizona or Utah—except it's too green!

Skirt above, around, and beneath ledges and knobs, traversing slopes that are

Bear grass dances in the wind on Little Baldy.

mile to the 4390-foot Silver Star summit. Plan on hanging around absorbing views of Hood, Rainier, Saint Helens, Adams and a plethora of minor but equally beautiful peaks and ridges.

When it's time to return, retrace steps 0.4 mile back to the major trail junction and follow the Silver Star Trail No. 180 (the old road) on a gentle descent (after a short 75-foot climb) through meadow upon meadow of brilliant wildflowers. The walking is leisurely and this route isn't as rocky as the roads coming up from the south. Pass the Chinook Trail in 1 mile and reach the beginning of Ed's Trail 0.6 mile farther. Your vehicle is 0.5 mile downhill from there.

EXTENDING YOUR TRIP
Sturgeon Rock (Hike 13), the Indian Pits (Hike 13), and Little Baldy (Hike 15) all make for great extended wanderings.

increasingly steep. At 1.5 miles pass through the trail's highlight landmark, a rock arch that strangely looks like two rock transformer robots butting heads.

Next, a short but very steep section of trail must be negotiated, requiring the use of hands. Just beyond, another short scramble awaits. It's best to avoid this trail in wet conditions. The way now descends about 75 feet before going back up to meet Trail No. 180 (the old road and your return) at a major junction at 2.1 miles. The trail veering southeast is the Bluff Mountain Trail to Little Baldy (Hike 15). The trail veering southwest is a shortcut to the Silver Road Trail and Sturgeon Rock (Hike 13). Head left up the old road and in 0.1 mile reach a junction.

Straight heads to the Indian Pits and Grouse Vista trails (Hike 13). Left leads 0.3

15 Little Baldy

RATING/ DIFFICULTY	ROUND-TRIP	ELEV GAIN/ HIGH POINT	SEASON
*****/3	8.4 miles	1600 feet/ 3940 feet	late-May–Nov

Maps: Green Trails Lookout Mtn No. 396, Bridal Veil No. 428; **Contact:** Gifford Pinchot National Forest, Mount Adams Ranger District, Trout Lake, (509) 395-3400, www .fs.fed.us/gpnf; **Notes:** FR 41 requires high-clearance vehicle; **GPS:** N 45 46.803 W 122 10.019

This is definitely the most spectacular trail within the Silver Star Roadless Area. Nearly the entire way is along a lofty ridge awash in wildflower splendor and exploding with views reaching in every direction. You'll easily fill your memory card trying to capture the nearly 100 flower species painting the way. And you'll stop numerous times, mouth agape, admiring the magnificent volcanoes surrounding you and the mighty Columbia flowing below.

GETTING THERE

From Vancouver, head north on I-5 to exit 11 and then follow State Route 502 east for 6 miles to Battle Ground. Turn left onto SR 503 and drive north 5.6 miles, turning right onto Rock Creek Road (which eventually becomes Lucia Falls Road). Continue east for 8.4 miles and turn right onto Sunset Falls Road. Follow this paved road for 7.3 miles to the Sunset Campground. Turn right onto Forest Road 41, proceeding through the campground to a bridge over the East Fork Lewis River. Turn

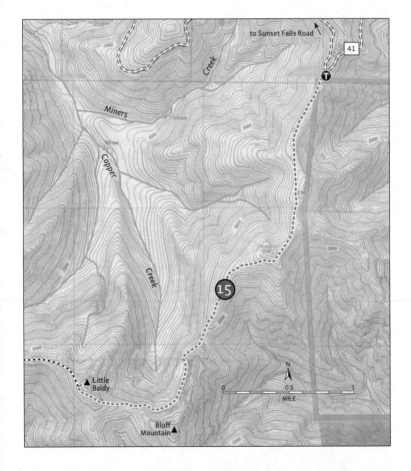

left and follow the potholed and very rough FR 41 for 9 miles to a high saddle. The unsigned trailhead is on the right (elev. 3540 ft).

ON THE TRAIL

As soon as you get out of your car and lace up your boots, your eyes will be fixed on a panorama of peaks for as far as you can see and on a phalanx of flowers too numerous to count. Enjoy a rare glimpse of Lookout Mountain, a locally prominent peak and known by few. Now look over to Silver Star Mountain and trace the ridge before you leading up to it. That's your cloud-catching route!

Begin by following an old jeep track, now the Bluff Mountain Trail, across the century-old Yacolt Burn, which devastated timber stocks but replaced them with fields of flowers. Crest a small knoll and look south to Oregon's Larch Mountain, Benson Plateau, and Nesmith Point. The flowers are profuse: paintbrush, star tulip, harebells, tiger lilies, avalanche lilies, lupine, penstemon, bistort, wooly sunflower, and bear grass. Especially bear grass—it lines the way dancing in the near perpetual breezes.

Continue along the rolling ridge, slightly climbing and dropping. At 1.5 miles reach a 3675-foot knoll and begin dropping. Look for deer and coyote tracks in the soft and rocky roadbed. Deer are profuse in the Silver Star area. At 2.2 miles the old road ends. Bear right, continuing on trail now and dropping, coming to a gap (elev. 3100 ft) swathed in huckleberry bushes at 2.5 miles.

Now resume climbing, crossing a scree slope before rounding some cliffs. Expect to encounter a few rough sections along the way as well as lingering snow patches in early summer. At 3.2 miles, come to a swath of mature forest—a real rarity in the Silver Star highlands. Cross a small creek and continue ascending, traversing yet another scree slope. At 3.6 miles reach a gap (elev. 3600 ft) shrouded in a stand of silver fir. Continuing now on lightly traveled tread, the trail traverses grassy and brushy slopes just beneath the rocky summit of Little Baldy. Before the trail crosses yet another scree slope, head right and carefully pick a route along the ridgeline, reaching Little Baldy's 3940-foot summit in about 0.25 mile.

Juniper and penstemon carpet the peak while a few Native American vision pits pock the high rocky slopes. And the view? It's stupendous! North to Saint Helens and Rainier. East to Lookout and Adams. South to Bluff, Hood, and Portland below. And west to the radiating flowery ridges of Silver Star. Stay long and savor it.

EXTENDING YOUR TRIP

You can continue on the Bluff Mountain Trail west for another 2 miles to Silver Star Mountain (Hikes 13 and 14). If transportation can be arranged and you're feeling adventurous, return via the rarely hiked rough-and-tumble view-packed Stairway Trail.

Opposite: North Bonneville and Ives Island from Beacon Rock

columbia river gorge, washington: west

Classic scenery and dramatic landscapes are what you'll experience in the Columbia River Gorge, a deep canyon cut by the West's mightiest river through one of its largest and most rugged mountain chains. Lacking the abundance of waterfalls streaming down Oregon's western half of the Gorge, Washington's side also lacks many of the crowds that congregate to see those cascades. With a southern exposure, many of the mountain trails here melt out earlier than Oregon's, and the wildflower shows rival or top any in the Beaver State.

Plenty of new trails and new land acquisitions have recently been made here, and almost all of them are easily reached by State Route 14, the old Evergreen Highway, offering a scenic and more relaxed drive than I-84. Charming Stevenson sits at the center of the Gorge in Washington State, home to the excellent Columbia Gorge Interpretive Center and a great base from which to explore. Beacon Rock State Park offers family-friendly camping, and Vancouver's wide array of amenities are less than an hour away from most of these trails.

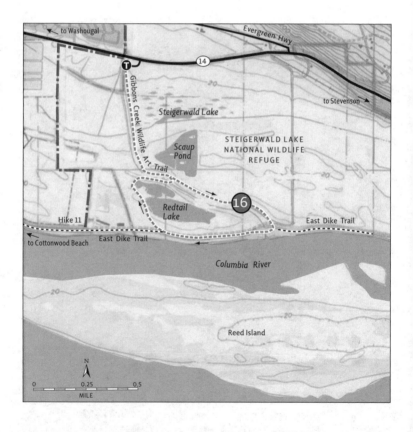

16 Steigerwald Lake National Wildlife Refuge

RATING/ DIFFICULTY	LOOP	ELEV GAIN/ HIGH POINT	SEASON
***/1	2.8 miles	None/ 10 feet	Year-round

Maps: USGS Washougal, trail map from refuge; **Contact:** Ridgefield National Wildlife Refuge Complex, (360) 887-4106, www .fws.gov/ridgefieldrefuges/steigerwaldlake; **Notes:** Wheelchair accessible. Dogs prohibited. Entrance gate open from 6:00 AM to 8:00 PM. Section of trail closed Oct 1–Apr 30 for wildlife protection; **GPS:** N 45 34.222 W 122 18.879

🚶 ♿ ❀ 🏠 *Follow this delightful new loop trail through a rich riparian world of wetland meadows, sloughs, cottonwood breaks, and shallow lakes that teem with birds. Steigerwald Lake National Wildlife Refuge occupies former farmland, now gorgeous open space at the extreme western edge of the Columbia River Gorge National Scenic Area. Here, urban yields to rural, bluffs overshadow floodplain, and a multitude of avian residents pass by, mate, nest, and reside.*

GETTING THERE
From Vancouver, head east on State Route 14 for 18.2 miles, turning right into a large parking area just after entering the Columbia River Gorge National Scenic Area. Privy available.

ON THE TRAIL
Opened in June of 2009, the Gibbons Creek Wildlife Art Trail is a pleasant path that meanders through the 1000-plus-acre Steigerwald Lake National Wildlife Refuge. Created in 1987, the refuge is managed to restore river bottomlands to benefit both resident and migrating birds. One of the unique features of this refuge is its location near the mouth of the Columbia River Gorge, the lowest gap through the Cascade Mountains, allowing birds more associated with the east side of the state to occasionally stray here. Look for kingbirds, phoebes, nighthawks, Lewis's woodpeckers, and burrowing owls. Of course there should be plenty of herons, geese, ducks, and kingfishers on hand for your visit as well.

While designated an art trail (like the one at Willapa National Wildlife Refuge),

Steigerwald Lake NWR protects important floodplain habitat for migrating birds.

ACTING TO SAVE THE GORGE

Though the sign is weathered, faded, and crowded by young trees, most travelers heading east into the Columbia River Gorge along Washington State Route 14 still manage to catch a glimpse of an old billboard protesting the establishment of the Columbia River Gorge National Scenic Area. Establishing the national scenic area was not without its controversies. But with strong backing from both sides of the political aisle, from then-current and former governors of both Washington and Oregon, from all four U.S. senators, and from nearly all congresspeople from both states, President Ronald Reagan signed the act into law on November 17, 1986. It established a national scenic area, the first of its kind, "to protect and enhance the scenic, natural, cultural and recreational resources of the Columbia River Gorge; and to protect and support the economy of the area by encouraging growth to occur in urban areas and allowing future economic development consistent with resource protection."

The national scenic area is managed in partnership by both states, six counties, the U.S. Forest Service, and a newly established Gorge Commission, which is funded equally by the two states and is comprised of twelve volunteers appointed by the counties and states. No small feat considering that the area consists of 292,500 acres of public and private lands spanning a distance more than 80 miles. A lifelong dream for many who cherish the natural, cultural, historical, and scenic significance of this great place, without this landmark act, surely the Gorge would have been relentlessly developed and subdivided during the boom years that followed. There are still interests who would like to see the act weakened—even abandoned—but watchdog organizations like the Friends of the Columbia Gorge (see "Befriending the Gorge" in the western Oregon section) work hard to make sure that doesn't happen.

Steigerwald has only just begun acquiring and commissioning pieces of art to be placed along the way. Plenty of wildlife, however, will be on hand regardless of the amount of art present.

The trail heads south across wet meadows, passing through a tunnel of willows. At about 0.3 mile reach a channel feeding into Steigerwald Lake. Scan the open water for waterfowl. Scan the tall grasses and cattails for songbirds. And enjoy the pretty backdrop of Gorge sentinels, Mount Pleasant and Larch Mountain.

Continue on the delightful trail, coming to a stately row of cottonwoods. Here the trail bends east to travel along Gibbons Creek, coming to a junction at 0.6 mile. The trail on the left is closed from October 1 to April 30 to protect wintering birds. If it's closed, head right. If it's open, continue straight, following along Gibbons Creek for 0.6 mile and reaching the East Dike Trail (Hike 11). Enjoy exceptional views here of the Columbia River, Reed Island, and Crown Point.

To continue the loop, turn right (west) on the East Dike Trail and proceed for 0.5 mile, reaching the western extension of the Gibbons Creek Wildlife Art Trail. Turn right and skirt Redtail Lake, a shallow body of water usually supporting a heavy concentration of birds.

The trail continues over an attractive boardwalk. It then bends east along cottonwood-lined Gibbons Creek, eventually crossing it to return to the junction with the eastern leg of the trail. Turn left and retrace your steps, returning to the parking lot in 0.6 mile.

17 Cape Horn

RATING/ DIFFICULTY	LOOP	ELEV GAIN/ HIGH POINT	SEASON
****/3	7 miles	1350 feet/ 1300 feet	Year-round

Maps: Green Trails Columbia River Gorge–West No. 428S, trail map from on-site map box; **Contact:** Columbia River Gorge National Scenic Area, (541) 308-1700, www.fs.fed.us/r6/columbia; **Notes:** Dogs permitted on leash. Lower half of loop closed Jan 1–July 1 to protect nesting peregrine falcons. Trail subject to change, particularly the lower half. Consult Columbia Gorge NSA for status; **GPS:** N 45 35.357 W 122 10.706

Soak up stunning nonstop views of river, mountain, and valley from one of the most prominent landmarks in the Columbia Gorge. Thanks to a new mostly volunteer-built loop trail you can now round Cape Horn—gingerly strolling along precipitous ledges, languidly lolling across hilltop pastures, weaving up and over oak-cloaked basalt cliffs, and frequently pausing to admire one of the finest natural landscapes in the American West.

Cape Horn offers some of the finest views in the Gorge.

GETTING THERE

From Vancouver, follow State Route 14 east for 26 miles, turning left onto Salmon Falls Road. Immediately turn right into a Park and Ride lot, and park. The trail begins on west side of Salmon Falls Road (elev. 500 ft). Privy available.

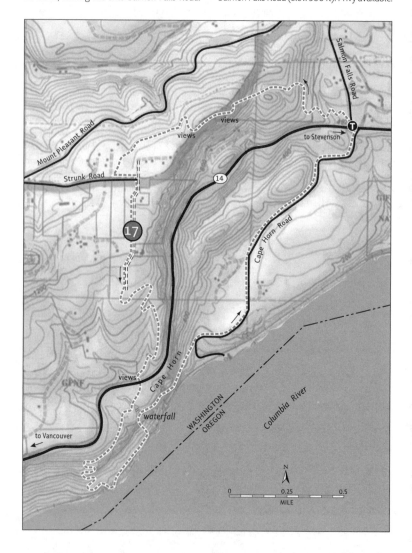

ON THE TRAIL

Built almost entirely by volunteers over the years, the trail is well used and well liked. However, because it was never constructed to proper standards nor reviewed by governing land agencies, the Forest Service is currently assessing options, which include closing and or relocating sections of this loop. Among the agency's concerns are hiker safety and possible conflicts with nesting peregrine falcons and other sensitive species. Be sure to check on the status of the trail before setting off.

Cross the Salmon Falls Road, entering mature forest saved from development by the Columbia Land Trust (see "Want to Protect Land around the Columbia? Buy It!" in the introduction). After dropping into a lush draw, begin climbing and reach a map box at 0.2 mile. Pick up a map and continue climbing, switchbacking up an increasingly steep ridge to Pioneer Point. At 0.5 mile bear left at a junction and, under a tunnel of greenery, walk parallel to a gravel road. At about 1 mile come to the first of several ledge-top viewpoints on 1300-plus-foot Pioneer Point, which give sweeping views across the Columbia and out to Oregon. Exercise caution and keep children and dogs close by.

Leave the ledges, heading to the right and dropping slightly to a gravel road. The trail resumes to the left and after a short distance comes to paved Strunk Road. Turn left and, after 300 feet, turn right onto a gravel road. Follow this through fields that up until 2008 sported a house but which are now home to the Nancy Russell Overlook thanks to the Friends of the Columbia Gorge (see "Befriending the Gorge" in the western Oregon section). Heading back into forest, bona fide trail resumes. Now slowly descending, soon reach a spectacular viewpoint above the high-

way. This is the classic Cape Horn view that motorists get. You have it all to yourself here.

Continue, and at about 3.5 miles reach SR 14. Until underpasses are in place, carefully cross the road to a now much rougher trail, dropping to oak-topped basalt bluffs above the Columbia River. In 0.25 mile, bear right. The trail to the left descends to a good viewpoint above a waterfall. The main trail continues, dropping and then traveling over basalt cliffs that themselves drop over 100 feet into the river below.

Now heading east, follow tread across a bluff where railroad tracks below enter a tunnel. The rugged topography and scenery here are absolutely stunning. The way now follows a rough-and-tumble up-and-down course across scree slopes and passes beneath a waterfall. Losing more elevation, the trail reaches the paved Cape Horn Road (elev. 150 ft) at about 5.7 miles. Head left, following this quiet country road 1.3 miles back to the trailhead. Use caution crossing SR 14.

18 Sams-Walker Nature Trail

RATING/ DIFFICULTY	LOOP	ELEV GAIN/ HIGH POINT	SEASON
***/1	1.2 miles	None/ 30 feet	Year-round

Maps: Green Trails Columbia River Gorge–West No. 428S; **Contact:** Columbia River Gorge National Scenic Area, (541) 308-1700, www.fs.fed.us/r6/columbia; **Notes:** NW Forest Pass required. Wheelchair accessible. Dogs permitted on-leash; **GPS:** N 45 36.708 W 122 03.109

One of the quietest trails in the Columbia River Gorge, Sams-Walker is perfect for leisurely morning and evening strolls and nature contemplation any time

Once a homestead, now a pastoral nature trail

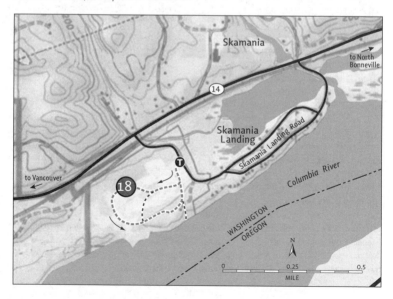

of day. Stroll along this virtually level, barrier-free trail through attractive oak and ash forest and riverside fields, listening to birdsong and watching for deer. Rife with history as well as wildlife, this natural area was home to Native peoples before it was homesteaded by German immigrants in the 1880s. Later, the Sams family raised fourteen children here on their dairy farm (and an eponymous Walker married into the Sams family, hence the trail's name).

GETTING THERE

From Vancouver, follow State Route 14 east for 33 miles, turning right (just before the Skamania General Store) onto Skamania Landing Road. After 0.3 mile come to the trailhead on your right (elev. 30 ft). Privy available.

ON THE TRAIL

While this trail is short, it's long on delights. Young children will especially like it. So will folks new to hiking and the outdoors. Take time to read the attractive interpretive plaques along the way. Then pause, reflect, and absorb. In springtime, Sams-Walker is alive with floral bouquets and avian symphonies. In early summer, it's abuzz with mosquitoes! Come fall, stately oak, ash, and maple add streaks of gold to this emerald easel.

The trail starts as a wide swath across a field of hip-high grasses. Take in good views of Oregon's Nesmith Point and Rock of Ages Ridge directly south across the Columbia. March across the field and look back at Hardy Ridge, Archer Mountain, and Hamilton Mountain.

In 0.2 mile the trail splits. Go right—you'll be returning from the left. At 0.3 mile the trail splits again. Unless you want to shorten this loop (and why would you do that?), continue

to the right, soon entering a mature forest of hardwoods and cedars. Emerge back in pasture and reach a picnic area on a bluff above the Columbia. Plummeting Horsetail Falls can be seen across the grand river.

Continue on the loop, ignoring the shortcut leading left, and traverse a grove of cottonwoods. Pass by a brushy side trail that heads right, but do take the second short side trail to the river overlook. Then, back on the main trail, pass some big oaks, perhaps a rabbit or two, and return to the trailhead.

EXTENDING YOUR TRIP

Looking for nearby, similar trails that are wheelchair accessible? Three miles to the west, visit the Saint Cloud Picnic Area (NW Forest Pass required) and take to its 0.4 mile of orchard-weaving trails. Two miles to the east in Beacon Rock State Park's Doetsch Day-Use Area, find a 1-mile paved interpretive trail.

19 Beacon Rock

RATING/ DIFFICULTY	ROUND-TRIP	ELEV GAIN/ HIGH POINT	SEASON
***/2	1.8 miles	600 feet/ 848 feet	Year-round

Maps: Green Trails Columbia River Gorge–West No. 428S, trail map from park website; **Contact:** Beacon Rock State Park, (509) 427-8265, www.parks.wa.gov; **Notes:** Dogs permitted on-leash. Trail frequently closed during winter storms; **GPS:** N 45 37.730 W 122 01.285

Follow a twisting trail of ramps and stairways to the top of the largest basaltic monolith in the Northwest. Then take in breathtaking views of the

Beacon Rock's trail is an engineering marvel.

Columbia River and its striking Gorge from this 848-foot core of an ancient volcano. Named by Lewis and Clark in 1805, the rock was bought by wealthy engineer and amateur botanist Henry J. Biddle in 1915, and he constructed this marvel of a trail. After his death, his children gave the rock to the state for a new park in 1932.

GETTING THERE

From Vancouver, follow State Route 14 east for 35 miles to Beacon Rock State Park. The trail begins on the south side of the highway, just past the campground entrance (elev. 250 ft). Privy available.

ON THE TRAIL

The trail starts right at the base of the imposing landmark. Follow the wide and well-trodden path around the western base

of the basaltic behemoth. Then commence climbing on a trail that is truly one of the engineering marvels of the hiking world. By way of a series of dangling catwalks and stairways and switchbacking ramps, the sturdy trail ascends the rock's sheer face. Iron casings and railings provide safety, but keep small children close by. Constructed from 1915 to 1918 by Biddle and his buddy Chas Johnson, and later reinforced by the Civilian Conservation Corps, the trail truly is a marvelous feat.

After twisting and turning for nearly a mile, the trail ends on top of the rock. Views are breathtaking, taking in the Bonneville Dam in the east all the way to Crown Point in the west. Watch trains chug and boats putter below. Imagine Lewis and Clark plying the river before you over 200 years ago. It was they who named the rock back on October 31, 1805. And it was here at Beacon Rock that they first noticed tidal influences in the river. Yet, nearly 150 miles inland from the Pacific it would still be some time before they exclaimed "Ocean in view!"

The airy viewing loft can be quite crowded on a sunny summer day, so be prepared to share.

20 Hamilton Mountain

RATING/ DIFFICULTY	ROUND-TRIP	ELEV GAIN/ HIGH POINT	SEASON
*****/4	8.2 miles	2100 feet/ 2438 feet	Year-round

Maps: Green Trails Columbia River Gorge–West No. 428S, trail map from park website; **Contact:** Beacon Rock State Park, (509) 427-8265, www.parks.wa.gov; **Notes:** Dogs permitted on-leash; **GPS:** N 45 37.951 W 122 01.213

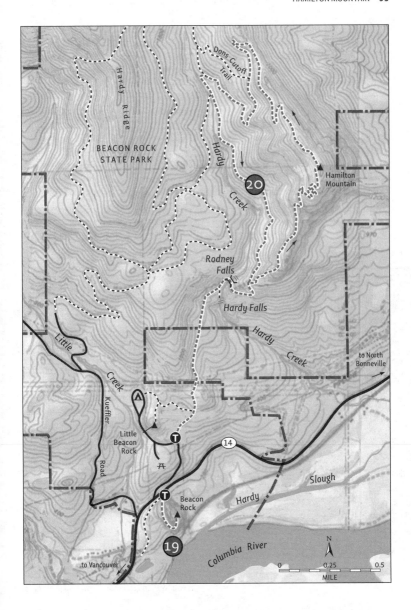

Dons Cutoff Trail

Hardy Ridge

BEACON ROCK
STATE PARK

Hardy Creek

20

Hamilton
Mountain

Rodney
Falls

Hardy Falls

Hardy Creek

to North
Bonneville

Little Creek

Kueffler Road

Little
Beacon
Rock

T

14

Slough

T

Beacon
Rock

Hardy

19

Columbia River

to Vancouver

N

0   0.25   0.5

MILE

⚙ 🎒 🏠 One of the most popular destinations on the Washington side of the Gorge, Hamilton Mountain lives up to its hype, delivering breathtaking views, dazzling wildflowers, and a pair of dramatic waterfalls. Amble below, along, and above basaltic cliffs, peering up and down the dramatic Gorge spread before you. Marvel at a seemingly impenetrable wall of Oregon peaks across the river that are dwarfed by glacial-robed Mount Hood rising above them. And delight in the trails and bridges leading you to all of this, the showy legacies of the 1930s-era Civilian Conservation Corps (CCC).

Impressive cliffs on Hamilton Mountain's south face

GETTING THERE

From Vancouver, follow State Route 14 east for 35 miles to Beacon Rock State Park. Just after the park headquarters, turn left toward the campground and reach the trailhead in 0.3 mile (elev. 475 ft). Privy available. Additional parking is available at the nearby picnic area.

ON THE TRAIL

While Beacon Rock is the crown jewel of the 5100-acre state park that shares its name, attracting scads of admirers from near and far, Hamilton Mountain is where the real hiking action is in the park. But don't expect solitude—you'd be better off exploring the park's Hardy Ridge (Hike 21) if that's your objective.

The trail starts at a lovely picnic area graced with structures built by the CCC. Beacon Rock is one of over 800 state parks nationally that was developed and enhanced by President Franklin D. Roosevelt's "Tree Army" during the Great Depression.

Enter a grove of large firs and immediately start climbing. At 0.4 mile, in a powerline swath, bear right at a junction with a trail leading to the campground. Continue climbing through attractive forest that's decorated by snowy-white Pacific dogwood bouquets in spring and garnished with golden vine maple leaves in autumn.

At 1.1 miles, come to a junction (elev. 960 ft) for the Hardy Falls Viewpoint spur. Affording not the best vista, the spur drops steeply 50 feet to a platform above the falls. Better waterfall viewings wait ahead, so carry on 0.1 mile to another junction. Left leads to Rodney Falls, an impressive 50-foot cascade that thunders through a tight chasm into a punchbowl basin named the Pool of Winds. Pool of Mist is what I prefer to call it—and you'll realize why soon enough!

After literally soaking in the view, continue on your way to Hamilton, dropping 50 feet to cross Hardy Creek on a hardy bridge. Then, steeply climb to reach a junction (elev. 1100 ft) with the Hardy Creek Trail at 1.6 miles. You'll be returning from the left, so proceed to the right, steadily climbing, switchbacking beneath and around steep ledges and cliffs, views expanding at each turn. Beacon Rock and the Bonneville Dam lie directly below. Mount Hood peeks above Oregon's steep and impressive Gorge Face. Look to the west too for a good view of Archer Mountain and a series of cinder cones scattered across the landscape. In late spring and early summer, paintbrush, phlox, larkspur, and others decorate Hamilton's steep slopes.

At 3.4 miles crest Hamilton's 2438-foot summit where a sign erroneously says 2480 feet. Brush obscures viewing to the south and west, but views are good to the east, especially to impressive Table Mountain.

Now, hike along Hamilton's north ridge, enjoying excellent views of Hardy Ridge. At 4.1 miles emerge on an open flat saddle (elev. 2100 ft), perfect for lunchtime, nap time, or just sitting and staring into the distance time. By this point, crowds have thinned out considerably, as many Hamilton hikers travel out and back instead of making the loop.

At 4.3 miles reach a junction with an old fire road. Follow it to the left, slowly descending through forest, passing Don's Cutoff (an alternative route—turn left at its terminus), and reaching the Upper Hardy Creek Trail (elev. 1500 ft) at 5.3 miles. Continue left, and after 0.1 mile veer left onto the Hardy Creek Trail. The trail leading right connects to the West and East Hardy Ridge Trails (Hike 21).

Now paralleling Hardy Creek, gently descend through lush forest, occasionally passing remnant burnt snags. At 6.6 miles arrive back on the Hamilton Mountain Trail.

Turn right and retrace familiar ground 1.6 miles back to the trailhead.

EXTENDING YOUR TRIP

For a slight variation on the return, take the campground spur trail 0.4 mile to the recently reopened (thanks to the Chinook Trail Association) Little Beacon Rock Trail. Follow this nice path through pika-hopping talus 0.2 mile to the mini monolith, Little Beacon Rock. Return to the main trail or turn left, hiking 0.2 mile through Hadley Grove (named for park's first superintendent) to the campground set in old-growth forest. Then follow the road 0.5 mile back to your vehicle.

21 Hardy Ridge

RATING/ DIFFICULTY	ROUND-TRIP	ELEV GAIN/ HIGH POINT	SEASON
***/3	7.6 miles	1860 feet/ 2700 feet	Year-round

Maps: Green Trails Columbia River Gorge–West No. 428S, trail map from park website; **Contact:** Beacon Rock State Park, (509) 427-8265, www.parks.wa.gov; **Notes:** Dogs permitted on-leash; **GPS:** N 45 38.469 W 122 01.935

One of Washington's most popular and beloved state parks, thousands of hikers take to Beacon Rock State Park's namesake rock and Hamilton Mountain trails every year. But very few venture over to Hardy Ridge and its network of trails. Though this area is a playground primarily for equestrians and mountain bikers, even few of them flock to these trails. The flowers on Hardy are as showy as anywhere in the park, the views from the ridge just as good as from Hamilton, and it's all experienced minus the masses.

GETTING THERE

From Vancouver, follow State Route 14 east for 35 miles to Beacon Rock State Park (1.8 miles west of Skamania). Just before the park headquarters, turn left onto Kueffler Road and proceed for 1 mile. Turn right (signed "Equestrian Trailhead"), coming to picnic grounds, an equestrian campground, and the trailhead in 0.3 mile (elev. 840 ft). Privy available.

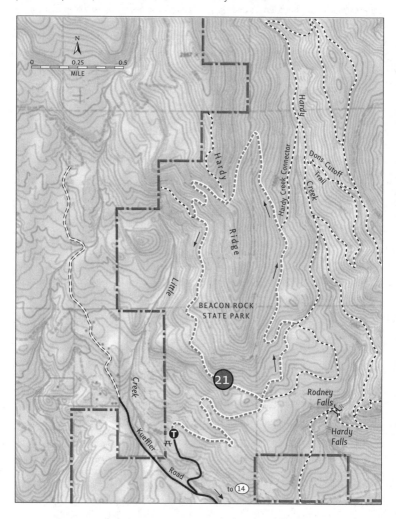

Proliferating wildflowers on Hardy Ridge

ON THE TRAIL

Starting on a park service road (closed to vehicles), wind your way up a hillside of deciduous trees that resemble an eastern hardwood forest, coming to a four-way junction (elev. 1350 ft) at 1.2 miles. You'll be returning on the left-hand trail, and the trail to the right makes a 1-mile loop back to the main road (trail). Continue straight. At 1.8 miles, come to another four-way junction (elev. 1550 ft). To the right is the previously mentioned 1-mile loop; straight ahead, the main trail continues to Hardy Creek and connects with the Hamilton Mountain loop (Hike 20). Bear left on the Hardy Ridge Trail. After a short climb, pass through a cool stretch of forest and arrive at another junc-

tion (elev. 1800 ft) at 2.7 miles. The trail to the right is a brand-spanking-new connector trail to the Upper Hardy Creek Trail, compliments of the Washington Trails Association (WTA). The WTA has greatly increased its presence in southwestern Washington over the past few years, maintaining and building new trails.

The loop continues straight and is now officially hiker-only. At 3.2 miles the way leaves old road for bona fide trail with new tread, once again the work of the WTA. In cool hemlock forest, switchback up steep slopes and come to a junction (elev. 2550 ft) among flowered outcroppings and great views at 3.9 miles. The trail to the right is an unofficial brushy way path along Hardy Ridge. If you like, wander up it 0.2 mile to a

2700-foot knoll for stunning views of the Columbia River, Larch Mountain, Nesmith Point, and Hamilton Mountain. Admire the floral arrangements in early summer.

Once content, complete the loop. Now heading west, gradually descend, passing more fine viewing and flower gardens. After about 0.4 mile, the good trail ends and you're on an old road that is both steep and rife with chest-high brush. Hopefully the park and the WTA will eventually rehabilitate this section. In about another 0.4 mile, the way emerges onto another road. Head left, now on much better tread and an easier grade, only dealing with high grasses (avoid in tick season), and reach the first four-way junction after 1.3 miles. Turn right and retrieve your vehicle in 1.2 miles.

EXTENDING YOUR TRIP

Skip the less attractive western half of this loop and retrace your way to the new Hardy Creek connector trail, and from there hike along Hardy Creek. Or combine your outing with Don's Cutoff Trail for a trip up Hamilton Mountain.

22 Aldrich Butte

RATING/ DIFFICULTY	ROUND-TRIP	ELEV GAIN/ HIGH POINT	SEASON
**/3	3.6 miles	1080 feet/ 1129 feet	Year-round

Map: Green Trails Columbia River Gorge–West No. 428S; **Contact:** Columbia River Gorge National Scenic Area, (541) 308-1700, www.fs.fed.us/r6/columbia; **Notes:** Hike begins at the Bonneville Hot Springs Resort, which has generously provided access. Respect patrons' privacy and resort premises. Access can be denied anytime. **GPS:** N 45 39.324 W 121 57.640

The views from Aldrich are dam good. So dam good that the U.S. military constructed a defense post here during World War II to watch over the Bonneville Dam below. A foundation and remnants of a gun mount are all that remains—and of course those fine views too. Survey Table Mountain, Hamilton Mountain, Tanner Butte, the Greenleaf Slough, and Hamilton Island from this oft-overlooked landmark in the heart of the Gorge.

GETTING THERE

From Vancouver, follow State Route 14 east for 38 miles and turn left on the Hot Springs Road (directly across from the Bonneville Dam access road, 1 mile east of North Bonneville town access). (From Portland, follow I-84 east to exit 44 at Cascade Locks and take the Bridge of the Gods—$1 toll—to SR 14. Turn left and drive 3 miles west, turning right onto Hot Springs Road.) Drive under the railroad tracks, and in 0.1 mile turn right, continuing for 0.7 mile to Bonneville Hot Springs Resort. Park in the large gravel parking lot located northwest of the resort (elev. 50 ft).

ON THE TRAIL

Until recently, hiking to Aldrich Butte involved starting on a rutted old road or following buzzing high-tension wires. But now, thanks to the Portland-based Mazamas and the Bonneville Hot Springs Resort, you can follow a new trail that bypasses the old less-than-scenic routes. Named the Dick Thomas Trail for the Mazama volunteer who constructed a good portion of the new tread, find the trail by walking 0.1 mile up a jeep track that takes off from the northwest corner of the parking lot.

The Dick Thomas Trail (look for a small trail sign on a lone ash) immediately takes off north, away from the service road heading west. Follow this good trail upward through lush forest, eventually coming to a marshy opening known as Carpenters Lake (elev. 550 ft) at 1 mile. Perhaps it was once, but with the absence of a little beaver carpentry, the lake is now merely a soggy grassy swale. Be sure to cast your eyes upward to Table Mountain and the Sacagawea and Papoose Rocks.

After crossing Carpenters' outlet creek on a small bridge, come to an old road (which sees some ATV use). Turn right, and after 0.1 mile come to another road. Turn left, following this road for 0.1 mile to another junction (elev. 625 ft). The road to the right continues to Table Mountain (Hike 23). You want to hang a left, following the old road up Aldrich Butte.

At about 0.2 mile, pass an unmarked side trail that heads to the right to Cedar Falls (be sure to have a map if you explore this and other unmarked trails and roads in the area). At 1.8 miles reach the 1129-foot summit.

Trees have been reclaiming the butte, growing within and around an old foundation and gun mount. But views are still good, particularly from just below the summit. Locate Dog and Wind Mountain, Tanner Butte, Gillette Lake, and Munra Point directly across the river. Of course, there's also a great view of the Bonneville Dam and city of North Bonneville. Aldrich's sun-kissed openings also harbor a few showy flowers, including arrowleaf balsamroot, which is pushing its western range here in the heart of the Gorge.

EXTENDING YOUR TRIP

For lonely wandering, follow the old road right at Carpenters Lake 0.8 mile to the Pacific Crest Trail (elev. 800 ft). From here you can head right 0.7 mile to the Greenleaf

Aldrich Butte was used as a defense post during World War II.

Overlook (Hike 26), or continue straight on the old road (eventually petering into trail) into the talus-strewn basin beneath Table Mountain. Experienced off-trail travelers may want to continue to Greenleaf Falls.

23 Table Mountain

RATING/ DIFFICULTY	ROUND-TRIP	ELEV GAIN/ HIGH POINT	SEASON
*****/5	9 miles	3425 feet/ 3400 feet	May–Nov

Map: Green Trails Columbia River Gorge–West No. 428S; **Contact:** Washington DNR,

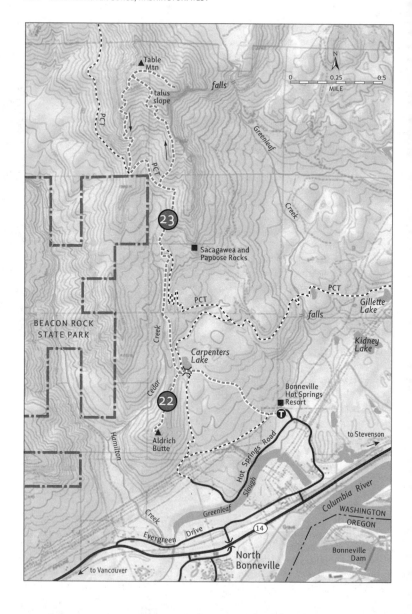

Pacific Cascade Region (Castle Rock), (360) 577-2025, www.dnr.wa.gov; **Notes:** Hike begins at the Bonneville Hot Springs Resort, which has generously provided access. Respect patrons' privacy and resort premises. Access can be denied anytime. Hike is extremely difficult and involves scrambling up a talus slope. Stay on designated trails to avoid disturbing endangered plants; **GPS:** N 45 39.324 W 121 57.640

⚙⭐ *An iconic peak within the Gorge, it was Table Mountain that gave birth to the Bridge of the Gods hundreds of years ago when half of it slid off in a massive landslide, damming the Columbia River. But what's left of the Table is impressive too: sheer cliffs, mystical rock formations, and a tabletop draped in alpine flowers, including several endangered ones. To be seated at this table, however, requires physical prowess and competence with negotiating rocky and steep terrain. Really steep! This is one of the toughest hikes in this book—and one of the most rewarding.*

GETTING THERE

From Vancouver, follow State Route 14 east for 38 miles and turn left on the Hot Springs Road (directly across from the Bonneville Dam access road, 1 mile east of North Bonneville town access). (If coming from Portland, follow I-84 east to exit 44 at Cascade Locks and take the Bridge of the Gods—$1 toll—to SR 14. Turn left and drive 3 miles west, turning right onto Hot Springs Road.) Drive under the railroad tracks, and in 0.1 mile turn right, continuing for 0.7 mile to Bonneville Hot Springs Resort. Park in the large gravel parking lot located northwest of the resort (elev. 50 ft).

The trail heads up a challenging talus slope.

ON THE TRAIL

The hike to Table Mountain is tough, and until recently, long. But thanks to the Portland-based Mazamas and the Bonneville Hot Springs Resort, you can follow a new trail to an old road, knocking miles off the old approach from the Bonneville trailhead (Hike 26). Locate a jeep road taking off northwest from the parking lot. Follow it 0.1 mile to the Dick Thomas Trail that veers right (look for a sign in a lone ash) from where a service road continues left.

Take this trail upward through lush forest, past Carpenters Lake (a marsh actually), for 1 mile to an old road, sometime ATV track (elev. 550 ft). Turn right and after 0.1 mile come to another road. Turn left, following this road for 0.1 mile to another junction (elev. 625 ft). The road left continues to Aldrich Butte (Hike 22). You want to continue on the road right.

Steadily climbing through deciduous forest, with Cedar Creek tumbling on your left, reach the Pacific Crest Trail (elev. 1400 ft) after 1.2 miles (2.4 miles from trailhead). Either bear left on the PCT, or continue straight for 0.2 mile on the road, once again meeting the PCT. Then follow the PCT to the right for another 0.2 mile to a kiosk that introduces you to the Washington DNR's 2837-acre Table Mountain Natural Resource Conservation Area—and the Heartbreak Ridge Trail that will take you through it.

Here, at an elevation of 1700 feet, you have roughly gained 1650 feet of elevation over a course of 2.8 miles. You will gain the next 1650 feet in 1.2 miles! The trail is that steep. While not really exposed, it can be dangerous if you're not careful, especially in bad weather and snow. It's best to go up the Eastway section, with its talus slope, and down the Westway section, which is slightly less steep. Best to have trekking poles too, and good gripping shoes.

User-built and only slightly modified since, the Heartbreak (more like lung-buster) Ridge Trail climbs at an insanely ridiculous grade straight up. After 0.6 mile, reach a saddle (elev. 2475 ft) beneath the impressive face of the mountain and teetering above a sheer drop-off above a jumbled pile of landslide debris. A memorial here marks the spot where a hiker tragically died in the spring of 2010.

The trail now drops 75 feet through windblown contorted firs and maples before commencing up a series of tight switchbacks. At 2700 feet, reach the base of a large talus slope. The trail goes straight up it. Reminiscent of the kind of trails you'd find in New Hampshire's White Mountains, it's a rock hop (stick to the left of the slope) for 300 vertical feet. Resume actual tread at the top of the talus and angle left back into forest for a short distance, reaching a junction (elev. 3200 ft) at 4 miles.

You'll be returning to the left, but first the summit awaits. Turn right onto the Overlook Trail section, following it 0.3 mile up Table's 3400-foot summit and out across flowered meadows to a vertigo-inducing, heart-pounding viewpoint directly above sheer 1000-foot-plus cliffs at the face of the mountain. Not a place for children, dogs (you didn't bring any along did you?), or the easily unnerved. But what a view! Hamilton, Benson Plateau, Chinidere, Defiance, Eagle Creek valley, the Columbia River, and—11,000 feet above—Mount Hood! Look north and east, too, to Adams, Rainier, Saint Helens, Greenleaf Peak, and the Soda Lake Peaks. Take time to smell the flowers—can you locate Howell's daisy? Endemic to the Gorge, the largest population of this threatened species is found on Table.

After you're through feasting on views and flowers, dismiss yourself from the Table and begin an arduous descent. Retrace your steps 0.3 mile back to the previous junction. Then continue right on the Westway section, steeply dropping mostly along an open ridge (with good views northwest to Lookout Mountain and Silver Star) and the edge of cliffs. Loose rock makes the descent tricky in spots and it's easy to twist an ankle. Take your time.

Reach the PCT (elev. 2000 ft) after 1.1 knee-jarring miles. Turn left and rejoice once again to be hiking on good tread and at a sane grade, reaching the Heartbreak Ridge Trail junction after 0.5 mile. From here its 2.8 familiar miles back to the trailhead. Consider a soak at the Hot Springs Resort upon completion!

EXTENDING YOUR TRIP

For a return variation, and if a car shuttle can be arranged, follow the PCT from the Heartbreak Ridge Trail 6.5 easy miles to the Bonneville trailhead (Hike 26).

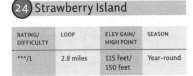

24 Strawberry Island

RATING/ DIFFICULTY	LOOP	ELEV GAIN/ HIGH POINT	SEASON
***/1	2.8 miles	115 feet/ 150 feet	Year-round

Map: Green Trails Columbia River Gorge–West No. 428S; **Contact:** City of North Bonneville Heritage Trails, www.nbtrails.net, and U.S. Army Corps of Engineers, Bonneville Lock and Dam (Portland District), (509) 427-4281, www .nwp.usace.army.mil; **Notes:** Dogs permitted on-leash; **GPS:** N 45 38.018 W 121 58.731

 *Wide-open lawns of tall, swaying grasses providing stunning views of towering surrounding peaks, let me take you down to Strawberry Island's fields, where the scenery is quite real! Retrace the footsteps of Lewis and Clark along a wildlife-rich slough and breathtaking bluff above the Columbia River, across what the intrepid explorers called Strawberry Island. And while the island is now known as Hamilton, wild strawberries still grow profusely upon it.*

GETTING THERE

From Vancouver follow State Route 14 east for 37 miles, turning right on the North Bonneville access road. (If coming from Portland, follow I-84 east to exit 44 at Cascade Locks and take the Bridge of the Gods—$1 toll—to SR 14. Turn left and drive 4 miles west, turning left into North Bonneville.) Then, immediately turn right onto Cascade Drive. After 0.4 mile, turn left onto Portage Drive, coming to the trailhead (elev. 35 ft) at ball fields in 0.2 mile. Privy available.

ON THE TRAIL

Several miles of excellent trails traverse Strawberry Island, connecting with North Bonneville's Heritage Trails, the Fort Cascades Trail, and the Hamilton Island fishing areas. The loop described here is a suggestion to get you on your way. Feel free to shorten or lengthen your stay—any distance will yield happy hiking results.

From the trailhead, immediately come to a four-way intersection. Head right (signed "Rail Pond") on a perfectly level path across

Inviting lawns and soothing views on Strawberry Island

fields edged by giant cottonwoods. At 0.6 mile come to a junction. Continue right along Hamilton Creek, entering thickets of blackberries and singing blackbirds. At 0.8 mile a short spur leads 0.1 mile right to Clark's Viewpoint on the western tip of Strawberry Island.

Now head east along the Columbia, enjoying excellent views of Munra and Nesmith points across the river. Watch for rabbits dining on grasses and bald eagles hoping to dine on rabbit!

At 1 mile come to a junction. The trail right leads 0.5 mile along the Columbia to the fishing access road, an alternative starting point. Head left, coming to another junction after 0.1 mile. The trail left leads 0.1 mile back to the Rail Pond Trail. Bear right and climb a wide-open grassy bluff, enjoying views of Beacon Rock, Hamilton Mountain, Aldrich Butte, Table Mountain and a wall of Oregon peaks and ridges. After 0.3 mile come to another junction. Continue straight, cresting the bluff and enjoying even wider views. The parallel trail on the right is equally scenic, with excellent river views.

After another 0.2 mile come to Big Tire Junction at the top (elev. 150 ft) of the crest. Right leads 0.15 mile to the parallel bench trail. Left leads 0.3 mile back to the trailhead. Continue straight for 0.7 mile, enjoying Columbia River breezes and vistas as you slowly descend to a three-way junction at the edge of the fishing access road (no trailhead parking here). Now turn left and once again head west. The trail splits at 0.1 mile. Both lead back to the trailhead. The trail left is more scenic and slightly longer, with some elevation gain. The trail right is direct and level, returning to your vehicle in 0.4 mile.

EXTENDING YOUR TRIP

Consider an easy stroll on the 2-mile paved Hamilton Island Trail. A brochure and map are available from the Heritage Trail kiosk located immediately off of Cascade Drive when you first turned into town.

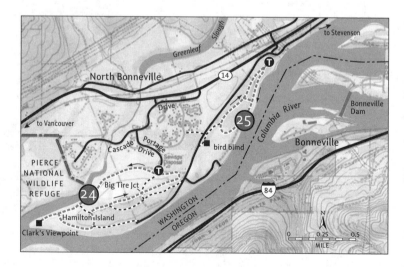

25 Fort Cascades Loop

RATING/ DIFFICULTY	LOOP	ELEV GAIN/ HIGH POINT	SEASON
**/1	1.2 miles	20 feet/ 40 feet	Year-round

Maps: Green Trails Columbia River Gorge–West No. 428S, interpretive map from on-site kiosk; **Contact:** U.S. Army Corps of Engineers, Bonneville Lock and Dam (Portland District), (509) 427-4281, www .nwp.usace.army.mil; **Notes:** Soft surface, but wheelchair accessible. Dogs permitted on-leash; **GPS:** N 45 38.661 W 121 57.481

Take this short and easy trail for a trip through Pacific Northwest history. While this riverbank locale just downstream from the Bonneville Dam now consists merely of a quiet young forest of oak and fir, it once boasted a town, military post, railroad, and a flurry of human activity. First floods in the late 1800s and then the construction of the dam in 1938 changed all of that. Grab an interpretive brochure at the trailhead and wander back in time.

GETTING THERE

From Vancouver, follow State Route 14 east for 38 miles and turn right on the Bonneville Dam access road (directly across from Hot Springs Road, 1 mile east of North Bonneville town access). (If coming from Portland, follow I-84 east to exit 44 at Cascade Locks and take the Bridge of the Gods—$1 toll—to SR 14. Turn left and drive 3 miles west, turning left onto dam access road.) In 0.1 mile turn right at the stop sign, onto the fishing access road, and proceed another 0.1 mile to Fort Cascades Historic Site (elev. 20 ft).

Civil-War-era gravesite at Fort Cascades

ON THE TRAIL

Start by stopping at the kiosk and reading the fine displays on this area's past exploration, transportation, settlement, military, and fishing history. While traces remain of these past pursuits, it is the change wrought by the Bonneville Dam that most sticks out here. The Cascades of the Columbia, a once formidable obstacle for travel along the river, no longer exist—having been harnessed for power and corralled for flood prevention.

Now grab for yourself an interpretive brochure and begin hiking to fourteen stops. At 0.1 mile the trail splits—head left, dropping down along the river and enjoying good views while learning about the flood of 1894. Pass a junction with a shortcut that heads right and a viewpoint spur that heads left. Soon come to the old Cascades townsite. Settled in 1850 while Washington was a territory, Cascades served as the Skamania county seat until 1893. A year later, the flood put a permanent end to the town.

Continue through quiet forest to a meadow that provides excellent viewing of Munra Point across the river. The trail then loops back, coming to a junction at 0.7 mile. The trail left continues 0.25 mile past a fish-monitoring station to a bird blind beside a marsh. It also connects to North Bonneville's trail system, leading around Hamilton Island (now a peninsula). The loop continues right another 0.5 mile, passing more historical relics, including parts of a narrow-gauge railway and an 1861 gravesite.

26 Gillette Lake and Greenleaf Overlook

Gillette Lake

RATING/ DIFFICULTY	ROUND-TRIP	ELEV GAIN/ HIGH POINT	SEASON
**/2	6 miles	500 feet/ 400 feet	Year-round

Greenleaf Overlook

RATING/ DIFFICULTY	ROUND-TRIP	ELEV GAIN/ HIGH POINT	SEASON
**/3	8.6 miles	875 feet/ 650 feet	Year-round

Map: Green Trails Bonneville Dam, OR No. 429; **Contact:** Columbia River Gorge National Scenic Area, (541) 308-1700, www.fs.fed.us /r6/columbia; **Notes:** NW Forest Pass required; **GPS:** N 45 39.028 W 121 55.988

This is an easy hike to a small quiet lake and a small ledge granting some good views. The lake and its surroundings aren't scenically exceptional, but their formations are. Here, about 700 years ago, large portions of nearby Greenleaf and Table Mountains slid off, depositing jumbled boulders and creating varying depressions, some of which eventually became lakes. The massive landslide even blocked the Columbia River's passage (see "The Gods Must Be Angry" in the western Washington section). Travel through this hummocky landscape, appreciating the sheer force of nature.

A pair of hikers along the PCT brave autumn rains.

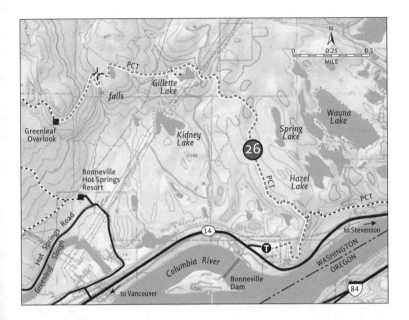

GETTING THERE

From Vancouver, follow State Route 14 east for 40 miles to the Bonneville trailhead, located on the left (elev. 100 ft). (From Portland, follow I-84 east to exit 44 at Cascade Locks and take the Bridge of the Gods—$1 toll—to SR 14. Turn left and drive 2 miles west to the trailhead, located on your right.) Privy available.

ON THE TRAIL

From the large trailhead area, follow the Tamanous Trail 0.7 mile to its terminus with the Pacific Crest Trail (elev. 300 ft). A delightful trail through attractive forest, especially during the autumn, it's named after the Great Spirit of several Northwest tribes. En route you'll pass a nice viewpoint out toward Oregon's Eagle Creek valley.

At the PCT junction, head left. The way right travels 1.4 miles to the Bridge of the Gods, skirting a couple of residences and paralleling the highway. The way left, your route, travels up and down over small ridges and passes and by many small pools and ponds. If you walk this way in midautumn, when the area pools are refilling from heavy rains, you'll need to watch your step: hundreds of rough-skinned newts will be migrating to pools and ponds to begin breeding. Unlike their higher-altitude brethren who mate during the summer, these temperate valley-residing newts breed during the winter.

Pass through an old cut and cross an old logging road. The forest around you is still a working forest, and you'll be crossing cuts of various ages. Don't despair, though—the trees grow back and there is plenty of attractive forest standing along the way. At 2.7 miles, cross a gravel road and powerline swath (elev. 400 ft). Gillette Lake lies just below. Not in the most attractive setting, the lake nevertheless is quite pretty, its northern shore graced with cascaras and its eastern shore decorated with talus.

The PCT drops gradually, reaching campsites and a short spur to the lake (elev. 275 ft) after another 0.3 mile. Bear left for the lake—for picnicking or, in warm weather, feet soaking. Or bear right (avoiding an unmarked route that goes straight) to continue hiking along the PCT to the Greenleaf Overlook.

Cross a pretty creek on a footlog and after another 0.25 mile reach a logging road in a fairly recent cut. Then resume hiking on trail and in attractive forest. Look for Pacific dog-

wood. Pass a small pond on the left, home to Pacific (western) pond turtles, a species threatened with extirpation in Washington State. Shortly afterward, drop into a cool ravine, crossing Greenleaf Creek on a wide and sturdy bridge.

Resume gentle climbing and at 4.3 miles reach the Greenleaf Overlook (elev. 650 ft), a mossy outlook set among tall firs. Enjoy nice views of the Bonneville Dam and the imposing emerald flank of steep Oregon ridges behind it.

EXTENDING YOUR TRIP

Continue north on the PCT for nearly another 3 miles to the Table Mountain Trail to tackle one of the rugged sources of the ancient landslide debris you just hiked over. But, if

THE GODS MUST BE ANGRY

One of the more attractive and well-known man-made structures in the Columbia River Gorge is the Bridge of the Gods, built in 1926 and spanning a narrow section of the river near Stevenson, Washington and Cascade Locks, Oregon. But much more intriguing is the natural bridge that the gods built many years prior.

Somewhere between AD 1000 and 1700 (geologists aren't sure of the exact date), a huge landslide occurred. Massive amounts of Table Mountain and Greenleaf Peak slid off, covering more than 5.5 square miles of the valley below and blocking the Columbia River. This natural dam, more than 200 feet high and 3.5 miles long, impounded the river and formed a lake 35 miles long. Eventually the river broke through it. Area First Peoples recount the event with numerous legends and stories.

One such, told by the Klickitat people, explains that two brothers named Pahto and Wy'east were quarreling over land in the valley. Their father, the great chief Tyhee Saghalie, shot two great arrows in opposite directions across the river, indicating where the sons would settle. In the process, the great arrows formed a bridge, allowing the family to periodically congregate. But eventually, peace was lost when the two sons fell in love with Loowit. They violently fought over her, causing the bridge to fall apart and creating the Cascade Rapids (since buried by the construction of the Bonneville Dam). Saghalie punished all three by turning them into great mountains: Mount Adams (Pahto), Mount Hood (Wy'east), and Mount Saint Helens (Loowit).

But Loowit had the last word in 1980 when she blew her top!

the summit of Table is your objective, it is much shorter and saner to approach it from the Bonneville Hot Springs Resort (Hike 23).

27 Bunker Hill

RATING/ DIFFICULTY	ROUND-TRIP	ELEV GAIN/ HIGH POINT	SEASON
**/3	4.4 miles	1250 feet/ 2383 feet	Mar–Dec

Map: Green Trails Wind River No. 397; **Contact:** Gifford Pinchot National Forest, Mount Adams Ranger District, Trout Lake, (509) 395-3400, www.fs.fed.us/gpnf; **Notes:** NW Forest Pass required; **GPS:** N 45 48.459 W 121 56.428

There's nothing revolutionary about this Bunker Hill, and you won't need to battle for it either—it'll all be yours. Named by two settlers for the famous site in Boston, this little peak stands watch above the Wind River valley and once served as a fire lookout. The tower is long gone and the trees are big, obstructing any viewing. But a little snooping around just below the summit will lead you to some ledges with a nice view south out to the Gorge.

GETTING THERE

From Stevenson, head east on State Route 14 for 3 miles, turning left (north) onto Wind River Road. Drive 8.6 miles on this good paved road and turn left onto Hemlock Road (signed for the Wind River Work Center). After 1.2 miles (just beyond the work center), turn right onto Forest Road 43 (signed for Canopy Crane). Proceed for 0.7 mile, turning right onto FR 417. In 0.1 mile pass the Pacific Crest Trail, where parking is extremely limited. Continue another 0.2 mile to a large parking area for the Whistle Punk Trail (elev. 1130 ft). Privy available. Park here and walk the road back to the PCT.

Bunker Hill offers limited but good views of the Wind River Valley.

ON THE TRAIL

Walk the road 0.2 mile back to the PCT, following along a fence line of a now unused section of the Wind River Nursery. Two decades of budget cuts and dwindling staff have reduced much of a once bustling area of the Gifford Pinchot National Forest into a "ghost forest." Follow the PCT north across the fallow nursery. Heavily forested Bunker Hill rises before you. Elk and deer frequent the field you're traversing.

The trail soon enters forest, crossing a wet alder and maple flat. At 0.5 mile from the trailhead, reach a junction (elev. 1220 ft). The PCT continues right, scooting along the base of Bunker Hill on its way to the Wind River. You

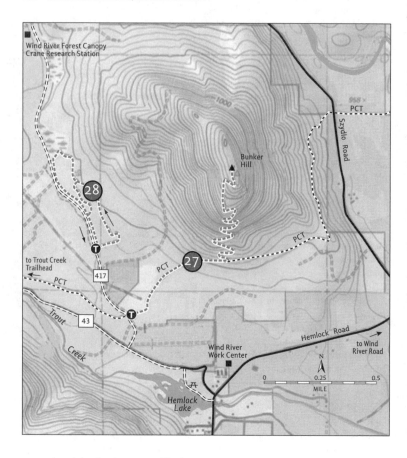

want to bear left to begin your switchbacking charge up Bunker Hill. Despite being a small peak, it's a good little climb, with a pitch that's steep from time to time. But the tread is good, weaving through some beautiful patches of old-growth Douglas-fir.

At 2 miles from the trailhead, reach the 2383-foot summit. All that remains of the fire lookout that once graced this peak are the concrete blocks that anchored it. If its views

you're interested in, head south along the ridge a few hundred feet, staying to the left and paralleling the trail to reach a small set of ledges just below the summit. From here, take in a nice view south of the Wind River valley and of Dog, Wind, Augspurger, and Huckleberry Mountains too. Oregon's Mount Defiance dominates the backdrop, and you'll be able to catch a glimpse of the Columbia River at its base.

28 Whistle Punk Trail

RATING/ DIFFICULTY	LOOP	ELEV GAIN/ HIGH POINT	SEASON
**/1	1.5 miles	70 feet/ 1200 feet	Mar–Dec

Map: Green Trails Wind River No. 397; **Contact:** Gifford Pinchot National Forest, Mount Adams Ranger District, Trout Lake, (509) 395-3400, www.fs.fed.us/gpnf; **Notes:** NW Forest Pass required. Wheelchair accessible; **GPS:** N 45 48.605 W 121 56.615

Enjoy a saunter back to a time when the forest was abuzz with whistle punks, high climbers, loaders, and steam donkeys. Hardscrabble loggers from northern Europe and the Midwest toppled trees 200 feet high and the rivers boomed with timber during the spring runoff. Learn about the logging practices of yesteryear, and embrace the silence and beauty of a regenerating forest and one spared from the ax.

GETTING THERE

From Stevenson, head east on State Route 14 for 3 miles, turning left (north) onto Wind River Road. Drive 8.6 miles on this good paved road and turn left onto Hemlock Road (signed for the Wind River Work Center). After 1.2 miles (just beyond the work center), turn right onto Forest Road 43 (signed for Canopy Crane). Proceed for 0.7 mile, turning right onto FR 417. In 0.3 mile come to the trailhead (elev. 1130 ft). Privy available.

ON THE TRAIL

This is a delightful loop trail of 1.5 miles, with an option to shorten it by 0.75 mile or tack on an additional 0.75 mile. Perfectly flat and wheelchair accessible, the way is littered with logging relics from the 1920s and lined with informative plaques about this bygone era. Start by walking up an old road and immediately come to a junction. You'll be returning on the road. Head right through a swamp of Oregon ash, a tree that Northwest forest ecologist Stephen Arno, in his book *Northwest Trees*, describes "as a typical eastern hardwood that got misplaced on the west side of the continent."

After traversing the wetlands, the trail weaves around various logging artifacts in various degrees of decay before taking to an old logging railroad bed. You can take a shortcut trail to the left, back to the road, or continue on the full loop. Following the old railbed, the trail eventually skirts an attractive wetland complete with an observation deck. Across the

Old logging relics litter the forest floor along the Whistle Punk Trail.

dogwood-dotted swamp, you may be surprised to see towering firs and cedar—trees hundreds of years old and spared from past harvesting.

Continue hiking, crossing a channel and enter that ancient forest, part of the Thornton T. Munger Research Natural Area. The trail returns to the old road that you started on. Turn left and head back to the trailhead to complete your loop.

EXTENDING YOUR TRIP

For a short and very interesting side trip, before following the loop back to your car, take the road right 0.4 mile through spectacular groves of ancient fir, hemlock, and cedar and come to the edge of the Wind River Forest Canopy

Mount Hood rises in the distance above the Columbia River Gorge.

Crane Research Station. From this spot, look up and catch a glimpse of the twenty-eight-story crane that was constructed in the early 1990s to allow scientists to study the canopy of the surrounding ancient forest. An interpretive display provides more insight. Return to the trailhead with a whole new appreciation of our ancient forests and logging heritage.

29 Sedum Point

RATING/ DIFFICULTY	ROUND-TRIP	ELEV GAIN/ HIGH POINT	SEASON
***/3	10 miles	2125 feet/ 3275 feet	May–Nov

Map: Green Trails Wind River No. 397; **Contact:** Gifford Pinchot National Forest, Mount Adams Ranger District, Trout Lake, (509) 395-3400, www.fs.fed.us/gpnf; **GPS:** N 45 48.684 W 121 57.383

Solitude is almost guaranteed along this overlooked section of the Pacific Crest Trail. Saunter through old-growth forest groves to a pair of excellent viewpoints—one north across the Trout Creek valley to the ancient forests of the Thornton T. Munger Research Natural Area, the other south down the Wind River valley out to the Columbia. And sedums? Yep, you'll see 'em! They're stonecrops, a ledge-clinging star-shaped yellow flower that sprouts from rosettes of fleshy leaves.

GETTING THERE

From Stevenson, head east on State Route 14 for 3 miles, turning left (north) onto Wind River Road. Drive 8.6 miles on this good paved road and turn left onto Hemlock Road (signed for the Wind River Work Center). After 1.2 miles (just beyond the work center), turn right onto Forest Road 43 (signed for

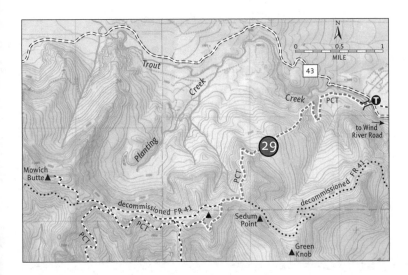

Canopy Crane). Proceed for 1.4 miles to the trailhead (elev. 1200 ft) on your left and parking for two vehicles—additional parking is available on the shoulder just beyond.

ON THE TRAIL

While this hike follows the Pacific Crest Trail, you'd hardly know it by this inconspicuous trailhead. The absence of signs or a reader board has led to more than a couple of cases of illegal mountain-bike use along this stretch. Surely there must be a few dollars somewhere to have a few signs posted?

Start by crossing Trout Creek on a sturdy arched bridge. Pass a riverside campsite and mosey through carpets of mossy greenery in a beautiful grove of old-growth forest. Begin climbing, crossing a few cascading creeks en route. Crest a ridge, and at 1.6 miles come to a ledge (elev. 1750 ft) granting excellent viewing north of Trout Creek cutting through a volcanic landscape. Immediately to the right

is Bunker Hill (Hike 27), an igneous plug. To the left is Trout Creek Hill, an ancient shield volcano like Oregon's Larch Mountain (Hike 69). See if you can locate the Wind River Forest Canopy Crane Research Station to the left of Bunker Hill. From this vantage you can see the twenty-eight-story crane hovering above a large grove of ancient forest.

The trail now turns southward, gently climbing along a ridge draped in uniform second growth. Occasionally pass a fire-scarred snag, evidence of past fires that resulted in this young forest.

After slightly descending into a small depression, the way gains elevation more steadily. Traverse a steep hillside, passing window views of Mount Adams and of the Indian Heaven Wilderness country. At 4 miles, pass through a lovely grove of big old firs, apparently spared from past fires. At 4.5 miles, intersect the decommissioned FR 41 (elev. 2950 ft). Continue on the PCT south another 0.4 mile, rounding a knoll. Leave the trail to the right, ascending steep meadows for 0.1 mile (careful to not damage delicate flowers) to a 3275-foot semi-open summit.

Views! Mount Adams and Hood! And the Wind River valley to the Gorge—Dog Mountain, Mount Defiance, Tanner Butte, and more. The flower show is good too—and there are even some sedums. But technically you're not on Sedum Point; that's the smaller knoll directly to your east, reached by following old FR 41 for 0.5 mile followed by a short scramble.

EXTENDING YOUR TRIP

For more good views and solitude, continue south on the PCT for another 0.4 mile, reaching a junction with the Sedum Ridge Trail. Turn right, and after a couple of hundred feet turn left onto long-closed FR 41. Follow this easy-to-walk old road 0.8 mile, turning right at a large berm onto another closed road. Continue for 0.75 mile to the 3513-foot summit of Mowich Butte. The lookout is long gone and vegetation is growing in, but there's still excellent viewing north to Adams, Saint Helens, the Trapper Creek country, and a slew of old volcanoes and craters in between.

MEXICO TO CANADA

Putting in a long, hard day on the trail can certainly be challenging, but it can be rewarding as well. Imagine putting in three, four, or five months on the trail. A small group of hikers from coast to coast do just that each year on one of America's eight national scenic (long-distance) trails. The granddaddy of them all, the 2175-mile Appalachian Trail (AT) is the most popular. Completed in 1937, it winds its way from Georgia to Maine.

Here in the Columbia River Gorge, the Pacific Crest Trail works its way 2650 miles from the Mexican to the Canadian border. Though it was officially completed in 1993, in 1968 the Pacific Crest Trail—or PCT as it is lovingly called—joined the AT as one of America's first national trails. Administered by the National Park Service, the National Trails System consists of congressionally designated trails. Inclusion in the system is based on the trail's cultural, historical, and scenic attributes as well as its draw for outdoor recreation.

The PCT, like most of the national trails, actually consists of many trails woven together to form one continuous corridor. While much of the PCT traverses deep wilderness far from population centers and roads, many good day-hiking opportunities exist where the trail crosses or comes close to travel corridors.

The PCT is well maintained and cared for and is looked after by several citizen groups like the Pacific Crest Trail Association (PCTA). In the Columbia River Gorge, take a day hike on this grand trail at Table Mountain (Hike 23), Gillette Lake (Hike 26), Bunker Hill (Hike 27), Sedum Point (Hike 29), Dry Creek Falls (Hike 83), Benson Plateau (Hike 84), Wahtum Lake (Hike 91), and Indian Mountain (Hike 93). You can walk across the Bridge of the Gods too, which is part of the trail, although it'll cost you $0.50 and there is no sidewalk—so use caution.

Opposite: East summit Soda Peaks

trapper creek wilderness

The southernmost federal wilderness in Washington's Cascade Range, Trapper Creek lies just a dozen miles north of the Columbia River Gorge. At just over 6000 acres it's not very large, but its importance is grand. Protecting nearly the entire Trapper Creek watershed, this wilderness provides exceptional and pristine habitat in an area that has been heavily and intensively logged. Trapper Creek houses superb stands of old-growth forest that are habitat for endangered northern spotted owls. The heavily forested wilderness contains one lake, many creeks, and several peaks that top 4000 feet and provide excellent viewing. Elk are numerous as are cougar, bobcat, and black bear. While

Trapper Creek ranks among Washington's smaller wilderness areas, it offers exceptional hiking. An excellent network of trails, including many built by the Portland-based Mazamas, traverses the wilderness. Created as part of the 1984 Washington Wilderness Act, an adjacent 4540-acre roadless area (the Bourbon Tract) of equal ecological importance was left out of the wilderness due to timber pressures at the time. The Bourbon Tract, with its extensive old growth, would make a nice addition to the Trapper Creek Wilderness.

30 Trapper Creek

RATING/ DIFFICULTY	ROUND-TRIP	ELEV GAIN/ HIGH POINT	SEASON
***/3	9 miles	1500 feet/ 2400 feet	Apr–Dec

Maps: Green Trails Lookout Mtn No. 396, Wind River No. 397; **Contact:** Gifford Pinchot National Forest, Mount Adams Ranger District, Trout Lake, (509) 395-3400, www.fs.fed.us/gpnf; **Notes:** NW Forest Pass required. Free wilderness permit required, self-issued at trailhead; **GPS:** N 45 52.914 W 121 58.804

Follow frolicking Trapper Creek up a deep valley into the heart of the wilderness bearing its name. Wind through magnificent groves of towering ancient firs. Let cascading side creeks captivate you and stand in awe at a plummeting waterfall at Trapper's upper reaches. Steep ridges and peaks hem you in and capture plenty of moisture-laden clouds. Trapper Creek receives in excess of 100 inches of precipitation a year. The result? A lush and verdant environment and some pretty impressive trees!

Massive ancient trees line Trapper Creek.

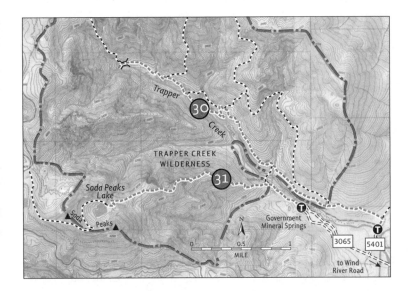

GETTING THERE

From Stevenson, head east on State Route 14 for 3 miles, turning left (north) onto Wind River Road. Drive 14.4 miles on this good paved road and turn left onto Forest Road 3065 (Mineral Springs Road). Continue for 0.4 mile, turning right onto FR 5401. In 0.5 mile come to the road end and trailhead (elev. 1200 ft). Privy available.

ON THE TRAIL

From the large parking area, enter thick, dark forest and immediately come to a junction. The trail right travels along Dry Creek through the Bourbon Roadless Area (Hike 33) to the Big Hollow Trail (Hike 34). You can make a superb 15-mile loop by combining these trails with the Trapper Creek hike.

Head left on the wide and well-graded Trapper Creek Trail. In 0.8 mile enter the wilderness and come to a major junction

shortly afterward. The trail right heads up Howe Ridge to 4207-foot Observation Peak (Hike 32). Strong hikers can combine it with the Trapper Creek Trail for a 13-mile loop. The trail left heads to a handful of cabins on a Forest Service road. Continue straight up the Trapper Creek Trail. After an easy 0.7 mile, cross a side creek and reach a junction (elev. 1400 ft) with the Soda Peaks Lake Trail (Hike 31). Continue right.

With Trapper Creek nowhere in sight, start climbing and pass showy Pacific dogwood trees among fire-scarred big firs and cedar snags. Even in this saturated valley, fire plays a major role in forest succession. At 2.5 miles, come to a junction with the Big Slide Trail (elev. 1900 ft). This side trail, along with others within the valley, was constructed by the Portland-based Mazamas. Many of these trails tend to be primitive and challenging. The Big Slide Trail climbs 700 feet in 0.7 mile to connect with the Howe Ridge Trail, offering a loop option on the return.

Head left and soon come to the Deer Cutoff Trail, another Mazamas-built side trail. Veer left and drop 300 feet into a spectacular grove of old-growth giants beside Trapper Creek. The valley now grows increasingly more rugged as the trail winds through more giant cedars, firs, and hemlocks and by a couple of mineral springs too.

At 3.3 miles reach the second junction with the Deer Cutoff Trail, and soon afterward intersect the Sunshine Trail (elev. 1900 ft), a very steep path that climbs up the southern face of Observation Peak. The Trapper Creek Trail, now much narrower and lightly traveled, continues to climb, crossing numerous side creeks and passing by pretty cascades. At about 4.5 miles the trail crosses Trapper Creek on a big bridge (elev. 2400 ft). This is a good spot to turn around after enjoying lunch on the bridge, watching the pristine waterway rush by below.

EXTENDING YOUR TRIP

Strong and adventurous hikers can continue farther along the Trapper Creek Trail. Beyond the bridge, the trail steeply climbs out of the valley, passing an overlook of breathtaking Trapper Falls, which plunges 100 feet. Eventually the climb eases as the trail reaches a broad, brushy ridge flush with huckleberries and frequented by elk. A tricky crossing of Trapper Creek is required to continue. Pass the Rim Trail and the Shortcut Trail before coming to a 3700-foot saddle at 7 miles, where the trail terminates at a four-way junction. Head left for Sister Rocks, right for Observation Peak (both Hike 35), or continue down the Big Hollow Trail to Dry Creek (Hikes 34 and 33, respectively) for a satisfying 15-mile loop.

31 Soda Peaks Lake

RATING/ DIFFICULTY	ROUND-TRIP	ELEV GAIN/ HIGH POINT	SEASON
****/5	7 miles	2460 feet/ 3760 feet	June–Nov

Maps: Green Trails Lookout Mtn No. 396, Wind River No. 397; **Contact:** Gifford Pinchot National Forest, Mount Adams Ranger District, Trout Lake, (509) 395-3400, www .fs.fed.us/gpnf; **Notes:** NW Forest Pass required. Free wilderness permit required, self-issued at trailhead; **GPS:** N 45 52.972 W 121 59.771

The only lake within the 6050-acre Trapper Creek Wilderness, Soda Peaks Lake sits in a cirque surrounded by majestic ancient trees. The way is tough—quite steep—but tenacious hikers will be rewarded with tranquility upon reaching this little subalpine gem. Gargantuan towering trees provide plenty of awe along the way, and a mighty fine viewpoint of the Trapper Creek watershed waits for those who want to push on a little farther.

GETTING THERE

From Stevenson, head east on State Route 14 for 3 miles, turning left (north) onto Wind River Road. Drive 14.4 miles on this good paved road and turn left onto Forest Road 3065 (Mineral Springs Road). Continue for 1.2 miles to Government Mineral Springs and parking. The trail begins near the Iron Mike mineral spring (elev. 1300 ft). Privy available.

ON THE TRAIL

Sure, take time to check out what remains of the Government Mineral Springs area before you embark on your hike. A hotel and resort were built here in 1910 to accommodate

Excellent views from high above Soda Peaks Lake

tourists seeking the medicinal waters of the region. A happening place during the prohibition years, the resort burned to the ground in 1934. The Civilian Conservation Corps was responsible for building the guard station in 1937, along with the campground, picnic area, and pump pavilion that still remain. Take a sip from Iron Mike, and then head north up the gated road, passing a row of leased cabins before coming alongside Trapper Creek.

The way then crosses a side creek, which once supplied the old resort with water, and then enters the Trapper Creek Wilderness.

Shortly beyond, 0.5 mile from your start, reach a junction with the Soda Peaks Lake Trail (elev. 1500 ft). The way right connects with the Trapper Creek Trail and was once the recommended way to begin this hike. Unfortunately, the old bridge is out and has not been replaced, requiring a difficult ford for much of the hiking season.

Continue left, immediately climbing—and steeply at that! Following tight switchbacks, steadily ascend a rib covered in salal, huckleberries, and old-growth greenery—some of the ancient giants defy gravity. Gaps in the forest canopy provide glimpses to a lush junglelike landscape that may very well harbor Sasquatch and legendary plane hijacker D. B. Cooper.

Continue the grueling climb out of the valley. Magnificent hemlocks and noble firs help divert your attention from the strenuous slog. Cross a small scree slope that's vibrant in autumn, and then commence to clamber once more. After 3 challenging miles, arrive at the forested shores of Soda Peaks Lake (elev. 3760 ft). Nice camp and picnic sites can be found by the outlet stream. Good huckleberry harvesting can be found throughout the basin. Linger long—you earned it and deserve it.

EXTENDING YOUR TRIP

If you're not wiped out, by all means continue up the trail, traversing the cirque that cradles the lake. About 0.8 mile from the lake, the trail reaches a saddle between the two Soda Peaks. Continue for another 0.25 mile, reaching a splendid viewpoint (elev. 4370 ft) that overlooks the lake, the Trapper Creek valley, and beyond. The trail continues, leaving the wilderness area to cross scree slopes with good views south and west before reentering forest. It terminates 1 mile later at FR 54 (elev. 3650 ft), an alternative

approach reached by following paved FR 54 from Stabler for about 12 miles.

32   Observation Peak via Howe Ridge

RATING/ DIFFICULTY	ROUND-TRIP	ELEV GAIN/ HIGH POINT	SEASON
****/5	13 miles	3000 feet/ 4207 feet	June–Nov

Maps: Green Trails Lookout Mtn No. 396, Wind River No. 397; **Contact:** Gifford Pinchot National Forest, Mount Adams Ranger District, Trout Lake, (509) 395-3400, www .fs.fed.us/gpnf; **Notes:** NW Forest Pass required. Free wilderness permit required, self-issued at trailhead; **GPS:** N 45 52.914 W 121 58.804

A long and winding trail to a former lookout site, this hike offers a good workout, solitude, and spectacular old-growth scenery capped with excellent views of Mounts Hood, Adams, and Saint Helens. Stare down, too, into the uncut thick forests of the Trapper Creek valley, one of the few remaining unblemished watersheds in the southern reaches of the Gifford Pinchot National Forest.

GETTING THERE

From Stevenson, head east on State Route 14 for 3 miles, turning left (north) onto Wind River Road. Drive 14.4 miles on this good paved road and turn left onto Forest Road 3065 (Mineral Springs Road). Continue for 0.4 mile, turning right onto FR 5401. In 0.5 mile come to the road end and trailhead (elev. 1200 ft). Privy available.

ON THE TRAIL

While this route to Observation Peak climbs 3000 feet, most of the way is well graded on good tread. Hikers looking for a shorter, much easier way to the 4207-foot former lookout site should take the Observation Trail from FR 64 (Hike 35). Hikers looking to make a long day hike or overnighter from either the Trapper Creek Trail (Hike 30) or Big Hollow Trail (Hike 34) should return via this route because of its gentle grade.

From the large parking area, enter thick, dark forest and immediately come to a junction. The trail right travels along Dry Creek through the Bourbon Roadless Area (Hike 33) to the Big Hollow Trail. You can make a superb 15-mile loop by combining these trails with the Observation Peak hike. Head left on the wide and well-graded Trapper Creek Trail, and in 0.8 mile come to a junction (elev. 1300 ft) after entering the wilderness.

Turn right onto Observation Trail No. 132 and begin climbing. Steadily yet gently, the well-graded trail winds its way up Howe Ridge, traversing steep slopes and darting in and out of creek-containing ravines. At about 2.5 miles, come to a nice campsite in a grove of big firs perched above a cascading creek (elev. 2300 ft). About 0.5 mile beyond, pass the Big Slide Trail, one of several primitive trails within the wilderness built by the Portland-based Mazamas. This path drops steeply to lose about 700 feet in 0.5 mile, where it connects with the Trapper Creek Trail.

Continue on the main trail, winding up the ridge. At about 4 miles cross a scree slope, which provides an excellent view over the valley to the Soda Peaks. At 4.6 miles the Sunshine Trail veers left for a steep and rough route to the valley below. Continue right, now traversing northeast-facing slopes, as waves of emerald ridges

A pair of hikers admire Mount Adams from Observation Peak.

are revealed through gaps in the forest canopy. At 5.9 miles reach a junction in a forested saddle (elev. 3800 ft). The way right leads to the Shortcut Trail to Trapper Creek (Hike 30), the Observation Trail to Sister Rocks (Hike 35), and the Big Hollow Trail to Dry Creek (Hikes 34 and 33, respectively). Head left instead, making one last climb to the 4207-foot summit of Observation Peak in 0.6 mile.

This is not the highest summit in the Trapper Creek Wilderness, but it's the one

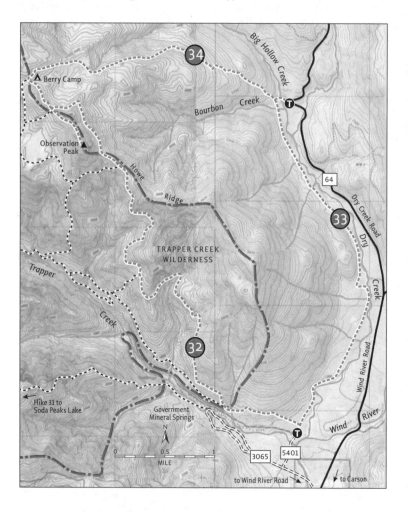

Dry Creek's extensive gravel bars invite lounging and exploring.

with the best views. Stand mouth agape at the showy, snowy, bulky volcanoes surrounding you: Rainier, Saint Helens, Adams, Hood, and Jefferson. Stare, too, at all of the little nubbles, buttes, and other volcanic remnants scattered across the landscape. Nothing remains of the lookout, which was decommissioned in the 1960s. But a carpet of wildflowers is rolled out on the summit for most of the summer.

33 Dry Creek

RATING/ DIFFICULTY	ROUND-TRIP	ELEV GAIN/ HIGH POINT	SEASON
**/2	8.4 miles	350 feet/ 1500 feet	Year-round

Map: Green Trails Wind River No. 397; **Contact:** Gifford Pinchot National Forest, Mount Adams Ranger District, Trout Lake, (509) 395-3400, www.fs.fed.us/gpnf; **Notes:** NW Forest Pass required; **GPS:** N 45 52.914 W 121 58.804

Saunter up a quiet valley floor sprinkled with groves of evergreen giants at the foot of the abrupt slopes of Howe Ridge. Following alongside a creek that at times disappears into a subterranean channel, marvel at rippling waters that yield to naked creekbed. While roads lie not far away, the valley exudes a feeling of remoteness and stillness. But look around, for these lush woods are anything but still, harboring a cornucopia of critters from flittering wrens to wintering elk.

GETTING THERE

From Stevenson, head east on State Route 14 for 3 miles, turning left (north) onto Wind River Road. Drive 14.4 miles on this good paved road and turn left onto Forest Road 3065 (Mineral Springs Road). Continue for 0.4 mile, turning right onto FR 5401. In 0.5 mile come to the road end and trailhead (elev. 1200 ft). Privy available.

ON THE TRAIL

From the large open parking area, enter thick, dark forest and immediately come to a junction. The trail left marches up the heart of the Trapper Creek valley, side trails radiating from it to the depths of the wilderness. Pay homage to Robert Frost, and head right on the trail less taken, wrapping around the base of Howe Ridge to traverse lush flats along Dry Creek. The entire way is within the 4540-acre Bourbon Roadless Area, which includes prime old-growth forest and elk and salmon habitat. Adding it to the adjacent Trapper Creek Wilderness is a must.

The trail is lightly traveled but well defined and nearly level for most of the way. After climbing about 50 feet or so up and over a bluff above the may-or-may-not-be visibly flowing creek, the trail takes to an old logging railroad bed. Come upon a few areas that permit good gravel-bar roaming and feet soaking.

At about 2 miles the trail makes a sharp left away from the creek but soon meets up with it once again—this time right alongside it. Enjoy this exceptionally pretty section of trail, with occasional viewing to the ridge opposite across the creek. The trail continues upstream, and after following an old skid road enters a grove of massive old Doug-firs.

At 4.1 miles reach Bourbon Creek (elev. 1500 ft), its intoxicating waters flowing down from Howe Ridge. You won't be wetting your feet here, but your feet are another story. The creek can be difficult to cross in high water and requires a little rock hopping even in the dry months. If forced to turn around, take solace in knowing that the trail terminates just 0.1 mile beyond at the Big Hollow Trail (Hike 34). Retrace your steps and enjoy the gentle trail, this time downstream.

34 Big Hollow

RATING/ DIFFICULTY	ROUND-TRIP	ELEV GAIN/ HIGH POINT	SEASON
***/4	9.2 miles	2700 feet/ 4207 feet	June–Nov

Maps: Green Trails Lookout Mtn No. 396, Wind River No. 397; **Contact:** Gifford Pinchot National Forest, Mount Adams Ranger District, Trout Lake, (509) 395-3400, www.fs.fed.us /gpnf; **GPS:** N 45 55.569 W 121 58.794

A quiet and lonely trail through the heart of the 4540-acre Bourbon Roadless Area, a de facto wilderness of primeval forest and clear rushing streams. The way is tough, hastily climbing a steep ridge dividing the Bourbon and Big Hollow Creek watersheds. An alternative approach to Observation Peak, this route helps you appreciate the deeply-cut valleys and formidable ridges of this wild corner of the Cascade Mountains.

GETTING THERE

From Stevenson, head east on State Route 14 for 3 miles, turning left (north) onto Wind River Road. Drive 14.4 miles on this good paved road, bearing right at the Government Mineral Springs turnoff (where the road becomes Forest Road 30). Continue on Wind River Road (FR 30) for another 2.1 miles, turning left onto Dry

Precarious log crossing over Big Hollow Creek

Creek Road (FR 64). Follow this paved, narrow road for 2.1 miles to the trailhead (elev. 1530 ft).

ON THE TRAIL

Taking off into a jungle of greenery, the trail drops a tad to cross lush bottomlands. At 0.2 mile reach Big Hollow Creek (elev. 1500 ft) just above its confluence with Bourbon Creek and then farther downstream its confluence with Dry Creek. Yep, in this hollow the Bourbon runs dry. Big Hollow Creek, however, usually runs pretty strong. A conveniently fallen tree crafted into an attractive albeit slightly discomforting to cross bridge spans the rushing waterway. Just beyond, in a mossy maple glade, is a junction with the Dry Creek Trail (Hike 33).

Veer right and immediately begin climbing. The grade doesn't mess around, opting to maximize elevation gain. At about 1 mile, wind through some big fire-scarred Doug-firs. Continue climbing through open old-growth forest, catching glimpses of ridges north and the Big Hollow below. At just past 2 miles, pass an old "Two Mile" marker in a tree (elev. 3050 ft). Not bad accuracy for back in the day!

Continuing through beautiful ancient forest, the grade eases, eventually coming upon a tributary of Big Hollow Creek (elev. 3400 ft) at about 3 miles. Prepare to get your feet wet or scout around for a better crossing. Then resume climbing but at a saner grade. Look for old insulators lining the way—this trail once provided the communication line to the lookout that no longer remains on Observation Peak.

At 3.5 miles come to a piped spring that once provided the lookout keepers with water and still provides backpackers with something to rehydrate their meals. Just beyond is a short cutoff trail on the left that leads to the Trapper Creek Trail (Hike 30). And just beyond that the Big Hollow Trail terminates at cozy Berry Camp at the junction with the Observation Trail (elev. 3760 ft).

You've worked hard to get this far, so you might as well continue a little farther to get a visual payoff. Turn left, following the Observation Trail for 1.1 miles to the 4207-foot summit of Observation Peak. Enjoy the view down into the Bourbon and Wind River valleys and out to surrounding glacial-clad volcanoes.

35 Sister Rocks and Observation Peak

RATING/ DIFFICULTY	ROUND-TRIP	ELEV GAIN/ HIGH POINT	SEASON
****/3	7 miles	1575 feet/ 4268 feet	late June– Oct

Map: Green Trails Lookout Mtn No. 396; **Contact:** Gifford Pinchot National Forest, Mount Adams Ranger District, Trout Lake, (509) 395-3400, www.fs.fed.us/gpnf; **GPS:** N 45 56.994 W 122 02.386

A backdoor, much easier approach to Observation Peak, this route also grants easy access to the higher and more stunning Sister Rocks. Reaching these two lofty and spectacular viewpoints involves traversing a high ridge beneath a forest of towering old-growth trees. Come in June for wildflowers, September for huckleberries, and all summer and fall for the opportunity to witness bears, elk, and other wild denizens of the Trapper Creek Wilderness.

GETTING THERE
From Stevenson, head east on State Route 14 for 3 miles, turning left (north) onto Wind River Road. Drive 14.4 miles on this good paved road (which becomes Forest Road 30), bearing right at the Government Mineral Springs turnoff. Continue on Wind River Road for another 2.1 miles, turning left onto Dry Creek Road (FR 64). Follow this narrow and brushy-in-spots road for 6.1 miles (the pavement ends at 4.1 miles), and turn left onto FR 58. Continue for 2.1 miles, bearing left at an unmarked junction at 1.8 miles, and reach the trailhead (elev. 3500 ft).

ON THE TRAIL
The trail immediately enters old-growth forest, part of the last large tracts of ancient forest in the southern reaches of the Washington Cascades. Look out at the surrounding clear-cuts—the moth-eaten hills and uniform second growth. Now enter the forest primeval and notice the difference—biological diversity! The Bourbon Roadless Area must be added to the nation's protected wilderness preserves.

The trail winds through magnificent hemlocks and firs, cutting through a carpet of clintonia, bunchberry, and trillium. While lightly traveled, the tread and trail are in excellent shape, a sharp contrast to the access road that grows closer and closer to washing out each season.

As you steadily climb, the forest transitions to silver fir at about 1 mile. At 1.2 miles, crest a ridge (elev. 4100 ft) and enter the Trapper Creek Wilderness. An excellent viewpoint to Mount Adams lies left. A boot-beaten but

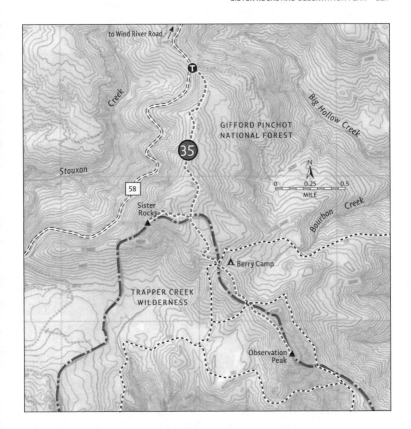

easy to follow path to Sister Rocks takes off right. Take it, meandering along a bear-grass-lined ridge to reach the juniper-lined ledges of Sister Rocks after 0.5 mile.

Once a site of a fire lookout, this 4268-foot peak offers breathtaking views of Mount Saint Helens, the Siouxon Roadless Area, the Soda Peaks and Trapper Creek watershed, and Mount Hood. All that remains of the lookout are broken glass and rusty nails (watch your dog). The old trail to this summit that came up from the west is also long gone.

After getting your fill of views, retrace your steps back to the main trail and head right to Observation Peak for another excellent vista. Following along a ridgeline, the trail loses a few hundred feet, reaching a 3750-foot saddle that boasts the snug Berry Camp 0.7 mile from the Sister Rocks way trail junction. Here, the Trapper Creek Trail (Hike 30) takes off right, while the Big Hollow Trail ventures left (Hike 34). A small, fairly reliable spring can be found just a short distance down the latter trail.

There are excellent views of Soda Peaks and Trapper Creek watershed from Sister Rocks.

Continue straight for Observation Peak. Notice the Pacific dogwoods en route, their blossoms among the showiest in the Northwest. A shy 0.5 mile from Berry Camp, the Shortcut Trail branches right to Trapper Creek. Just beyond is another junction. Left winds down the long and lonely Howe Ridge (Hike 32). Go right, regaining those lost few hundred feet and reaching the 4207-foot summit of Observation Peak within 0.6 mile. The story here is the same as Sister Rocks, in that a fire lookout once graced this peak. Nothing remains but the extended views from Mount Rainier to Mount Hood that the lucky lookout keeper used to wake up to on a regular basis. That is, when it wasn't raining! Savor the scenery.

Opposite: Looking east from Coyote Wall

columbia river gorge, washington: east

Plentiful sunshine, copious wildflowers, fascinating geological formations, and hillsides of magical oak forests are what await you in the eastern reaches of Washington's Columbia River Gorge. Site of many new additions to the national scenic area, the trail system here continues to grow—adding legions of admiring hikers who return to this region over and over again. Many of the trails remain open all winter. Summer can be hot. Fall is lovely. But spring is the best time to visit, despite the abundance of ticks looking for hosts. Some of the best flower shows in the entire Northwest unfurl here in spring and early summer. White Salmon and Bingen offer visitor services, while Columbia Hills and Maryhill State Parks are ideal for setting up base camp.

36 Wind Mountain

RATING/ DIFFICULTY	ROUND-TRIP	ELEV GAIN/ HIGH POINT	SEASON
***/3	2.8 miles	1230 feet/ 1907 feet	Mar–Dec

Map: Green Trails Bonneville Dam No. 429 (trail not shown); **Contact:** Columbia River Gorge National Scenic Area, (541) 308-1700, www.fs.fed.us/r6/columbia; **GPS:** N 45 42.862 W 121 45.205

🏠 *Though this conical peak is a well-recognized landmark within the Gorge, few folks have actually hiked it. Overshadowed by nearby Dog Mountain in both height and popularity, Wind lacks the famous floral shows of that iconic peak. But its 1907-foot summit, hovering over the Columbia River, does grant some delectable views, and Wind Mountain has something Dog can't bark about. The summit is an archeological reserve with numerous*

Wind Mountain with its Indian vision pits rises directly above the Columbia River.

rock pits once used by young Native Americans for vision quests. It's a sacred place that continues to enlighten folks from all backgrounds.

GETTING THERE

From Vancouver, follow State Route 14 east for 50.5 miles, turning left onto Wind Mountain Road. (From Portland, follow I-84 east to exit 44 at Cascade Locks and take the Bridge of the Gods—$1 toll—to SR 14. Turn right and proceed 8.5 miles to Wind Mountain Road. From Hood River, take exit 64 off I-84 and cross the Columbia River on a toll bridge—$0.75—turning left, or west, onto SR 14. Drive 15.7 miles to Wind Mountain

Road.) Follow Wind Mountain Road, bearing right at 1 mile and reaching Girl Scout Road at 1.4 miles, where you turn right. Drive 0.2 mile to the pavement's end at a clearing; park here (elev. 875 ft).

ON THE TRAIL

Begin by walking down the dirt road east for 0.1 mile. Here, beside a parking area (elev. 775 ft) for perhaps two vehicles, locate the unsigned but very obvious trail on your right. The way is short but steep in a couple of sections. The tread is narrow but well built.

The trail begins by making a long traverse across Wind's steep and thickly forested eastern slope. At about 0.6 mile, the way rounds a shoulder (elev. 1200 ft) and swings west through open forest. A short spur (use caution) leads to an overlook on the left.

Now steeply climbing, the trail crosses a large scree slope before returning to forest just below the summit. A large interpretive sign explains the significance of the numerous rock pits dug into the summit scree slopes. Archeologists believe the pits were constructed by Native Americans between

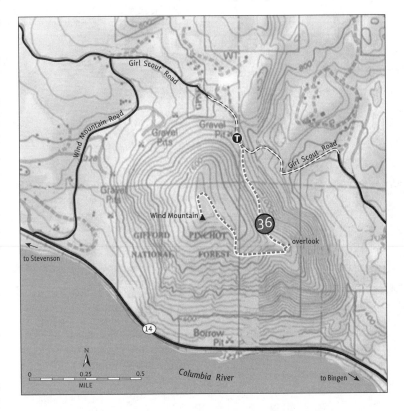

200 and 1000 years ago and were used for spirit questing.

Make the final short climb to the 1907-foot summit, being mindful not to leave the trail lest you damage this important archeological and cultural site. Aside from the rock pits, views from the summit are also intriguing. Look west over Home Valley and Carson and out to Table Mountain and Beacon Rock. Turn east for good views of Augspurger, Dog, Wygant, and Defiance. Nick Eaton forms an imposing wall south across the river. Sit and listen to the wind whistle through the surrounding contorted firs.

Conical Wind Mountain as viewed from Dog Mountain's open slopes

37 Dog Mountain

RATING/ DIFFICULTY	LOOP	ELEV GAIN/ HIGH POINT	SEASON
*****/4	7.3 miles	2900 feet/ 2945 feet	Mar–Dec

Map: Green Trails Hood River No. 430; **Contact:** Columbia River Gorge National Scenic Area, (541) 308-1700, www.fs.fed.us/r6 /columbia; **Notes:** NW Forest Pass required; **GPS:** N 45 41.956 W 121 42.464

 The most spectacular hike on the Washington side of the Columbia Gorge, Dog Mountain offers much to bark about. Straddling the transition zone between swirling clouds and golden rays of sunshine, Dog affords a beautiful perspective of the multifaceted Gorge. The view straight down to the river and over the cone of Wind Mountain is beyond breathtaking. And the flowers! You'll find the most stunning floral show sprawled across the sun-kissed meadows of this riverside peak. But there's a hitch. The way is steep making this a dog of a hike. And its popularity means you're never far from the pack.

GETTING THERE

From Vancouver, follow State Route 14 east for 54 miles to the trailhead (elev. 100 ft). Privy available. (From Portland, follow I-84 east to exit 44 at Cascade Locks and take the Bridge of the Gods—$1 toll—to SR 14. Turn right and proceed 12 miles to the trailhead. From Hood River, take exit 64 off I-84 and cross the Columbia River on a toll bridge—$0.75—turning left, or west, onto SR 14. Proceed 12.2 miles to the trailhead.)

ON THE TRAIL

Three trails ascend Dog Mountain: the old Dog Mountain Trail, the new Dog Mountain Trail, and the Augspurger connector. The old trail is the steepest and least interesting. The new trail is steep but full of views. The connector, while considerably longer than the other two, is quiet and only steep in sections. My suggestion? Up the new for maximum views and down the connector for minimal knee discomfort.

From the trailhead at the east end of the gargantuan parking area, begin climbing. The tread is wide—all the better to keep you from rubbing against the poison oak that grows in profusion here. Keep an eye out for rattlesnakes too, as they are occasionally spotted on Dog's lower reaches.

Passing under scrubby oaks and elegant pines, the way relentlessly climbs. After about 0.6 mile reach a junction (elev. 750 ft). The old trail heads left. Keep right on the new trail and, now in thick forest, continue ascending steeply. The grade finally begins to ease, and at 1.8 miles you can take a break at a grassy knoll (elev. 1600 ft), panting over some excellent views. But to quote a 1970s BTO song, "You ain't seen nothing yet!" And you ain't seen the end of the climbing either. Look up!

The way reenters forest and meets up once again with the old trail at about 2.3 miles (elev. 1970 ft). Continue straight, on a grade that can best be described as insanely steep. After 0.4 mile of true grit, once again break out of the forest and enter the famed flowered upper slopes of the mountain. Sensory overload! From spring through summer, you'll see a sprawling carpet of dazzling flowers: balsamroot, paintbrush, lupine, desert parsley, cluster lilies, and a myriad of others compete with a gorgeous backdrop of conical Wind Mountain and the buttressed ridges of Oregon's Mount Defiance, Nick Eaton Ridge, and Benson Plateau rising above the river. It's quintessential Columbia Gorge majesty.

At 2.9 miles, reach a junction on an open bluff unofficially known as the Puppy (elev. 2500 ft), where there was a fire lookout from 1931 until 1967. The right-hand trail makes a gradual ascent to the summit. It's forested and badly overgrown. Skip it and head left, traversing more meadow and skirting over and beneath small cliffs, enjoying nonstop views.

At 3.2 miles, reach a junction with the Augspurger Trail connector (elev. 2800 ft), your return route. But first continue right for 0.1 mile, and then turn left on a short spur to reach the 2945-foot Dog Mountain summit. The actual summit is forested and lies just to the east. Don't waste your time crashing brush looking for it. Instead, plop your butt down and soak up the view—from Hood to Saint Helens to Silver Star—one of the finest in the Gorge. You earned it.

When ready to descend, retrace your steps to the Augspurger Trail connector. Follow this lightly traveled path across windblown meadows, steadily losing elevation. Downward momentum is temporarily halted with a short ascent up a small knoll, and then once again it's downward, back into the forest to reach the Augspurger Trail (elev. 2250 ft) after about 0.8 mile.

The way right leads to Augspurger Mountain (Hike 38). The way left heads back to your vehicle. Languidly descend, traversing scree slopes and cool forests of mature trees. Enjoy nice views of Wind Mountain along the way. The grade is mostly gentle on this former section of the Pacific Crest Trail. At about 3.9 miles from the summit reach the trailhead.

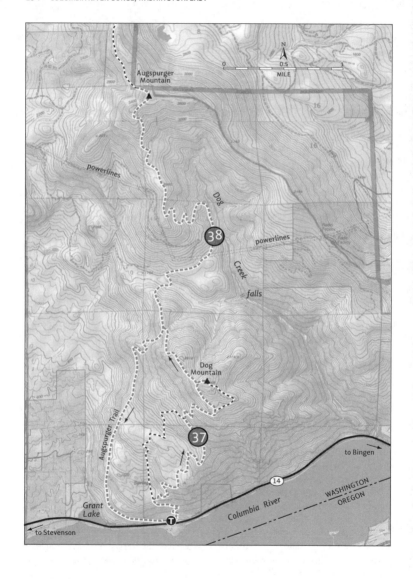

Augspurger
Mountain

N

0   0.5   1
MILE

powerlines

Dog

38

powerlines

Creek

falls

Dog
Mountain

Augspurger Trail

37

to Bingen

14

WASHINGTON
OREGON

Columbia River

Grant
Lake

T

to Stevenson

38 Augspurger Mountain

RATING/ DIFFICULTY	ROUND-TRIP	ELEV GAIN/ HIGH POINT	SEASON
****/5	13.8 miles	4180 feet/ 3660 feet	Apr–Nov

Map: Green Trails Columbia River Gorge–West No. 428S; **Contact:** Columbia River Gorge National Scenic Area, (541) 308-1700, www .fs.fed.us/r6/columbia; **Notes:** NW Forest Pass required; **GPS:** N 45 41.960 W 121 42.509

Perhaps the loneliest mountain accessible by trail on the Washington side of the Gorge—ironic too, due to its easy access right off State Route 14 and its close proximity to Dog Mountain, one of the most popular peaks in the Gorge. The views from Augspurger are also sprawling and plentiful—some of the best in the Gorge. Likewise for wildflowers. And you'll get it all to yourself. So what's the scoop? The way is long, with a lot of elevation and a section of encroaching greenery that scares people away. But the brush is ephemeral and the trail is in excellent shape—what are you waiting for?

Mount Adams above a ridge of wildflowers

GETTING THERE

From Vancouver, follow State Route 14 east for 54 miles to the trailhead (elev. 100 ft). Privy available. (From Portland, follow I-84 east to exit 44 at Cascade Locks and take the Bridge of the Gods—$1 toll—to SR 14. Turn right and proceed 12 miles to the trailhead. From Hood River, take exit 64 off I-84 and cross the Columbia River on a toll bridge—$0.75—turning left, or west, onto SR 14. Proceed 12.2 miles to the trailhead.)

ON THE TRAIL

From Dog Mountain's mall-size parking lot, locate the Augspurger Trail and immediately leave the crowds behind. On a very gentle grade, the trail wraps around Dog Mountain, traversing several scree slopes that provide nice views out to Wind Mountain and the Columbia. Once part of the Pacific Crest Trail, Augspurger fell off most hikers' radar once a new route closer to a bridged crossing of the Columbia was laid around Table Mountain.

At 2.9 miles come to a junction (elev. 2250 ft) with a trail leading right to Dog Mountain—a trail I have dubbed the Augie-Doggie (remember him?) connector. The Augspurger Trail continues left, descending into a seemingly impenetrable thicket of thimbleberries. This discourages many of the few who considered carrying on to Augspurger Mountain. Don't let it dissuade you. The head-high brush chokes the trail for less than 0.2 mile. The tread is good. Fight your way through—and sing: bears love thimbleberries. Once through, rejoice and continue descending into a saddle (elev. 1780 ft), crossing a small creek in a grove of big hemlocks and firs.

Start climbing again, and reach a dirt service road (elev. 1900 ft) at 3.7 miles. Turn right and follow the road, passing under high-tension wires and coming to trail again at 4.4 miles (elev. 2300 ft). Through a forest of tall firs and shrubby vine maple carpeted in vanilla leaf, make a long traverse high above Dog Creek yelping below. Then switchback up a ridge and break out onto a flowered basalt ridge. Views! Flowers! Keep climbing—they get better. Rising above adjacent powerlines, the trail crests a 2950-foot knoll at 5.2 miles. The Columbia River flows into the west beneath Beacon Rock and Table Mountain. To the south, it's Dog, Defiance, Nick Eaton, and Hood. This is a good place to call it quits, but the views do get better.

Continue along the ridge spine, passing an array of floral arrangements and hanging gardens and then undulating between forest and view-granting meadows. Bear scat is prevalent—be bear aware here. A few minor brushy sections are encountered, but the tread remains good. After some short steep switchbacks, round a false summit, and at 6.8 miles reach the actual summit (elev. 3660 ft) cloaked in trees. Disappointed? Don't be—continue on the trail just another 0.1 mile, descending 150 feet to spectacular flower-dotted meadows and jaw-dropping views—among the best in the Gorge. West is the mighty Columbia River, the Wind River valley, Trapper Creek Peaks, and Silver Star. North, Saint Helens and Adams rise above the Indian Heaven Peaks, Grassy Knoll, Big and Little Huckleberry Mountains, and the Big Lava Bed. Enjoy a view that very few of the millions of hikers who visit the Gorge each year will ever see.

EXTENDING YOUR TRIP

The trail continues descending, reaching a dirt road at 2 miles. You mean there's a short way here? The roads leading to the north trailhead are a nightmare—and besides, you would have missed all the great meadows along the way. If funding becomes available in the future, the Forest Service would like to connect this trail to Grassy Knoll (Hike 39).

39 Grassy Knoll and Big Huckleberry Mountain

Grassy Knoll

RATING/ DIFFICULTY	ROUND-TRIP	ELEV GAIN/ HIGH POINT	SEASON
*****/3	4.4 miles	1050 feet/ 3648 feet	Mid-Apr–Nov

Big Huckleberry Mountain

RATING/ DIFFICULTY	ROUND-TRIP	ELEV GAIN/ HIGH POINT	SEASON
*****/4	11.2 miles	2460 feet/ 4209 feet	June–Nov

Maps: Green Trails Wind River No. 397, Willard No. 398; **Contact:** Gifford Pinchot National Forest, Mount Adams Ranger District, Trout Lake, (509) 395-3400, www.fs.fed.us /gpnf; **GPS:** N 45 47.858 W 121 44.470

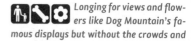 *Longing for views and flowers like Dog Mountain's famous displays but without the crowds and*

The Big Lava Bed

strenuous approach? Then plant yourself down on the Grassy Knoll Trail. Shrouded in a kaleidoscope of wildflowers, this former lookout site also offers jaw-slacking views from Hood to Adams. And a rocky craggy knoll on the way grants an eagle's-eye perspective of the massive and appropriately named Big Lava Bed. If you're feeling energetic, set out for Big Huckleberry Mountain via more knolls that you'll extol for their far-reaching views, dazzling floral displays, and lack of human visitors.

GETTING THERE

From Stevenson, head east on State Route 14 for 3 miles (6 miles from the Bridge of the Gods), turning left (north) onto the Wind River Road. Then proceed 4.1 miles and turn right (just after Wind River Bridge) onto Bear Creek Road. Follow this at-first paved road for 7.1 miles (it becomes gravel Forest Road 6808 at 3.6 miles), and reach an unsigned junction. Turn left on bumpy-but-okay-for-cars FR 68, coming to another junction at 2.1 miles at Triangle Pass. Bear right immediately to reach the trailhead (elev. 2800 ft).

ON THE TRAIL

Starting across an open patch of ridge, get a taste of what lies ahead in the form of larkspur, paintbrush, desert parsley, and more. Then enter forest and steadily climb. The well-maintained trail works its way through beautiful old growth before skirting above an old gravel pit. At 1.2 miles emerge on a rocky knoll (elev. 3620 ft) that grants exceptional viewing over the sprawling Big Lava Bed, with Mount Adams and Little Huckleberry Mountain hovering above. One of the South Cascades' most striking land-

forms, this massive flow originated from a crater some thousands of years ago. Now lodgepole pines and other hardy plants grow within the contorted, jagged, hardened lava, which emits magnetic forces known to thwart compass and GPS systems. Best to

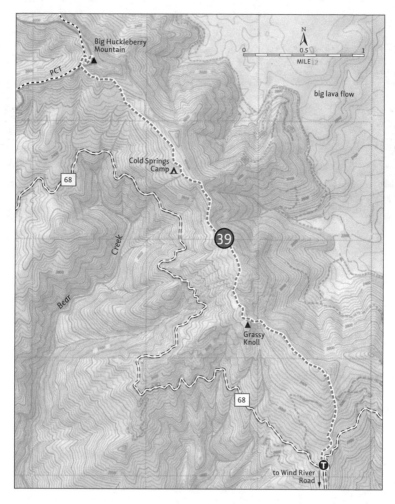

appreciate this place from above—but keep children and dogs away from the cliff edges.

Reenter forest and descend 200 feet before steeply climbing to the broad, appropriately named Grassy Knoll (elev. 3648 ft) at 2.2 miles. All that remains of the lookout are the foundation posts. But a tower isn't necessary to take in the stupendous views. Gaze south to hulking Augspurger Mountain, conical Wind Mountain, icy Mount Hood, and the shimmering Columbia. Stare west across Sedum Ridge to Silver Star, and turn northeast to capture Mount Adams. And don't forget to cast your glances downward to a myriad of flowers, including daffodils, no doubt planted years ago by a lookout keeper.

Wax content and call it a hike. Or if you're compelled to burn more calories, carry on following the trail northward. The way continues up a broader knoll bursting with even more flowers (elev. 3800 ft) and then drops to a saddle (elev. 3675 ft), which itself grants excellent views both east and west. The trail then steeply climbs an open sun-kissed slope (notice the balsamroot?), topping out at about 3875-feet before gently descending across forested slopes to Cold Springs Camp (elev. 3850 ft) at 3.9 miles.

Refill water bottles and climb another 75 feet or so before once again descending. Then, on bear-grass-lined trail, skirt beneath some ledges (elev. 3650 ft) and cross two small creeks before climbing steeply to meet the Pacific Crest Trail (elev. 4000 ft) at 5.4 miles.

Turn right and then turn right again onto the short but steep spur to Big Huckleberry Mountain. After 0.2 mile emerge on the 4209-foot summit, which also once sported a fire lookout. Views here aren't as widespread as from Grassy, but there's still some decent looking out—and flowers—and a more than likely chance you'll be alone. Contemplate why Little Huckleberry Mountain across the Big Lava Bed is more than 500 feet higher than Big Huckleberry!

40 Weldon Wagon Road

RATING/ DIFFICULTY	ROUND-TRIP	ELEV GAIN/ HIGH POINT	SEASON
***/3	5.4 miles	1290 feet/ 1900 feet	Year-round

Map: Green Trails Columbia River Gorge–East No. 432S; **Contact:** Washington DNR, Southeast Region (Ellensburg), (509) 925-8510, www.dnr.wa.gov; **Notes:** Crosses private property. Do not stray from trail right-of-way; **GPS:** N 45 48.170 W 121 28.171

Follow an old wagon road high onto a ridge that harbors an exceptional stand of Oregon white oak. Built from 1908 to 1911 to transport White Salmon valley–grown apples to market, the road long ago fell out of use. But it has since been resurrected as a trail—and one of the Gorge's least traveled and unusual ones at that. Come for the flower show in spring and the views of Mount Hood year-round. Foraging turkeys and deer will keep you company.

GETTING THERE

From Stevenson, drive State Route 14 east for 22 miles, turning left onto SR 141A. (From Portland, drive I-84 east to exit 64 in Hood River and take the toll bridge—$0.75—into Washington. Turn left, or west, on SR 14 and drive 1.6 miles, turning right, or north, onto SR 141A.) In 2.2 miles bear left (north) onto SR 141, and after 3.8 miles turn right in Husum onto Indian Creek Road (the turnoff is just before a bridge over Rattlesnake

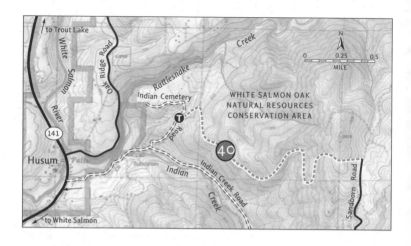

A lone oak along the Weldon Wagon Road

Creek). Follow this good gravel road 0.6 mile, bearing left onto Indian Cemetery Road. Proceed for another 0.4 mile to an unmarked jeep track on the right. This is the trailhead (elev. 650 ft). Park at the wide pullover on the left.

ON THE TRAIL

Begin on an old jeep track. At 0.2 mile, the Weldon Wagon Road Trail (signed) takes off right. A Klickitat County right-of-way, the trail nevertheless traverses private property at both its eastern and western reaches. Stay on the trail and respect the property owners' privacy and rights.

The way immediately gains elevation, winding through a mixed forest of pine, oak, and Doug-fir. At 0.7 mile leave forest for field. The old road continues, meandering across sunny south-facing slopes that radiate with blossoms in April and May. Views grow too—especially to the west, of the White Salmon River valley. Royal oaks resembling interpretive dancers and supple gymnasts, with their branches and limbs contorted and juxtaposed, line the way and punctuate the slopes. The scene looks more like it belongs in the Central Valley of California or in the Basque Country of northern Spain.

Continuing higher, the grade steepens, crossing a slope now denuded of trees. Mount Hood comes into view as well as Nestor Peak, Monte Carlo, and Monte Cristo. At 1.8 miles, high on the ridge (elev. 1570 ft), a large sign announces your entrance into the Washington DNR White Salmon Oak Natural Resources Conservation Area (NRCA). Encompassing over 300 acres, it protects one of the finest representations of this plant community within the state.

At 2.2 miles you'll enter the oak forest (elev. 1700 ft) the NRCA was created for. This is a good turnaround spot if views were your objective. The trail continues in forest, bending north and then east, skirting private property. Traverse stands of oak, crunching leaves and acorns as you pass. A major food source to deer, the acorns also provide sustenance to woodpeckers and the state's threatened western gray squirrel.

At 2.5 miles, crest the ridge (elev. 1900 ft) and leave the NRCA, passing a large "boundary bearing" oak. Slightly descend, traveling along the edge of a Christmas tree farm to reach the trail's eastern terminus (elev. 1860 ft) on Sandborn Road at 2.7 miles. A collection of old farm equipment here should pique your interest.

Storm clouds reflect off of channels lining the old lake bed.

Maps: USGS Camas Prairie, trail map from refuge's website; **Contact:** Conboy Lake National Wildlife Refuge, (509) 546-8300, www.fws.gov/conboylake; **Notes:** Dogs permitted on-leash; **GPS:** N 45 57.936 W 121 20.788

41 Conboy Lake National Wildlife Refuge

RATING/ DIFFICULTY	LOOP	ELEV GAIN/ HIGH POINT	SEASON
**/1	3 miles	Minimal/ 1875 feet	Mar–Dec

Situated north of the Gorge on a high plateau above the White Salmon and Klickitat Rivers at the southern base of Washington's second-highest summit, Conboy Lake is a fascinating and little-known locale. Nearly completely drained by nineteenth-

century settlers, the lake is now more of a marsh but is still rich in wildlife. A 6500-acre national wildlife refuge protects remnants of the lake as well as surrounding grasslands and pine groves. A tranquil trail introduces you to its wonders.

GETTING THERE

From Stevenson, drive State Route 14 east for 22 miles, turning left onto SR 141A. (From Portland, drive I-84 east to exit 64 in Hood River and take the toll bridge—$0.75—into Washington. Turn left, or west, on SR 14 and drive 1.6 miles, turning right, or north, onto SR 141A.) In 2.2 miles, bear left (north) onto SR 141 and follow it north for 16 miles, turning right onto Warner Road (near milepost 21). After 0.8 mile, turn left onto Sunnyside Road and continue for 1.4 miles, turning right onto the Trout Lake Highway. Drive 6.8 miles east, turning right onto Wildlife Refuge Road (signed for the refuge headquarters). Reach the trailhead (elev. 1840 ft) in 0.8 mile.

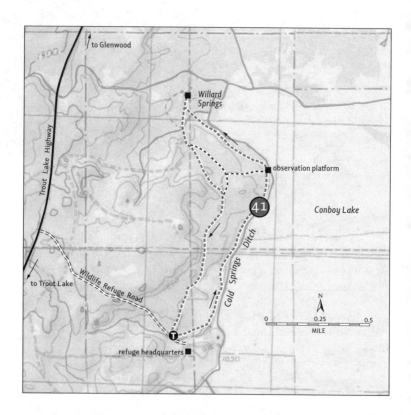

ON THE TRAIL

The Willard Springs Trail starts in a beautiful grove of ponderosa pine and Douglas-fir. The trailhead kiosk says this loop is 2 miles—it's closer to 3 but is easy and enjoyable nonetheless. Head right (although you're welcome to head left), skirting the refuge headquarters compound and arriving at what was once the lake's western shoreline. A channel now flows along the old lakeshore, while the former lakebed is a seasonal wetland especially pronounced in early spring. Teeming with birds, Conboy Lake is a bird-watcher's hot spot and one of only two places in the state where greater sandhill cranes nest. The refuge also harbors the Oregon spotted frog, an amphibian whose numbers have greatly diminished across its West Coast range.

Now heading north, the trail parallels the old lakeshore and travels through pine groves and clusters of aspen. Watch for turkey, deer, elk, coyote, and beaver when not scanning the grasses and reeds for songbirds and waterfowl. The near-level trail occasionally brushes up alongside the channel, offering excellent viewing out to the lake expanse.

At about 1 mile, reach an observation platform with a view out to Washington's second-highest summit, 12,276-foot Mount Adams. The trail continues north, passing a giant ponderosa pine before reaching a junction. The trail left is a shortcut to the return leg. Carry on right, through lodgepole pine and grassy wetland prairie. Look for camas—it was once profuse here, sustaining the Klickitat people and leading early settlers to name the area Camas Prairie.

At about 1.4 miles, reach a junction. The trail left is your return. But first head right for 0.2 mile to reach Willard Springs, which bubbles from basalt beneath a field. Are there any critters enjoying a drink of fresh springwater?

Retrace your steps back to the junction and continue right, soon coming to another junction. Go either way—the two paths quickly meet up again—and then follow an old road through gorgeous open pine forest back to the trailhead.

EXTENDING YOUR TRIP

Be sure to visit the 1891 hewn-log home near the refuge headquarters, and wander around the open area it graces.

42 Coyote Wall

RATING/ DIFFICULTY	ROUND-TRIP	ELEV GAIN/ HIGH POINT	SEASON
****/3	6 miles	1630 feet/ 1750 feet	Year-round

Map: Green Trails Columbia River Gorge–East No. 432S; **Contact:** Columbia River Gorge National Scenic Area, (541) 308-1700, www.fs.fed.us/r6/columbia; **Notes:** Dogs permitted on-leash. Trails are subject to change. Contact management agency for status. Area receives heavy mountain-bike use; **GPS:** N 45 42.002 W 121 24.192

A dramatic fold of sheer basalt cliffs, stately oak forests, and rolling open meadows that radiate with wildflower brilliance in the spring, the Coyote Wall howls to be hiked. Roam along the edge of the lofty wall, watching for thermal-riding raptors and nesting swallows. Amble across fields of dreamy blossoms. And scan the Gorge spread out below from the golden Columbia Hills in the east to the lofty cloud-catching emerald peaks in the west.

Stunning flowers and scenery from the Coyote Wall

GETTING THERE

From Bingen, drive State Route 14 east for 3.3 miles, turning left (just after milepost 69) onto Courtney Road. (From Portland, drive I-84 east to exit 64 in Hood River and take the toll bridge—$0.75—into Washington. Turn right, or east, onto SR 14.) From Courtney Road, make an immediate left turn into a parking area (elev. 120 ft).

ON THE TRAIL

As is the case with the adjacent Catherine Creek Area, the Forest Service has been busy acquiring lands here, while mountain bikers (and some hikers) have been busily building unauthorized trails on them. The Forest Service is in the process of implementing management plans for these ecologically as well as recreationally important parcels. The outcome will most certainly mean the closing and removal of many of the user-built trails. One such trail—affectionately known as the Syncline to the fat tire set—is a valley trail that makes for a popular loop. It crosses private lands and the Forest Service has targeted it for closure so the recommended hike described here excludes it.

Cross Courtney Road to a gated road that once served as the main highway on the Washington side of the Columbia. Walk crumbling pavement east, soon coming to an old "cow catcher" at the popular trail slated to be closed. Continue on the old highway, rounding Locke Lake (formed by causeways) and skirting beneath the impressive and formidable face of the Coyote Wall. Notice the big boulders that have come down off of it. Don't loiter!

After walking 0.6 mile on the old highway, come to an obvious well-used old jeep track that takes off left and now serves as a trail (elev. 175 ft). Take it. The road continues towards the Labyrinth (Hike 43), not a bad destination if you miss the turn.

A confusing network of user (mainly mountain bike) trails radiate from the main track. Avoid them and stick to the main trail, which traverses rolling countryside eastward and then makes a sharp switchback west. After heading west a short distance, the trail once again switchbacks east. Stay on it, switchbacking up over grassy and basaltic ledges dotted with ponderosa pines. Or take the secondary path left, which heads directly along the cliffy edge of the Coyote Wall. At about 1.5 miles they meet near a fence line.

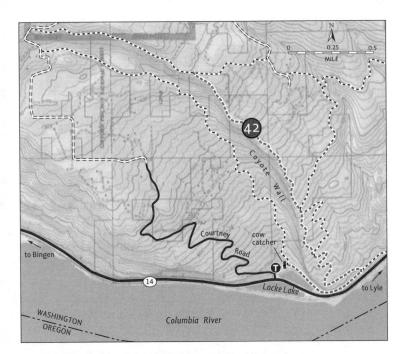

Staying on the old jeep track (double track in mountain biker talk), head straight up the broad grassy eastern slope of the Coyote Wall. Ignore a double track heading northeast. A user trail hugs left along the exposed edge of the wall. While providing stunning views, it can also be dangerous. One mountain biker perished here a couple of years back. More than likely this trail will be removed. Scan the eroded tracks going up and down and across this beautiful landmark. This is what unregulated and unplanned development looks like. Talk about coyote ugly!

When your eyes aren't fixated on the sheer basalt cliffs angling toward the river, they'll be flicking back and forth from east to west taking in an incredible Columbia

Gorge panorama that encompasses both its sunnier and wetter aspects. And in the spring, your nose will be on the ground admiring a bevy of blossoming beauties.

At about 2.7 miles, the track leaves meadows and cliff rim for forest and comes in 0.3 mile to long closed, now trail Atwood Road (elev. 1750 ft). Retrace your steps or, if the valley trail hasn't been closed yet, consider an 8-mile loop (see Extending Your Trip). Hopefully in the near future, the Forest Service can sign the official trails to alleviate some of the confusion hikers are bound to encounter here.

EXTENDING YOUR TRIP

To make a loop, follow the mostly forested Atwood Road Trail west for 1.2 miles to a gate by a house (elev. 2050 ft). Continue walking west on a dirt road, which merges with Courtney Road (stay left), passing great views and coming in 1 mile to a gated, closed road (FR Spur 230, elev. 1700 ft). Follow this spur, passing an old foundation, and then at 0.6 mile make a left onto another track and a quick left after that onto a well-used single track. Return to the cow catcher 2.2 miles later.

43 Catherine Creek: The Labyrinth

RATING/ DIFFICULTY	LOOP	ELEV GAIN/ HIGH POINT	SEASON
****/3	4.3 miles	780 feet/ 850 feet	Year-round

Map: Green Trails Columbia River Gorge–East No. 428S; **Contact:** Columbia River Gorge National Scenic Area, (541) 308-1700, www.fs.fed.us/r6/columbia; **Notes:** Dogs permitted on-leash. Trails are subject to change. Contact management agency for status; **GPS:** N 45 42.337 W 121 22.998

A spectacular area of sunny skies, legendary flower fields, and outstanding rock formations, the Catherine Creek Area is one of the crown jewels of the Columbia Gorge. And the Labyrinth is one of Catherine Creek's most stunning places. As the name suggests, you'll follow a path through a maze of basaltic rock formations. But there's more—waterfalls, a high open grassy slope granting striking views of the Columbia, placid oak woodlands, and mysterious Native American talus pits. Spring is best with its blossoms, but the area is gorgeous any time of year.

GETTING THERE

From Bingen, drive State Route 14 east for 3.3 miles and turn left (just before milepost 71) onto Old Highway No. 8. (From Portland, drive I-84 east to exit 64 in Hood River and take the toll bridge—$0.75—into Washington. Turn right, or east, onto SR 14 and drive 5.8 miles to the left turn onto Old Highway No. 8.) Immediately park at a pullout on the west side of the road (elev. 70 ft).

ON THE TRAIL

Like at the adjacent Coyote Wall (Hike 42), while the Forest Service has been busy acquiring lands here at Catherine Creek, hikers and mountain bikers have been busily building unauthorized trails on them. But the Forest Service is finally implementing management plans for these ecologically as well as recreationally important parcels. In the process, many of the user-built trails will be removed. That's a good thing, because unregulated recreation can be damaging to sensitive ecosystems. The loop described here should pretty much remain intact; main trail junctions are marked on the map in this book, but others are not. Be sure to check with the management agency for updates on trail status.

Start by heading west on the old highway, long closed to vehicles and littered by rockfall. Stare up at the basalt ledges looking for swallow nests. At 0.2 mile, cross a creek beneath a pretty waterfall. At 0.5 mile, after passing through a road cut, turn right onto an unmarked but obvious trail. Now begin steadily climbing beneath and around basalt ledges and talus slopes. Flowers add vibrant colors to the coarse volcanic rock. Lizards and ground squirrels scurry and flit about. And poison oak grows profusely here, so stay on the trail and consider wearing long pants.

Causeways form Rowland Lake on the Columbia River.

Ignore a trail heading left, continuing right instead over some small ledges. Check out the mini Devils Tower now in view. Pass big oaks and a small cave. At 0.8 mile come to a waterfall in a miniature version of Arizona's Oak Creek Canyon. Negotiate a steep (and potentially slick) section, and pass more wonderful basalt monuments, columns, and domes.

Cross the creek and continue to climb, coming to a junction (elev. 600 ft) at 1.2 miles. The short spur right leads to an excellent viewpoint east over the Columbia. Just beyond, another spur trail veers right to good viewing. At 1.4 miles, just after climbing another ledgy area, bear right at a junction (elev. 750 ft). Pass a barbed-wire fence and walk beneath a telephone line. The trail soon splits—either direction will work, as they soon meet up and emerge on a high, open grassy slope with stunning views of the river,

Rowland Lake, Columbia Hills, and the Tom McCall country in Oregon.

At 1.8 miles reach a junction (elev. 850 ft). The trail left steeply climbs to the Atwood Road Trail, which can be followed west to the Coyote Wall or east to the main Catherine Creek trailhead (Hike 44). The recommended loop continues right, traversing steep slopes and a gully housing a small creek. Upon reentering forest at 2.1 miles, come to a junction (elev. 825 ft). Proceed right, switchbacking down across meadows and eventually returning to forest. At 2.7 miles emerge in a valley (elev. 640 ft) strewn with basalt talus piles. Look closely and notice pits dug among the piles. Similar to the pits on Silver Star (Hike 13) and Wind Mountain (Hike 36), these were once used by young Native men for vision quests.

Then follow an old road, ignoring side paths (authorized and unauthorized), and

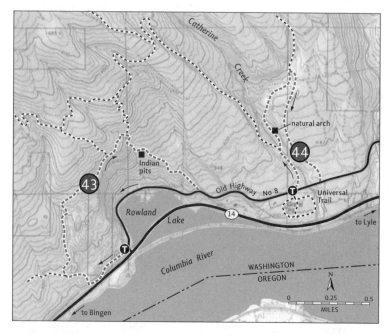

reach Old Highway No. 8 (elev. 240 ft) at 3.3 miles. Turn right and walk 1 mile along the narrow but lightly trafficked road, skirting Rowland Lake and returning to your vehicle.

EXTENDING YOUR TRIP
Combine your Labyrinth hike with the Coyote Wall (Hike 42) by using the Atwood Road Trail and the old highway.

44 Catherine Creek: Natural Arch

RATING/ DIFFICULTY	LOOP	ELEV GAIN/ HIGH POINT	SEASON
****/2	2.3 miles	370 feet/ 600 feet	Year-round

Map: Green Trails Columbia River Gorge–East No. 428S; **Contact:** Columbia River Gorge National Scenic Area, (541) 308-1700, www.fs.fed.us/r6/columbia; **Notes:** Dogs permitted on-leash. Trails are subject to change. Contact management agency for status; **GPS:** N 45 42.627 W 121 21.731

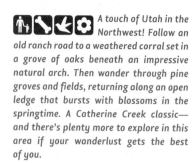

A touch of Utah in the Northwest! Follow an old ranch road to a weathered corral set in a grove of oaks beneath an impressive natural arch. Then wander through pine groves and fields, returning along an open ledge that bursts with blossoms in the springtime. A Catherine Creek classic—and there's plenty more to explore in this area if your wanderlust gets the best of you.

GETTING THERE

From Bingen, drive State Route 14 east for 3.3 miles and turn left (just before milepost 71) onto Old Highway No. 8. (From Portland, drive I-84 east to exit 64 in Hood River and take the toll bridge—$0.75—into Washington. Turn right, or east, onto SR 14 and drive 5.8 miles to the left turn onto Old Highway No. 8.) Continue for 1.4 miles to the trailhead (elev. 250 ft), located on your left. Privy available.

ON THE TRAIL

Since the late 1980s the Forest Service has been acquiring lands here at Catherine Creek, but the agency has only recently started to implement management plans for this ecologically rich area. Many of the crisscrossing trails here were illegally built by recreationists, and the Forest Service has targeted several of them for removal. The loop described here will be altered as the Forest Service reroutes sections away from fragile areas—check with the agency for updates.

From behind the gate, two old roads diverge across the open grassy countryside. Take the one right (signed "020") and saunter across a bedrock flat decorated with asters and swaying grasses. To protect nesting western meadowlarks, it is imperative to keep your dog under control here. The way soon meets up with Catherine Creek in a small canyon, coming to a junction at 0.3 mile. Left, the old Atwood Road climbs and heads toward the Coyote Wall (Hike 42). It's possible to follow it and return on another old road along Rowland Ridge for a nice loop of about 4 miles.

For the arch, bear right and cross Catherine Creek, coming to an old corral and ranch ruins

Catherine Creek's natural arch

at 0.5 mile (elev. 320 ft). Here in oak and pine forest surrounded by basalt walls, among chirping birds and flitting ground squirrels, you'll feel miles from the hurried transportation corridors of the Gorge just minutes away. Now look up to your right for the impressive basalt arch. A side trail up a scree slope offers better viewing.

The loop continues through forest patches and lupine fields, coming to a junction at 1.2 miles just after passing a powerline (elev. 570 ft). It's possible to continue left for explorations up Tracy Hill, although navigation may be confusing. The loop, however, follows a well-defined trail to the right, climbing up on an open ridge (elev. 600 ft) and then slowly descending to parallel Catherine Creek and pass above the arch. Flowers are profound in spring, the air fragrant with lupine. Views of the Columbia are sublime. At 2.1 miles reach Old Highway No. 8 (elev. 230 ft). Follow it 0.2 mile to the right, back to your car.

EXTENDING YOUR TRIP

While in the area, definitely walk the 0.8-mile paved wheelchair-accessible interpretive trail across the road (the Universal Trail). Four miles to the east via Old Highway No. 8 is the Balfour–Klickitat Day-Use Area (NW Forest Pass required). Find a lovely 0.7-mile paved wheelchair-accessible trail there, on a bluff above the confluence of the Klickitat and Columbia rivers.

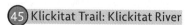

45 Klickitat Trail: Klickitat River

RATING/ DIFFICULTY	ONE-WAY	ELEV GAIN/ HIGH POINT	SEASON
**/2	10.5 miles	200 feet/ 350 feet	Year-round

Maps: USGS Lyle, USGS The Dalles North, USGS Klickitat, excellent trail map from conservancy website; **Contact:** Klickitat Trail Conservancy, www.klickitat-trail.org; **Notes:** Dogs permitted on-leash; **GPS:** N 45 41.793 W 121 17.408

    The Klickitat Trail winds 31 miles from the Columbia River through spectacular canyons to the Klickitat Valley—a high plateau between the golden Columbia Hills and piney Simcoe Mountains. This hike explores the trail's western reaches along the wild and scenic Klickitat River. Follow the churning glacial-born river above a basalt chasm, past whitewater rapids, and below a flank of oak-studded hills that burst with brilliant wildflowers in the spring.

Ledges along the Klickitat River

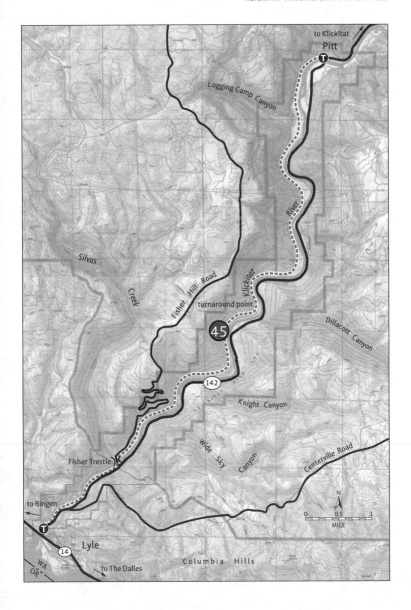

to Klickitat
Pitt

Logging Camp Canyon

River

Klickitat

Silvas

Creek

Fisher Hill Road

turnaround point

45

142

Dillacott Canyon

Knight Canyon

Wide Sky Canyon

Centerville Road

Fisher Trestle

to Bingen

Lyle

14

WA
OR

to The Dalles

Columbia Hills

N

0   0.5   1
MILE

GETTING THERE

The trailhead is on State Route 14 in Lyle, located just before the junction with SR 142 (elev. 150 ft). Privy available. (From Portland, drive I-84 east to exit 64 in Hood River and take the toll bridge—$0.75—into Washington. Turn right, or east, on SR 14 and drive 10.7 miles to Lyle and the trailhead.)

ON THE TRAIL

A spectacular rail trail that nearly met its demise due to a contingent of threatening opponents, the Klickitat Trail is alive and well today due to the untiring efforts of the Klickitat Trail Conservancy (KTC) and others. Managed cooperatively by the KTC, U.S. Forest Service, and Washington State Parks, it is absolutely imperative that you adhere to all posted regulations—particularly keeping your dog leashed and not leaving the trail right-of-way onto adjacent private property. Tensions over the trail have simmered, and you can help assuage the concerns of abutting property owners by being a good steward.

An excellent 10.5 mile one-way hike requires a car shuttle to pick you up at the Pitt trailhead (10 miles north on SR 142). Otherwise, an out and back will do from either direction.

From a brand-new trailhead (opened 2010), head north on a wide and smooth trail. The 1.6 miles between Lyle and the Fisher Trestle will eventually be paved to allow for wheelchair access. The remainder of the trail will remain natural surfaced. Paralleling SR 142 and passing a few homes, the trail gently climbs out of the Columbia River valley. At about 0.9 mile, cross a dirt road leading left, down to a county park on the Klickitat River. At 1.6 miles, leave the Columbia Gorge Natural Scenic Area and cross the Klickitat River on a high (recently restored)

trestle. Stare down into "the Narrows," a deep basalt chasm. Notice, too, planking suspended above the roiling river. Native Americans dipnet fish from the planking, one of only two areas within the Columbia drainage where this practice continues.

Cross Fisher Hill Road (an alternative trailhead) and continue north, passing tribal land. With SR 142 now on the opposite side of the river, enjoy miles of roadless, houseless, semi-wild walking. The tread can be rough at times, with rocky sections, but the grade is always gentle. Views are continuous of river rapids and steep oak-covered hills. One of only a few federally protected Wild and Scenic rivers in Washington, the Klickitat is coveted by kayakers (watch for them) and teeming with birds. Look for mergansers riding the currents and kingfishers scrutinizing the currents for bounty.

At about 5.5 miles, the way is routed around a small washout before passing through a stretch of ponderosa pines away from the river. This is a good turnaround spot if you're hiking out and back. Otherwise, continue and at 7 miles pass a lone homestead connected to the outside world by cable crossing.

The trail then once again brushes up along the river, retreats into forest, and then emerges along the river once again. Here at about 8 miles is a particularly attractive area of ledge along the riverbank—a fine spot for a siesta. Beyond, the trail bypasses a washout before reaching some homes at 9.3 miles. Be sure to close any gates you pass through.

At 10.5 miles come to SR 142 at the community of Pitt, which was once a pit—literally—having been named for a railroad company gravel pit used to help build the railway grade. Trailhead parking (elev. 350 ft) and privy are just across the road.

EXTENDING YOUR TRIP

Continue up the Klickitat Trail for another 3 miles to the old mill and railroad town of Klickitat, with plenty of historical structures and a neat inn.

46 Klickitat Trail: Swale Canyon

RATING/ DIFFICULTY	ROUND-TRIP	ELEV GAIN/ HIGH POINT	SEASON
***/3	11.4 miles	450 feet/ 1550 feet	Mar–July, Oct–Nov

Maps: USGS Wahkiacus, USGS Stacker Butte, excellent trail map from conservancy website; **Contact:** Klickitat Trail Conservancy, www.klickitat-trail.org; **Notes:** Dogs permitted on-leash. Trail closed approximately July 1–Oct 1 because of fire danger; **GPS:** N 45 43.409 W 121 01.854

 *Hike across a windy open plateau following alongside a gurgling creek, slowly descending into a deep canyon of pine groves, dogwood patches, and in springtime, a mosaic of wildflowers. Your passage to this wild and remote depression north of the Columbia Hills is via the Klickitat Trail, a 31-mile long former railroad bed. Quite a contrast from the western half of the trail along the Klickitat River (Hike 45), Swale Canyon's absence of roads and houses provides a completely different hiking experience.*

GETTING THERE

From the junction of State Routes 14 and 142 in Lyle, drive SR 14 east for 0.4 mile and turn left onto Centerville Road (Highway). (From Portland, drive I-84 east to exit 64 in Hood River and take the toll bridge—$0.75—into Washington. Turn right, or east, on SR 14 and drive 10.7 miles to the SR 142 junction in Lyle.

Hikers descending into Swale Canyon

Continue east on SR 14 for another 0.4 mile to Centerville Road.) Follow this good paved road for 14.5 miles, turning left onto gravel Harms Road. Reach the trailhead in 0.5 mile (elev. 1550 ft). Privy available.

ON THE TRAIL

The Klickitat Trail almost didn't become a reality because many abutting property owners didn't believe the public had a right to a public right-of-way. But due to the tireless efforts of the Klickitat Trail Conservancy (KTC) and others, the trail prevailed. The 15 miles of trail from Wahkiacus to Warwick are managed cooperatively by the KTC and

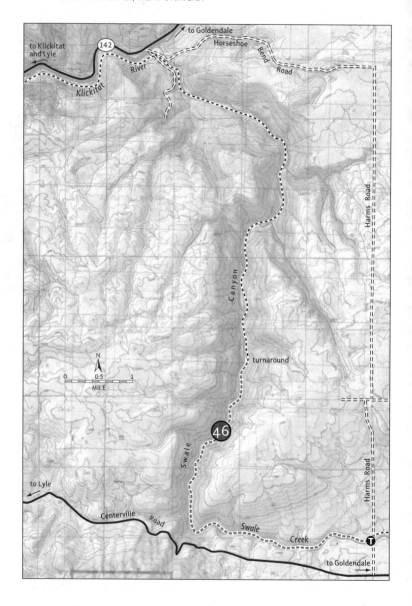

Washington State Parks. It is absolutely imperative that you adhere to all posted regulations—particularly keeping your dog leashed and not leaving the trail right-of-way onto adjacent private property. Be sure to close all gates you pass through too. Tensions over the trail have simmered, and you can help assuage the concerns of property owners by being a good steward.

If you can arrange a car shuttle at the Wahkiacus trailhead (elev. 550 ft), then you can make a 13-mile one-way trip. (From Lyle, travel 16.2 miles north on SR 142, turning right onto Horseshoe Bend Road, and continuing 0.1 mile south to the trailhead located at the junction with Schilling Road.) But the last 3 miles aren't very appealing, passing several structures (some decrepit) with owners of said structures permitted to drive on this section of trail. Most hikers will prefer this out-and-back option instead, enjoying the best part of the trail—twice!

Starting from the western edge of the Klickitat Valley (actually a plateau between the Columbia Hills and Simcoe Mountains), begin your long slow descent following Swale Creek into Swale Canyon. In springtime, the wetland pools at the head of the canyon teem with croaking frogs and singing birds. Also enjoy views up to Stacker Butte. Then cross the first of many attractively restored trestles, compliments of KTC volunteers. Mountain bikers appreciate the smooth passage now at the creek crossings. You will, too!

Pass basalt ledges as you wind down into the canyon. The surroundings are both harsh and beautiful. Shade is at a premium, so slather on the sun screen and get out the cap. Sage intermixes with willow and dogwood along the creek. At about 2.5 miles, finally some trees—an oak grove and ponderosa pines. At 5.7 miles, about 0.5 mile be-

fore the fourth trestle, is a lovely turnaround spot along the creek (elev. 1100 ft)—smooth sun-kissed rocks invite you to sit, snack, and soak before heading back.

EXTENDING YOUR TRIP

If you're still intrigued by what lies farther, at 8.4 miles is a particularly long and attractive trestle; 0.25 mile beyond that is an interesting old vehicle put out to pasture; at 9 miles the trail skirts a trestle laid waste by a rock slide; and at 10 miles is the first of the several aforementioned structures. Other nearby options include the 1.6 miles of trail east from Harms Road to Warwick (a future trailhead), which are quiet and delightful. Across open range, skirt a wildlife-rich marsh and catch a glimpse of Mount Adams. Also, the 3 miles of trail west from the Wahkiacus trailhead along the Klickitat River to the missing trestle make for nice, lonely walking. Interesting too, you'll pass a mineral spring and remains of an old dry-ice factory.

47 Lyle Cherry Orchard

RATING/ DIFFICULTY	ROUND-TRIP	ELEV GAIN/ HIGH POINT	SEASON
****/3	5 miles	1100 feet/ 1100 feet	Year-round

Map: Green Trails Columbia River Gorge–East No. 432S; **Contact:** Friends of the Columbia Gorge, www.gorgefriends.org; **Notes:** Beware ticks, rattlesnakes, and poison oak!; **GPS:** N 45 41.185 W 121 15.950

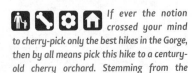 *If ever the notion crossed your mind to cherry-pick only the best hikes in the Gorge, then by all means pick this hike to a century-old cherry orchard. Stemming from the*

Columbia River, this trail winds through a basalt gap to a sprawling grassy bench. It then traverses wide-open slopes ripe with views before topping out at the old orchard sitting plumb above the Gorge. Harvest your reward of pastoral vistas and cherish the tranquility.

GETTING THERE

From the junction of State Routes 14 and 142 in Lyle, drive SR 14 east for 1.4 miles to the unmarked trailhead (just after passing through the small tunnels), located on the left at a wide pullout (elev. 100 ft). (From Portland, drive I-84 east to exit 64 in Hood River and take the toll bridge—$0.75—into Washington. Turn right, or east, on SR 14 and drive 10.7 miles to the SR 142 junction in Lyle. Continue east on SR 14 for another 1.4 miles to the trailhead.)

ON THE TRAIL

Starting in a narrow draw hemmed in by basalt walls, follow good tread upward through a stunted oak forest and reach the remnants of the old Columbia River State Highway in about 0.2 mile, where there's a sign and signup box. Take a minute to sign in and go over the trail's rules. Owned by the Friends of the Columbia Gorge (see "Befriending the Gorge" in the Western Oregon section), this beautiful property was purchased by the Russell Family to protect it from being developed. Nancy Russell (who died in 2008 from Lou Gehrig's disease) founded the Friends of the Columbia and was one of the driving (and most influential) forces behind the establishment of the Columbia River Gorge National Scenic Area in 1986.

Continue upward on slightly rugged tread, crossing scree and reaching a fantastic overlook (elev. 430 ft) of the Columbia at 0.5 mile. If the river views don't move you, the blossoms will. In early spring, death camas, prairie star, grass widows, and others begin working their magic on the landscape.

At 1 mile, reach a broad open bench and a junction (elev. 725 ft). The orchard lies right—upward—but feel free to divert on the side

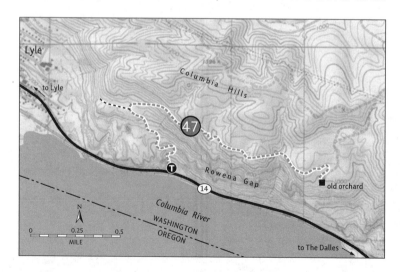

Hikers enjoy sweeping views on the way to the Lyle Cherry Orchard.

trail across the breezy bench, pulling a Julie Andrews. Otherwise, continue climbing, now more steeply and steadily across grassy slopes. Views grow with each step—the Rowena Plateau is fully revealed and snowy sentinel Mount Hood eventually makes a cameo.

Reenter forest and at about 1.5 miles pass an old pasture pool and, shortly afterward, an old stile (elev. 1100 ft). The way then loses about 50 feet of elevation, regains it, and at 2.3 miles comes to an old road. Turn right slightly descending to reach an old homestead site and the cherry orchard (elev. 1050 ft) in 0.2 mile. Not much remains of the orchard, but look around—there are still a couple of big old cherry trees holding on to life. The views, however, especially east toward The Dalles are like the rest of this hike—the pick of the crop!

48 Stacker Butte

RATING/ DIFFICULTY	ROUND-TRIP	ELEV GAIN/ HIGH POINT	SEASON
****/3	5 miles	1150 feet/ 3200 feet	Mar–Nov

Map: Green Trails Columbia River Gorge–East No. 432S; **Contact:** Washington DNR, Southeast Region (Ellensburg), (509) 925-8510, www.dnr.wa.gov; **Notes:** Dogs prohibited; **GPS:** N 45 41.692 W 121 05.551

Hike to a lofty, windswept, flower-carpeted, views-in-every-direction-for-as-far-as-you-can-see high point on the eastern fringe of the Columbia Gorge. Centerpiece of the 3594-acre Columbia Hills Natural Area Preserve, a land of oak and pine woodlands, grasslands, and rare plants, Stacker Butte stacks up among the area's finest hiking destinations.

GETTING THERE

From Lyle, drive State Route 14 east for 8 miles to the junction with US 197. (From The Dalles, follow US 197—exit 87 on I-84—north for 3.3 miles, turning right, or east, onto SR 14.) Continue on SR 14 for 0.9 mile, turning left onto gravel Dalles Mountain Road. (If coming from the east, follow SR 14 west for 16.5 miles from its junction with US 97.) Proceed 3.4 miles on Dalles Mountain Road (entering the Dalles Ranch unit of Columbia Hills State Park), and turn left just before an old ranch. Pass interpretive displays and continue on this at times rough dirt road for 1.4 miles to a gate. Park here, being sure not to block the gate (elev. 2050 ft). The hike begins on the gated road.

ON THE TRAIL

While this hike consists of walking a service road to a ridge sporting towers of various form and function, in no way does that diminish the journey. The road is rarely traveled and you'll hardly notice the towers. You'll be too busy looking out at nonstop horizon-spanning views. And if you come in April or May, you'll be awestruck by one of the finest floral shows in the entire Pacific Northwest. Balsamroot, lupine, paintbrush, phlox, larkspur, desert larkspur, and others paint this Columbia Hills peak in a radiant array of color.

Before beginning, remember that your four-legged friend is not permitted here, and

Lupine and arrowleaf balsamroot paint the Columbia Hills purple and yellow.

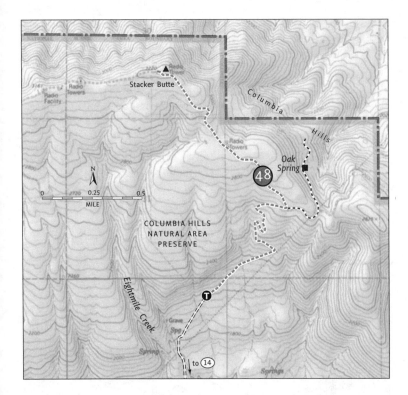

keep your feet from wandering off the road. Travel is permitted only on the preserve's roadways to help protect one of Washington's last large remnants of Idaho fescue and houndstongue hawkweed grassland communities. The preserve also harbors these three rare plants: obscure buttercup, Douglas' draba, and hot-rock penstemon.

The road climbs steadily across wide-open slopes. Did you remember the sunscreen? Wind shell? Views grow increasingly better with each step. From March to May, the flowers are profuse. And while busy admiring and identifying flora, don't forget the area's fauna, among them scampering ground squirrels, melodious meadowlarks, and flittering butterflies.

At 1.1 miles (elev. 2600 ft), a jeep track on the right diverts to Oak Spring, one of the many springs that dot the Columbia Hills. Feel free to wander this road. The main road continues left, cresting the ridge (elev. 2875 ft) and reaching a large tower at 1.75 miles. The summit is now in view. Continue climbing another 0.75 mile to reach Stacker Butte's 3200-foot summit, occupied by an oddly arranged and intriguing aviation tower.

Cast it a glance, and then let your eyes run wild across the horizons: South to The Dalles, endless wheat fields, and Mount Hood pointing to the heavens. West to the heart of the Gorge, with Mount Defiance shadowing surrounding peaks and ridges. East to massive wind towers sprouting across the landscape like giant voodoo needles jabbing Mother Earth. Question if this type of development is truly a green energy source. And finally set your sights north to Mount Adams, the Simcoe Mountains, and directly below to the Swale Canyon—a large rift in the Goldendale plains.

49 Horsethief Butte

RATING/ DIFFICULTY	ROUND-TRIP	ELEV GAIN/ HIGH POINT	SEASON
***/2	1.2 miles	200 feet/ 498 feet	Year-round

Map: Green Trails Columbia River Gorge–East No. 432S; **Contact:** Columbia Hills State Park, (509) 767-1159, www.parks.wa.gov; **Notes:** Dogs permitted (but not recommended) on-leash. Watch for rattlesnakes; **GPS:** N 45 39.013 W 121 06.018

A prominent landmark along the Columbia, Horsethief Butte has played host to Native Americans, Lewis and Clark, countless budding climbers, and scads of inquisitive hikers, but probably no horse thieves. Created by ancient lava flows and carved by floods of biblical proportions, the butte is an excellent place to contemplate the region's fascinating natural history.

GETTING THERE
From Lyle, drive State Route 14 east for 8 miles to the junction with US 197. (From The Dalles, follow US 197—exit 87 on I-84—north for 3.3 miles, turning right, or east, onto SR 14.) Continue on SR 14 for 2.8 miles (1.1 miles beyond the Horsethief Lake campground entrance). The trailhead is on

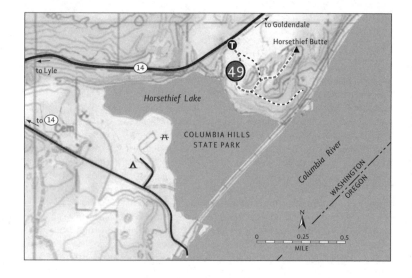

A starkly beautiful riverbank at Horsethief Butte

the right side of the highway (elev. 300 ft). (If coming from the east, the trailhead is 14.5 miles from the US 97 junction.) Park on north side of the road and use caution crossing the highway. Privy available.

ON THE TRAIL

The U.S. Army Corps of Engineers, romanced by 1950s Western movies, bestowed the name Horsethief on this basaltic monolith. While rustlers probably never used the cavernous butte as a lair, Native peoples frequented it for spiritual rituals. The butte, as well as other parts of the sprawling Columbia Hills State Park, contains numerous pictographs (paintings) and petroglyphs (carvings), among the oldest in the North-

west. Respect all artifacts and area closures within the park.

The hike to the just-shy-of-500-feet butte is short, but you can easily spend hours exploring its many aspects and treasures. In spring, the stark walls are decorated with bouquets of flowers. Lizards and snakes (namely bull snakes, a nonvenomous species oft mistaken for a rattler) sun and scurry on the warm ledges. The butte is popular with practicing rock climbers too, the folks responsible for a confusing arrangement of paths leading to and within it.

At just over 0.1 mile come to a junction. Head right, skirting along the base of the butte. In spring this sandy, rocky bench comes alive with death camas. After about

0.2 mile come to another junction. The trail right continues along the butte's base to an overlook above the railroad tracks and Horsethief Lake. It's worth the diversion.

For the big views, however, head left and climb up scree to a gap in the butte along a labyrinth of paths. Feel free to explore. To reach the top of the butte, look for a somewhat trodden way heading southeast up a narrow cleft. You'll need to use your hands, but it's not difficult nor dangerous. Once over this obstacle, follow a path angling northeast to the butte's summit. Enjoy superb views of the Columbia River, Columbia Hills, and Horsethief Lake with Mount Hood rising behind it.

EXTENDING YOUR TRIP

There's a lot more to explore in the 3338-acre Columbia Hills State Park. Miles of old ranch roads traverse the property, inviting wanderings. Less than 1 mile east of the trailhead is an old road leading north to a nice waterfall. You can also arrange for a guided hike to the enchanting pictograph, She-Who-Watches. Or check out the interpretive displays and old farm machinery at the Dalles Mountain Ranch (follow driving directions for Stacker Butte, Hike 48).

50 Crow Butte

RATING/ DIFFICULTY	ROUND-TRIP	ELEV GAIN/ HIGH POINT	SEASON
***/2	2 miles	380 feet/ 670 feet	Year-round

Map: USGS Crow Butte; **Contact:** Crow Butte Park (Port of Benton County), (509) 875-2644, www.crowbutte.com; **Notes:** $5 day use fee per car. Dogs permitted on-leash. Watch for rattlesnakes; **GPS:** N 45 51.063 W 119 51.206

 *A broad, grassy basaltic butte in the middle of nowhere—this landmark has much to crow over. Situated on a 1500-acre island in the Columbia River, in the shadow of the Horse Heaven Hills, birdlife here is prolific both in numbers and species. The views are good too, from the river below to the golden hills, plains, and fields embracing it.*

GETTING THERE

From the junction of US 97 and State Route 14, near Maryhill State Park, drive SR 14 east for 54 miles to Sonava Road at milepost 155 and turn left. (If coming from the east, take exit 131 off of I-82 and drive west on SR 14 for 26 miles and turn right on Sonava Road.) Then immediately turn right onto Butte Road and drive under SR 14, reaching the park day-use area in 2 miles. Park and walk to the campground. The trailhead is located near campsite no. 42 (elev. 290 ft). Privy and water available in the park.

ON THE TRAIL

Once administered by Washington State Parks, Crow Butte—along with a handful of other mostly eastern Washington parks—was removed from the state park system during the Locke administration's budget woes in the years just after 2000. It's a darn shame that our state park legacy was so easily discarded. Fortunately, most of the jettisoned parks have been maintained in some form or another as parks by other agencies. The 275-acre Crow Butte Park is now administered by the Port of Benton County.

Locate the wide trail that takes off for the 670-foot butte near campsite no. 42. Leaving the park's manicured and shaded lawns, the trail enters a grassy, near treeless environment fully exposed to sun and wind. Spring and fall are ideal times to visit, with agreeable temperatures and plenty of migrating birds. The butte is a bird-watcher's paradise, with a dizzying array of species: Bullock's orioles, loggerhead shrikes, black-headed grosbeaks, Caspian and Forster's terns, American avocets, black-necked stilts, least and western sandpipers, dunlins, Virginia rails, and marsh and rock wrens, among others.

At 0.2 mile come to a junction. The trail right, an excellent side trip, takes off for the west ridge and a secluded sandy beach on the Columbia. Consider extending your trip upon your return from the butte. For the butte, continue straight on a much lighter-traveled route. Traverse a slope of phlox, prickly pear cactus, and arrowleaf balsamroot. At 0.75 mile the trail pretty

A seemingly featureless horizon from Crow Butte

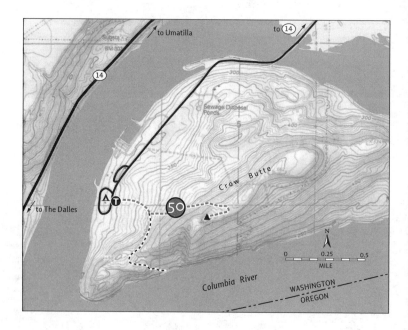

much peters out upon reaching the butte's northern ridge. Light tread continues right, however across basalt outcroppings lined with balsamroot. Follow it for 0.25 mile to the 670-foot summit. While powerlines extend across the butte, the view is quite sublime—from the broad vast flats east to the golden hills north and emerging uplands west. Watch raptors ride the thermals above.

You are standing on sacred land to the Umatilla peoples. While the surrounding wilds continue to convert to vineyards, wheat fields, and industrial parks, a landscape of no "improvements" is vital for nature to survive. Much of the vast "nothingness" of the Columbia Hills deserves to be protected as strongly as any westside old-growth forest grove.

Opposite: Balch Creek Canyon

portland metro

Perhaps in no other major metropolitan area in America is nature so close and integrated as in Portland. A leader in land-use planning, maintaining green belts, and developing trails, Portland is the type of big city that a big-city shunner can love. And there's much to love about Portland if you're a hiker. The city itself has more than 10,000 acres of parkland, including one of the largest urban parks in the country. You can hike through deep forests, on quiet islands, along undeveloped shorelines teeming with wildlife, and crest peaks with outstanding views—all without leaving the city limits.

51 Sauvie Island: Warrior Rock Lighthouse

RATING/ DIFFICULTY	ROUND-TRIP	ELEV GAIN/ HIGH POINT	SEASON
***/1	6.5 miles	None/ 10 feet	Year-round

Inviting beach on the Columbia River

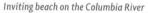

Map: USGS Saint Helens; **Contact:** Sauvie Island Wildlife Area, (503) 621-2488, www.dfw.state.or.us; **Notes:** $7 parking permit or $22 annual pass. Dogs permitted on-leash; **GPS:** N 45 48.507 W 122 47.895

 Hike on Oregon's largest island among stately cottonwoods and sandy beaches to one of its two noncoastal lighthouses. En route watch barges and tugs and all kinds of other watercraft ply the Columbia. It's a scene right out of the Mississippi—until you cast your eyes upward to Mount Saint Helens in the distance. The birding is good too—with more than 150,000 migratory ducks and geese taking to the island each fall and winter—so don't forget your binoculars.

GETTING THERE

From downtown Portland, follow US 30 (NW Saint Helens Road) west for just shy of 11 miles, turning right onto the Sauvie Island

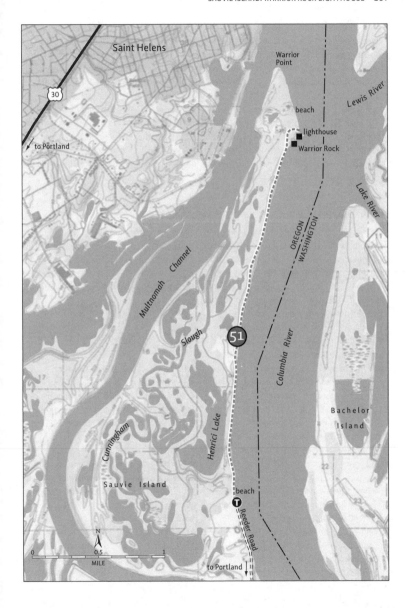

Bridge. (From Vancouver, take exit 306 on I-5, following Interstate Avenue S, and turn right, or west, onto US 30–Bypass, or Lombard Street. Drive 4 miles to Saint Johns Bridge and turn right onto US 30, reaching Sauvie Island Bridge in 3.5 miles.) Follow Sauvie Island Road, passing Cracker Barrel Grocery in 0.3 mile (where parking permits can be purchased), and turn right onto Reeder Road at 2.1 miles. Then follow Reeder Road for 12.7 miles (pavement ends at 10.5 miles) to its end and trailhead (elev. 10 ft). Privy available.

ON THE TRAIL

There's so much to love about Sauvie Island. Located a mere 10 miles from downtown Portland, this 24,000-plus-acre island, with its population of just over 1000, is nearly all wildlife preserve and agricultural land. And this island is rife with history too. On October 28, 1792, Lieutenant William Broughton, sailing for Captain George Vancouver, visited the rocky tip of the island, where he was met by twenty-three canoes carrying 150 Chinook Indians dressed in war attire. He quickly made peace and subsequently named the point Warrior Rock (he also named Mount Hood for his admiral). Lewis and Clark came through in 1805 and 1806. And in 1836, French Canadian Laurent Sauvé began managing several dairy farms for the Hudson's Bay Company at nearby Fort Vancouver. The island bears his name.

Start by walking out on the fine sandy beach and heading north. If the weather is nice, you'll have a hard time resisting lounging. After 0.25 mile, head up on the riverbank, picking up an access road for the wildlife management area, and proceed right. At 0.5 mile, bear right onto the more lightly traveled older road. Follow this delightful route under a canopy of giant cottonwoods to the light-

house at 3.25 miles. Several trails diverge left and right, offering access to beaches and sloughs. Soothing birdsong fills the air, occasionally interrupted by the harsher sounds of large vessels plying the river.

After coming to a small meadow, the way bends right to end at the lighthouse, built in 1930. The currents are pretty strong here, being close to the confluence with Washington's Lewis River. Views are good up and down the Columbia. Directly across the river is the Ridgefield National Wildlife Refuge.

EXTENDING YOUR TRIP

Walk a nice beach just to the north of the lighthouse and snoop around the tip of the island for views of the city of Saint Helens across the Multnomah Channel.

52 Sauvie Island: Oak Island Loop

RATING/ DIFFICULTY	LOOP	ELEV GAIN/ HIGH POINT	SEASON
***/1	2.9 miles	None/ 10 feet	Mid-Apr– Sept

Map: USGS Sauvie Island; **Contact:** Sauvie Island Wildlife Area, (503) 621-2488, www .dfw.state.or.us.; **Notes:** $7 per day parking pass or $22 annual pass. Dogs permitted on-leash. Trail closed Oct 1–Apr 15; **GPS:** N 45 42.834 W 122 49.252

Oak Island is actually a peninsula, not an island, but it is graced with plenty of stately Oregon white oaks. Nearly surrounded by the bird-bursting waters of Sturgeon Lake, this delightful loop is a great place for scoping out the island's mascot, the wood duck. And while you're at it, look for swans, herons, geese, kestrels, warblers, eagles, ospreys, sandhill cranes—

nearly 250 species of birds inhabit this island throughout the year.

GETTING THERE

From downtown Portland, follow US 30 (NW Saint Helens Road) west for just shy of 11 miles, turning right onto the Sauvie Island Bridge. (From Vancouver, take exit 306 on I-5, following Interstate Avenue S, and turn right, or west, onto US 30–Bypass, or Lombard Street. Drive 4 miles to Saint Johns Bridge and turn right onto US 30, reaching Sauvie Island Bridge in 3.5 miles.) Follow Sauvie Island Road, passing Cracker Barrel Grocery in 0.3 mile (where parking permits can be purchased), and turn right onto Reeder Road at 2.1 miles. Continue for 1.2 miles, turning left onto NW Oak Island Road. Proceed 4.1 miles (pavement ends at 3 miles; go straight at an intersection at 3.7 miles) to the road's end and the trailhead (elev. 10 ft). Privy available.

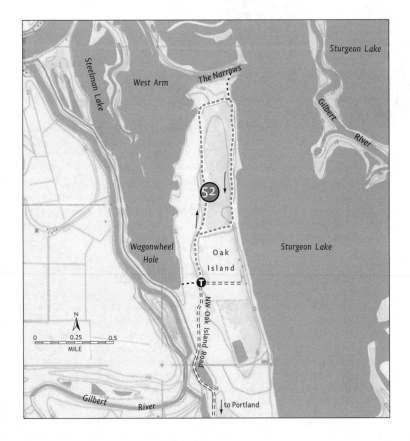

Oak leaf signs mark the way.

ON THE TRAIL

Nearly half of Sauvie Island, 12,000 acres in all, is managed as a wildlife area by the Oregon Department of Fish and Wildlife. Here on the island's wilder northern half, you'll find a saturated landscape of sloughs, wetlands, and shallow lakes. Sturgeon Lake is the largest body of water on the island, and this hike allows you to explore it up close and personal.

Pass a gate and proceed straight, ignoring a right-branching road that leads to a residence and a brushy trail on the left to the Wagon-wheel Hole on Sturgeon Lake (although you may want to explore that later). Pass a colorful nature trail sign, which will probably be empty of trail guides in both English and Spanish, and walk down an old road lined with snowberry and rose (as pretty and fragrant in spring by any other name). Admire big old gnarled oaks

too, and watch for raucous scrub jays in the brushy understory. At 0.3 mile come to a junction. You'll be returning on the right, so continue straight across a large grassy expanse. In spring look for camas lilies.

The trail bends right, in essence circling an "upland" of oak forest. At 1.3 miles a faint path leads left to The Narrows, a strait of water connecting Sturgeon Lake with its West Arm. Explore if you desire. Then head south, enjoying views over the lake and out to Silver Star, and Mounts Adams and Saint Helens in the distance.

At 2.2 miles the trail bends right. With farmland now on your left, pass a memorial and at 2.6 miles return to a familiar junction. Head left for 0.3 mile back to the trailhead.

53 Sauvie Island: Wapato Access Greenway

RATING/ DIFFICULTY	LOOP	ELEV GAIN/ HIGH POINT	SEASON
**/1	2.4 miles	50 feet/ 35 feet	Year-round

Maps: USGS Sauvie Island, trail map at trailhead; **Contact:** Oregon State Parks, (503) 986-0707, www.oregon.gov/OPRD/PARKS; **Notes:** Dogs permitted on-leash; **GPS:** N 45 39.616 W 122 50.316

A lovely little park protecting an expansive wetland known as Virginia Lake, the Wapato Access Greenway also protects shoreline along the Multnomah Channel. Cooperatively maintained by the Audubon Society of Portland, Wapato Access has been deemed an IBA—important bird area. Eight colorful posts displaying a native bird species grace the way. Read the brochure available at the trailhead about the posts and their significance for bird monitoring.

GETTING THERE

From downtown Portland, follow US 30 (NW Saint Helens Road) west for just shy of 11 miles, turning right onto the Sauvie Island Bridge. (From Vancouver, take exit 306 on I-5, following Interstate Avenue S, and turn right, or west, onto US 30–Bypass, or Lombard Street. Drive 4 miles to Saint Johns Bridge and turn right onto US 30, reaching Sauvie Island Bridge in 3.5 miles.) Follow Sauvie Island Road for 2.7 miles to the trailhead (elev. 10 ft), located on your left.

ON THE TRAIL

Before French Canadian Laurent Sauvé began managing dairy farms for the Hudson's Bay Company, the island now named after him was known as Wapato. An arrow-leaved aquatic plant, the wapato produces tubers that were an important staple to First Peoples in the region. Look for it along shallow Virginia Lake.

Walk the entrance trail for 0.2 mile to access the Wapato Loop Trail at a picnic pavilion. En route pass the first of eight IBA posts, this one denoting a Bullock's oriole. Turn left and immediately come to a junction. The spur right leads 350 feet to a wooden viewing platform above Virginia Lake. More of a marsh, the lake dries up by late summer, but birding remains good year-round.

Continue along the loop, and at 0.6 mile come to another junction. The spur left leads 375 feet to Hadley's Landing Dock on the Multnomah Channel. The loop continues along the channel under a canopy of cottonwoods and ash. While the area is peaceful, traffic can be heard whizzing by on US 30 across the channel. And depending on

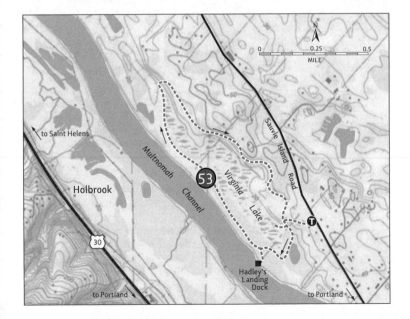

Virginia Lake

when you visit, mosquitoes may be whizzing around your ears.

Enjoy nice views along the channel that appear almost Lousiana-esque. Travel through a savanna-like setting next, crossing a small boardwalk at the northern tip of the Virginia Lake complex. The way then rolls a little, skirting a farm and passing by a couple of big oaks. At 2.2 miles return to the picnic pavilion, closing the loop. Turn left and return 0.2 mile to the trailhead.

EXTENDING YOUR TRIP

About 1.5 miles south of the Wapato Access Greenway, be sure to stop at the Howell Territorial Park, a 120-acre Metro park protecting an 1850s farmhouse, pioneer orchard, and large wetland.

54 Forest Park North

RATING/ DIFFICULTY	LOOP	ELEV GAIN/ HIGH POINT	SEASON
**/2	8.1 miles	465 feet/ 950 feet	Year-round

Map: Green Trails Forest Park No. 426S; **Contact:** Portland Parks and Recreation, (503) 823-7529, www.portlandonline.com /parks, and Forest Park Conservancy, forest parkconservancy.org; **Notes:** Dogs permitted on-leash; **GPS:** N 45 35.337 W 122 47.412

With more than 5000 acres of gently forested hills separated by lush ravines, Portland's Forest Park ranks as one of the largest natural areas within a major city, granting metro dwellers access to 70 miles of trails and old fire roads (see "Seeing the Forest Park for the

Trees" in the Portland Metro section). The park is a pretty safe place visited by scads of good folks, though views are practically nonexistent and it's safe to say that the landscape isn't very dramatic. This hike in the northern reaches of the park is just as popular with hikers and trail runners as the southern, more accessible areas, but some stretches are more lonely, offering a reprieve from the masses. Chances are good, too, of spotting some of Forest Park's wilder denizens.

GETTING THERE

From downtown Portland, follow US 30 (NW Saint Helens Road) west for 7.5 miles and turn left (just after going under Saint Johns Bridge) onto NW Bridge Avenue. Drive 0.2 mile and turn right onto Germantown Road. (From Vancouver, take exit 306 on I-5, following

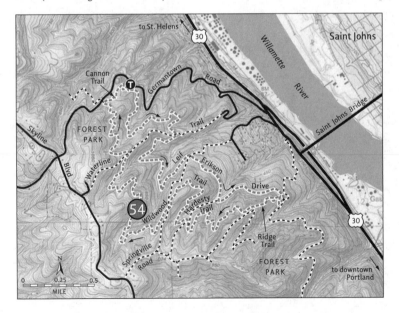

Interstate Avenue S, and turn right, or west, onto US 30–Bypass, or Lombard Street. Drive 4 miles to Saint Johns Bridge, turn right on NW Bridge Avenue, and in 0.3 mile turn left onto Germantown Road.) Follow Germantown Road 1.3 miles to the Leif Erikson trailhead (elev. 675 ft). Privy available.

ON THE TRAIL

This hike combines portions of Forest Park's two longest trails: the 30-mile Wildwood Trail and the 11-mile Leif Erickson Drive (now a trail). The former is hiker only; the latter is open to mountain bikes. Rogue mountain bikers have become a problem in the park, building bootleg trails and riding on hiker-only

Fern-lined trail in Forest Park

trails. Unleashed dogs are also a problem, and the parks department has recently become more active in fining violators.

Head southeast on the well-graded and delightful 11-mile-plus Leif Erickson Drive, a closed road coveted by bicyclists and runners. Soon pass milepost 11, the first old concrete post marking every quarter mile along the way. At 0.25 mile ignore an unmarked side trail. At just over 1 mile pass the unmarked Tolinda (a.k.a. Waterline) Trail (elev. 750 ft), which allows for a short loop if you're pressed for time.

Continue along the gently graded road, passing several small creeks and coming to a junction at 2 miles with the Springville Road, now a trail (elev. 725 ft), offering another shorter loop option. Pass an old house foundation smothered in English ivy. This invasive species is prevalent in Forest Park. Park employees and volunteers continue to remove it, though at times this seems a futile effort.

Just beyond, at 2.4 miles, reach a junction with the Hardesty Trail, yet another option for shortening this loop. Continue forward for nearly another mile, coming to the Ridge Trail (elev. 660 ft) at 3.3 miles. This is the recommended turnoff—take it right, steeply zigzagging up the rib of a ridge to reach the Wildwood Trail (elev. 910 ft) at 3.7 miles.

Here, at milepost 21 on the 30-mile-long Wildwood Trail, turn right and head northwest. Other than the sound of industrial Portland clanging and humming from far below, enjoy a fairly peaceful natural environment. The trail rounds ridges and darts in and out of ravines under an emerald canopy of alder, maple, and fir and through a verdant carpet of salal, ferns, and Oregon grape. The tread is good but can get quite muddy in spots in winter.

After climbing to 940 feet, slowly descend into a nice ravine of cedars and the junction

SEEING THE FOREST PARK FOR THE TREES

It was as far back as the late 1800s, during Portland's nascent days, that the Reverend Thomas Lamb called for the creation of a municipal park commission to design parks for the growing urban center. In 1903, the commission employed the world-famous Olmsted brothers of Massachusetts (who were instrumental in the creation of the National Park Service, among many notable achievements) to design a city park system. Among the Olmsteds' recommendations was acquisition of the Tualatin Mountains along Portland's western limits for a wild wooded park. "No use to which this tract of land could be put would begin to be as sensible or as profitable to the city as that of making it a public park," they concluded.

The first parcels of what would become Forest Park were 52 acres donated by prominent lawyer, Frederick Van Voorhies Holman. But formation of the great park was slow, with many setbacks—including oil speculation, logging, and a land boom that led to a road being built through the mountains (now the Leif Erikson Drive trail).

But visionary citizens and civic leaders persevered. In 1948, 4200 acres of the area was dedicated as Forest Park. Today the park consists of 5100 acres, giving Forest Park the distinction of being the largest forested natural area within the city limits of a major metropolitan area in the United States. The park is a great pride of the city with more than 70 miles of trails. And folks can join the Forest Park Conservancy (forestparkconservancy.org) to "maintain, preserve, protect, and improve" this incredible backyard wilderness.

with the Hardesty Trail (elev. 840 ft) at 4.9 miles. At 5.3 miles traverse an attractive stretch of forest and travel on tread reinforced with old tires (talk about re-treads!). At 5.7 miles reach the loop's high point at 950 feet and, just beyond, the junction with the Springville Road.

Staying fairly high along the ridgeline, skirt two ravines that harbor seasonal creeks, and reach the Tolinda Trail at 7.2 miles (elev. 900 ft). Follow the Wildwood Trail another 0.6 mile to just before the Germantown Road trailhead (an alternative start) turning right onto the brand-new-not-on-most-maps-yet Cannon Trail (elev. 800 ft). Built by the Friends of Forest Park, this 0.3-mile trail allows you to return to the Leif Erikson trailhead to complete this 8.1-mile loop without walking on the busy Germantown Road.

EXTENDING YOUR TRIP

Describing Forest Park's entire trail system is beyond the scope of this book, but there are miles of hiking options in this city gem. Get a good map and enjoy exploring.

55 Forest Park South: Balch Creek Canyon

RATING/ DIFFICULTY	ROUND-TRIP	ELEV GAIN/ HIGH POINT	SEASON
***/1	2.4 miles	300 feet/ 425 feet	Year-round

Map: Green Trails Forest Park No. 426S; **Contact:** Portland Parks and Recreation, (503) 823-7529, www.portlandonline.com /parks, and Forest Park Conservancy, forest parkconservancy.org; **Notes:** Dogs permitted on-leash; **GPS:** N 45 32.158 W 122 42.746

Old stone house remains in Balch Canyon

 *Balch Creek slices through the Tualatin Mountains, Portland's green backdrop also known as the West Hills, via a gorgeous ravine. While much of the 5000-plus-acre Forest Park consists of a fairly monotonous landscape of rolling hills covered by second and third growth, the scene is dramatically different here within the park's southern reaches. Hikers of all ages and abilities will delight over this perhaps most scenic and diverse trail within the park, with Balch Creek's waterfalls, old-growth groves, and the ruins of an eloquent old stone building that once offered rest to weary walkers.*

GETTING THERE

From downtown Portland, follow NW Vaughn Street west (take exit 3 off of I-405—the US 30 exit—to NW Vaughn. Turn left onto NW 26th Avenue. After one block, turn right onto NW Upshur Street and continue 0.4 mile to the road's end and trailhead at Lower Macleay Park (elev. 125 ft). Privy available, but parking is limited. An alternative start is the Hike 56 trailhead, from which you can access the canyon by hiking north 0.75 mile on the Wildwood Trail.

ON THE TRAIL

In 1897 Donald Macleay, a prominent Portland businessman and proud Scot, gave the City of Portland a sizeable chunk of property to commemorate the sixtieth year of Queen Victoria's reign—and to protest high property taxes. He preferred donating his land as a park to paying the taxes on it. Portland's first major park, however, came with a couple of provisions, one which stated that "the city shall provide conveyance for carrying patients from area hospitals through the park during the summer." Paths were subsequently widened to accommodate wheelchairs, and the first 0.3 mile of this trail along Balch Creek is now paved for universal access. Macleay Park has since been absorbed into the greater Forest Park complex and is one of the more attractive parts of this backyard wilderness.

Follow the Lower Macleay Trail under a neat, high old bridge and come to the creek, which disappears into an old wooden catch. Downstream from here the creek is submerged beneath industrial flats all the way to the Willamette River. Upstream, it's a delightful bubbling waterway. Cross the creek, entering the heavily wooded canyon, and come to the pavement's end in 0.3 mile.

Continue upstream, passing charming little falls and rapids. Cross the creek once more at a pretty little waterfall. Take time to notice the forest too—some of Portland's biggest and oldest trees adorn this canyon, and a beautiful split-rail fence adorns the trail.

At 0.8 mile come to a massive Douglas-fir, an official City of Portland Heritage Tree. At 0.9 mile reach the 30-mile-long Wildwood Trail at the old stone house (elev. 340 ft). The intriguing and elegant building may have you pondering its origin: Inn? Country

cottage? Tea house? Nope, it was a pee house! Built by the Works Progress Administration in 1936, the structure served as a public restroom until 1962.

Continue straight on the Wildwood Trail, upstream for another 0.3 mile to a bridge crossing over Balch Creek (elev. 425 ft). From here the trail climbs out of the canyon, making this a logical turnaround spot. Now enjoy the ravine downstream.

EXTENDING YOUR TRIP

Hike too short? Extend it into a 5.3-mile lollipop loop. From the old stone house, hike 1.6 miles north on the Wildwood Trail, turning left for 0.25 mile on the Birch Trail, which

A pair of hikers inspect an old-growth giant.

leads to NW 53rd Drive (elev. 860 ft). Follow the road left for 0.25 mile to Holman Fire Road (gated to vehicles), continuing 0.8 mile back to the Wildwood Trail. Turn right and retrace familiar ground back to the trailhead. More options exist—get your map out!

56 Macleay Park: Pittock Mansion

RATING/ DIFFICULTY	ROUND-TRIP	ELEV GAIN/ HIGH POINT	SEASON
***/2	2.3 miles	400 feet/ 950 feet	Year-round

Map: Green Trails Forest Park No. 426S; **Contact:** Portland Parks and Recreation, (503) 823-7529, www.portlandonline.com /parks, and Forest Park Conservancy, forest parkconservancy.org; **Notes:** Dogs permitted on-leash; **GPS:** N 45 31.620 W 122 43.667

Why drive to one of Portland's premier landmarks and viewpoints when you can hike there? A nice loop can be made from the Balch Creek canyon to the Pittock Mansion, from which you can relish the architectural beauty of the century-old French Renaissance National Historic landmark and the bird's-eye view of the Rose City and its rolling emerald environment. Not to mention a few volcanoes to gape at too!

GETTING THERE

From downtown Portland, follow NW Vaughn Street west (take exit 3 off of I-405—the US 30 exit—to NW Vaughn). Turn left onto NW 23rd Avenue and follow it for nine blocks, turning right onto Lovejoy Street. Lovejoy eventually bends right (northwest) to become NW Cornell Road. Continue 1.4 miles, and shortly after the second tunnel turn right to reach the Macleay Park trailhead (elev. 550 ft). Privy available.

ON THE TRAIL

This hike could easily be a history primer about two of early Portland's most prominent citizens. The hike starts in land donated to the city in 1897 by prominent businessman Donald Macleay, which established the beginning of what would become the 5100-acre Forest Park. And it ends at the now city-owned Pittock Mansion, built in 1909 as the twenty-two-room elaborate estate of Henry Pittock, publisher of the state's largest newspaper, the *Oregonian*, and his wife Georgiana, one of the founders of the city's Rose Festival. The Pittock Mansion is now one of the city's most visited landmarks. Most of the eighty thousand annual visitors drive to it from the south. But you'll hike to it from the north and earn the views from the mansion's manicured grounds.

The hike starts on the Wildwood Trail on the south side of Cornell Road. Use caution crossing this busy road. From here, just above Balch Creek (elev. 350 ft), the lowest point on the Wildwood Trail, to the mansion at more than 900 feet, is the greatest dramatic relief along the 30-mile-long trail. Within 200 feet, come to a junction with the Upper Macleay Trail, your return route. Continue left on the Wildwood Trail.

The way gently climbs, traversing a hillside shaded by mature forest. At 0.6 mile bear right at a junction with the Cumberland Trail (elev. 620 ft), which continues east to the Kings Heights neighborhood. In another 0.1 mile bear right at the junction with the Macleay Trail, and 0.1 mile after that continue straight at the junction with the Upper Macleay Trail (elev. 700 ft), which will be your return route.

The Wildwood Trail now climbs more steeply, following a series of short switchbacks. At 1.3 miles emerge at the parking lot for the mansion (elev. 950 ft). There's an admission charge to tour the building, but you can roam the grounds for free. Do it— the views of the city, the Tualatin Mountains (a.k.a. West Hills), and out to Washington State are excellent!

Return 0.5 mile to the Upper Macleay Trail and turn left (west). Traversing a steep hillside, the trail gently descends 0.5 mile through beautiful old-growth groves before meeting back up with the Wildwood Trail. Be careful crossing the road back to your vehicle.

EXTENDING YOUR TRIP

From the trailhead, you're within walking distance to the Audubon Society of Portland's 150-acre sanctuary, where you'll find 4 miles of kid-friendly trails, an interpretive center, a nature store, and a wildlife care center. Dogs are prohibited. Visit audubon portland.org for more information.

57 Tryon Creek State Natural Area

RATING/ DIFFICULTY	LOOP	ELEV GAIN/ HIGH POINT	SEASON
***/2	2.1 miles	330 feet/ 250 feet	Year-round

Map: Trail map from nature center or park website; **Contact:** Oregon State Parks, (541) 567-5032, www.oregon.gov/OPRD/PARKS; **Notes:** Dogs permitted on-leash; **GPS:** N 45 26.497 W 122 40.529

While Forest Park is often touted as Portland's premiere nature park, Tryon Creek is my choice. Lacking the brigades of zooming mountain bikes, trail runners, and roving dogs that often descend upon the at times monotonous terrain of Forest Park, Tryon

Creek is peaceful, varied, and graced with a family-friendly trail system that allows for multiple loop options. And it's all centered on a pretty little creek that meanders through an emerald ravine in a 670-acre park right within the city limits.

GETTING THERE

From Portland, follow I-5 south to exit 297. Turn right onto Barbur Boulevard (State Route 99W), and after 0.1 mile turn right onto SW Terwilliger Boulevard. Continue for 2.3 miles to the park entrance and trailhead (elev. 250 ft). Privy and water available.

ON THE TRAIL

Before taking to the trails of Tryon Creek, check out the staffed nature center. Aside from learning about the park's flora and fauna, gain an appreciation of how this sprawling greenbelt came to be. Back in the 1960s the area was slated to become a housing development, but thanks to the Friends of Tryon Creek the state was convinced instead to preserve it as a park. The Friends are still quite active, operating a nature store and educational and stewardship programs.

The park has about 8 miles of hiking trails, 3.5 miles of equestrian trails, and a 3-mile paved bike path. Feel free to combine them and roam at will, crafting your own loops and routes. While the park's myriad of trails may seem confusing, junctions are well marked and the park map (available for free at the nature center) is accurate and indispensable. The loop described here captures the essence of the park and consists solely of hiker-only trails.

Start by following the Maple Ridge Trail west from the nature center. At 0.2 mile, bear left at a junction with a spur that leads to the North Horse Loop. After another 0.1 mile

Lush vegetation grows along Tryon Creek.

come to a junction with the Middle Creek Trail. Take it right for 0.15 mile, dropping down into the lush emerald ravine containing Tryon Creek (elev. 125 ft) and a major trail convergence zone.

Cross the salmon-bearing waterway on High Bridge, one of several delightful bridges spanning Tryon and its tributaries. Turn left, continuing on the Middle Creek Trail and following Tryon Creek downstream. In winter, enjoy good views of the creek. In spring, woodland flowers—particularly trilliums—brighten the surrounding slopes. By summer a thick, verdant jungle obstructs much of the creek from sight.

At about 0.2 mile from High Bridge, veer right onto the Cedar Trail, making a big horseshoe bend around a quiet ravine housing—yep, you guessed it—cedars. Climbing out of the Tryon Creek valley, cross the West Horse Loop in about 0.2 mile, and after crossing Park Creek (elev. 250 ft) reach a junction with the Hemlock Trail 0.35 mile farther.

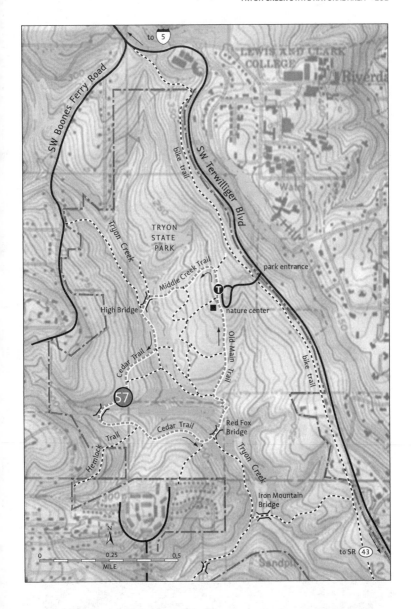

Continue left on the Cedar Trail, dropping to a small creek crossing (elev. 165 ft) and then climbing to follow a ridge (elev. 230 ft) above Tryon Creek before dropping back toward it. At 0.4 mile from the last junction, reach a junction with the Red Fox Trail. Turn left on Red Fox, ignoring the South Creek Trail at 0.1 mile and reaching the Red Fox Bridge on Tryon Creek (elev. 110 ft) shortly afterward.

Continue on the Red Fox Trail, climbing steeply out of the ravine to reach the Old Main Trail in 0.1 mile (elev. 220 ft). Turn right and follow this wide trail 0.3 mile back to the nature center.

EXTENDING YOUR TRIP

There are several options for extending your trip. Consider the North Creek Trail, a delightful and quiet 0.4-mile path along Tryon Creek, and the South Creek Trail to the Iron Mountain Bridge, another 0.4-mile creekside journey. The Center Trail, snaking along the north rim of Tryon's ravine, and the Big Fir Trail are also lovely paths.

58 Oaks Bottom Wildlife Refuge

RATING/ DIFFICULTY	ROUND-TRIP	ELEV GAIN/ HIGH POINT	SEASON
**/1	2.8 miles	60 feet/ 100 feet	Year-round

Map: USGS Lake Oswego; **Contact:** Portland Parks and Recreation, (503) 823-7529, www .portlandonline.com/parks; **Notes:** Dogs permitted on-leash; **GPS:** N 45 29.136 W 122 39.005

Drive, bike, or take the bus to this 168-acre wildlife refuge located in the heart of the city. Once destined to become an industrial site, in 1988 Oaks Bottom became Portland's first formally dedicated urban wildlife refuge. Oaks aren't abundant here, but cottonwoods are, along with eagles, waterfowl, and great blue herons, Portland's official bird. And expect a lot of surprises, too, from a charming historical amusement park to a beautiful giant mural.

Grove of oaks

GETTING THERE

From downtown Portland, follow State Route 99W (SW Pacific Highway) to Ross Island Bridge. (From Vancouver, follow I-5 south, taking exit 299A to the bridge.) Cross the bridge, following US 26 east (Powell Boulevard)

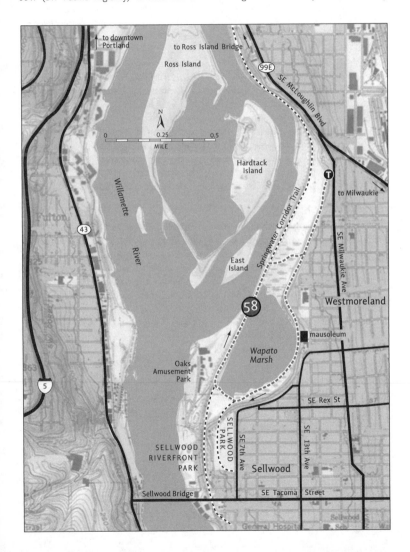

and immediately turn right (south) onto SR 99E (SE McLoughlin Boulevard). In just over 1 mile, exit to the right onto SE Milwaukie Avenue, driving south 0.1 mile to the trailhead (elev. 100 ft).

ON THE TRAIL

Follow the paved path, immediately leaving an urban environment and descending into an area of meadows, woodlands, and wetlands. At 0.3 mile reach a junction (elev. 40 ft). Head left on the dirt trail—you'll be returning on the paved path on the right. Pass another side trail right (which leads back to the paved path) and, in forest, skirt the base of a bluff. Above are houses and civilization. Now rolling and dipping, and occasionally crossing a small bridge, the path winds along the edge of a sprawling wetland.

An imposing building, a mausoleum actually, soon interrupts the mostly natural scene. But the walls facing the refuge became the country's largest hand-painted outdoor mural in 2009, depicting native wildlife and vegetation and allowing the seven-story building to "fit in." Children will love it. Can you identify all of the critters on the wall?

The trail continues around the wetland, coming close to water's edge a couple of times and allowing you to put those binoculars to work. See any pintails, mallards, coots, or wigeons?

At 1.4 mile emerge in a meadow on the south end of the refuge. Ignore a trail heading left to Sellwood Boulevard and another trail heading left toward Sellwood Park. Continue 0.2 mile across the meadow, passing beneath a railroad underpass and coming to the paved Springwater Corridor Trail and the Oaks Amusement Park. Opened in 1905 and now run by a nonprofit, the small and delightful Oaks Park is one of the oldest continuously run amusement parks in the country. Admission to the grounds is free and the rides are modestly priced. Treat the kids or continue hiking by following the Springwater Corridor Trail north. A former rail line extending from just south of downtown all the way to Boring, it weaves together several parks and greenbelts, including Powell Butte (Hike 59).

After hiking 0.7 mile on this popular biking and running trail, come to a junction. A short trail leads left through mature forest to nice overlooks on the Willamette River of East and Hardtack Islands. Check it out, or return right (east) on the paved path, passing the Tadpole Pond frog study area, and come to a familiar junction in 0.2 mile. Turn left and walk 0.3 mile to the trailhead.

EXTENDING YOUR TRIP

Adjacent Sellwood Park offers a good view of Oaks Bottom and nice strolling among manicured grounds. Nearby Sellwood Riverfront Park and Willamette Park have nice paved paths along the Willamette River. And across the river, check out Marquam Nature Park's 9 miles of trail, including one to 1073-foot Council Crest, the highest point in Portland.

59 Powell Butte Nature Park

RATING/ DIFFICULTY	ROUND-TRIP	ELEV GAIN/ HIGH POINT	SEASON
***/1	2.1 miles	150 feet/ 620 feet	Year-round

Map: Trail map from trailhead kiosk or park website; **Contact:** Portland Parks and Recreation, (503) 823-7529, www.portlandonline.com/parks; **Notes:** Wheelchair accessible. Dogs permitted on-leash. Unpaved trails closed during heavy rainfall; **GPS:** N 45 29.420 W 122 29.831

Enjoy outstanding views of four snow-capped volcanoes, scads of emerald dormant lava domes, and pastoral rolling countryside, all from this extinct volcano right within the Portland city limits. Easily amble up a paved path to a century-old walnut orchard atop the butte. Then languidly loop the summit, taking in soothing vistas in every direction. Miles of radiating trails invite further exploring.

GETTING THERE

From Portland, follow I-205 to exit 19 and head east on Powell Boulevard (US 26) for 3.2 miles. Turn right onto 162nd Street and proceed 0.4 mile to the large parking lot and trailhead (elev. 470 ft). Privy available.

ON THE TRAIL

Before heading up to the open fields of Powell Butte, take a moment to read about the fascinating history of this place at the trailhead kiosk. One of three extinct volcanic cinder cones within the Portland city limits, Powell Butte once housed an orchard and dairy farm. In the 1960s the city began using it as reservoir with aboveground water tanks. In 1980 the city moved water storage underground and expanded its capacity in 2010. In 1990 the entire area became a 600-plus-acre nature park, providing excellent habitat for a myriad of birds and mammals. About half of the park is open fields and a third is closed to public entry for wildlife protection.

Follow the paved Mountain View Trail, gently meandering up the butte and crossing

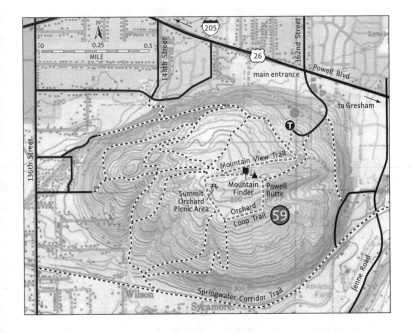

Old walnut trees grace Powell Butte.

old fence lines and hedgerows en route. At 0.6 mile the Meadowland Trail branches right. Five hundred feet farther, reach the Orchard Loop Trail (elev. 620 ft). It makes no difference which direction you choose to walk this 0.8-mile loop around the open summit of the butte. Just be sure to avoid any side trails (all junctions are well marked)—unless you want to head down them! Particular points of interest along the loop are a century-old walnut orchard and a mountain finder that points out prominent peaks and how far away they are. On a clear day, count on seeing Mount Saint Helens, Mount Adams, Larch Mountain, Mount Hood, Silver Star Mountain, and Mount Jefferson as well as more than fifty volcanic cones dotting the surroundings.

Linger long, exploring side trails, or return to your vehicle fully content with a touch of nature and good mountain views without ever leaving the city.

EXTENDING YOUR TRIP

There are more than 9 miles of trails in the park open to hikers, mountain bikers, and equestrians. The allowed use for each trail is indicated on the park's map and trail signs. Avoid using unofficial paths, as volunteers are aggressively restoring these blighted boot tracks. Trails in the park's western reaches traverse attractive forestlands, a nice contrast to the butte's meadows.

60 Mount Talbert

RATING/ DIFFICULTY	LOOP	ELEV GAIN/ HIGH POINT	SEASON
**/2	2.8 miles	525 feet/ 750 feet	Year-round

Maps: USGS Gladstone, trail map from park website; **Contact:** North Clackamas Parks and Recreation District, (503) 742-4353, www.oregonmetro.gov; **Notes:** Dogs prohibited; **GPS:** N 45 25.239 W 122 33.177

Rising above busy Clackamas Town Center and congested I-205 is a little green island virtually unknown to many of the thousands of shoppers and commuters that pass by it every day. One of a string of extinct volcanoes and lava domes between the Columbia and Clackamas rivers, 750-foot Mount Talbert is the largest undeveloped butte in northern Clackamas County.

Providing important habitat for a myriad of fauna and flora, Mount Talbert also offers hikers over 4 miles of fine, uncrowded trails.

GETTING THERE

From Portland, follow I-205 to exit 14 and head east on Sunnyside Road. Immediately turn right (south) onto SE 97th Avenue and continue for 1 mile, turning left (east) onto SE Mather Road. In 0.2 mile reach the trailhead, located on the left (elev. 325 ft). Privy available.

ON THE TRAIL

A fairly new preserve, Talbert contains a nice interlinking trail system complete with attractive interpretive signs. Before taking to the Mather Road Trail, consider checking out the short Prairie Loop to the right—especially in the spring, when camas and woolly sunshine are in bloom.

The Mather Road Trail immediately enters a forest of fir and oak, climbing 0.4 mile to a junction with the Park Loop Trail (elev. 490 ft). You'll be returning on the left, so head right. In 0.1 mile bear left at a junction—the trail right leads 0.3 mile to a neighborhood. Junctions are well-marked with signs that bear trail maps. The way now gently climbs, traversing beautiful oak forest carpeted with flowers in the spring. Look for western gray squirrels and rubber boas, a docile nonvenomous rubbery-looking snake.

At 0.6 mile come to another junction (elev. 600 ft). The Park Loop Trail continues to

Mount Talbert supports healthy stands of Oregon white oak.

the right, to Sunnyside Road. Veer left on the Summit Trail, gently rounding the 750-foot summit through woods and terrain that resemble Appalachia. At 1 mile, after passing some big oaks, come to a small clearing on the summit with a view east of rolling greenery at the edge of the rural/urban divide.

The trail then descends, coming to a junction with the West Ridge Trail at 1.3 miles (elev. 570 ft). Head left if you prefer a shortcut back to the trailhead. The recommended loop continues right, descending into a fern gully and coming to the Park Loop Trail at 1.6 miles (elev. 390 ft). Turn left and follow the Park Loop Trail, skirting along the preserve's western boundary.

At 2.1 miles bear left at a junction (elev. 340 ft), remaining on the Park Loop and climbing, passing a seasonal brook. Look for Pacific dogwood, more easily noticed in

spring when it's blooming. At 2.3 miles, at the edge of an oak grove, bear right at a junction (elev. 490 ft) with the West Ridge Trail, reaching the Mather Road Trail 0.1 mile farther. Then turn right and head downhill 0.4 mile back to the trailhead.

EXTENDING YOUR TRIP
Compare and contrast Mount Talbert with Portland's nearby extinct volcanoes. Mount Tabor is the home of a beautiful city park. Rocky Butte contains a natural area and the Grotto, a Catholic shrine and botanical garden. And Powell Butte (Hike 59) is a nature park with miles of trails and excellent views.

61 Oxbow Regional Park

RATING/ DIFFICULTY	LOOP	ELEV GAIN/ HIGH POINT	SEASON
***/2	4.5 miles	200 feet/ 210 feet	Year-round

Maps: USGS Sandy, trail map from the park website; **Contact:** Metro, (503) 663-4708, www.oregonmetro.gov/oxbow; **Notes:** Day-use fee $5 per vehicle (pay at entrance, credit cards accepted). Dogs prohibited; **GPS:** N 45 29.474 W 122 17.792

Born of glacial ice on Oregon's highest summit, the Sandy River flows for more than 50 miles on its way to the Columbia. Captain Clark (of Lewis and Clark fame) attempted to wade it back in November of 1805 but, as he noted in his journal, to his dismay he "found the bottom a quick sand and impassable." But you don't need to worry about crossing the Sandy when you have miles of lovely trail to hike beside it in this 1200-acre park. A small gorge, big trees, inviting sand bars, and high bluffs are added incentives.

GETTING THERE

From Portland, take the Troutdale exit (exit 17) off of I-84 and follow the frontage road for 0.6 mile, turning right onto SW 257th Avenue. Continue south on this major arterial for 2.9 miles turning, left onto NE Division Street. (Alternatively, reach this junction from exit 19 on I-205, following NE Division Street east.) Continue east for 2.7 miles, bearing right on Oxbow Drive. Then in 2.3 miles turn left onto Oxbow Parkway. Proceed 1.6 miles to the park entrance station, and then continue 1.5 miles on the park road, turning left into a large parking area beside the group picnic area (elev. 100 ft). Privy available.

ON THE TRAIL

With nearly fifty Wild and Scenic rivers, Oregon leads the nation. The Sandy is one of them, with its upper and lower sections designated Wild and Scenic to forever remain free flowing. Metro's Oxbow Regional Park protects 1200 acres of prime riverbank, bluff, and riparian forest on the lower Sandy where it exits a small gorge into a series of oxbows. Mere minutes from metropolitan Portland, the park is popular with anglers, rafters, kayakers, campers, equestrians, and hikers. Laced with 15 miles of trail, you can easily spend days exploring Oxbow. This loop hike is a nice introduction.

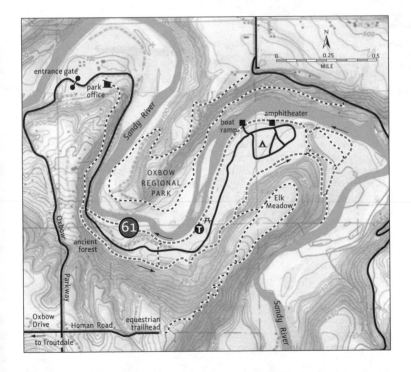

Old-growth forest along the Sandy River

From the group picnic area, head west along a bluff above the river and immediately enter a substantial grove of old-growth forest. Sticking close to the river, ignore several side trails that lead left, and after 0.5 mile come to trail marker "C" at a small parking area (alternative trailhead). Continue along the river for 0.2 mile, crossing the park road and coming to a trail junction at marker "B." The trail to the right parallels the road for 0.8 mile, passing a plaque commemorating the cleanup after the great flood of 1996.

Head left instead and travel east, paralleling the road and gently climbing, passing through magnificent groves of ancient cedars and firs. At 1.2 miles come to an unmarked junction—bear right. Soon come to another unmarked junction (elev. 200 ft)—bear left. Soon after that come to marker "E," where the trail diverges. Go either way—the paths soon meet up. At 1.7 miles, after a small climb and dip, intersect a closed-to-traffic dirt road at marker "F." For a shortened loop, head left 0.1 mile back to your vehicle—otherwise, continue right and in 0.1 mile reach marker "G" at a junction (elev. 210 ft).

Turn left, back onto trail (now open to bikes and horses), gently descending through attractive second-growth forest. Ignore side trails leading left to the campground, and at 2.6 miles come to marker "N" (elev. 125 ft). Turn right and after 0.3 mile come to a junction at marker "J" (elev. 100 ft). The trail right follows the river a short way before petering out. Turn left and follow the river downstream, passing gravel bars and spots along the riverbank that encourage lounging.

Stick to the trail closest to the river, ignoring side trails left that lead to the campground. Come to marker "M" at 3.6 miles, climbing a bluff (elev. 130 ft) to the campground. The trail then drops off the bluff, arriving at the boat ramp (elev. 90 ft) at 4 miles. Climb again, crouching to get beyond a large fallen tree, and then pass through picnic areas perched above the river. Following restored tread, hike along the bluff edge, enjoying excellent views of the Wild and Scenic Sandy River and reaching your vehicle at 4.5 miles.

EXTENDING YOUR TRIP

Follow that previously crossed closed-to-traffic dirt road 0.4 mile up to Elk Meadow on Alder Ridge (elev. 400 ft). From there, hike a 1.4-mile nearly level loop, brushing the rim of a gorge above the river. Catch some good but limited views. The trail is popular with equestrians and can be muddy.

Opposite: Looking west over Sand Island from Angels Rest

columbia river gorge, oregon: west

Classic scenery and dramatic landscapes are what you'll experience in the Columbia River Gorge, a deep canyon cut by the West's mightiest river through one of its largest and most rugged mountain chains. And on the Oregon side of the river in the Gorge's western half, nothing epitomizes this region more than waterfalls. Perhaps nowhere else in the country is there such a high concentration of cascades, including Multnomah, the state's highest. And a high concentration of trails too, some of the oldest and best loved in America, delivering you to old-growth forests, mossy ravines, thundering chasms, breathtaking overlooks, historical sites, and lofty summits. And this entire splendor is within an hour's drive of more than two million people!

62 Sandy River Delta

RATING/ DIFFICULTY	ROUND-TRIP	ELEV GAIN/ HIGH POINT	SEASON
**/1	6.7 miles	Minimal/ 30 feet	Year-round

Maps: Green Trails Columbia River Gorge–West No. 428S, trail map from trailhead kiosk; **Contact:** Columbia River Gorge National Scenic Area, (541) 308-1700, www.fs.fed.us/r6/columbia; **Notes:** Dogs permitted off-leash within the delta but on-leash only along Confluence Trail; **GPS:** N 45 32.757 W 122 22.427

The Sandy River Delta is quite possibly the largest dog park in the Pacific Northwest, where hundreds of Portlanders and their four-legged companions come to frolic rain or shine, year-round. But if you're not fond of all of these fur balls, it's best to wag your tail elsewhere. Otherwise, enjoy

Boardwalk leading to bird blind

exploring a virtually level 1400-acre parcel of beach, slough, meadow, and deciduous forest on the western front of the Columbia River Gorge National Scenic Area.

GETTING THERE
From Portland, follow I-84 east and take exit 18. After 0.2 mile turn right at a stop sign and proceed under the freeway. In another 0.2 mile turn left on a dirt road and drive 0.2 mile to a large parking area and trailhead (elev. 20 ft). Privy available.

ON THE TRAIL
Once a cattle ranch, the 1400-acre Sandy River Delta property was acquired by the U.S. Forest Service in 1991. The flat, lush bottomland was formed by mudflows traveling down the Sandy River from Mount Hood. In this unique part of the Columbia River Gorge National Scenic Area, the Forest Service has been eradicating

invasive plants and working on a management plan to help restore this ecosystem to a more natural state. Plans call for closing sensitive areas to recreation and removing the old dam that shut off a channel of the river. The good news for hikers is that the Forest Service has constructed a 1.3-mile hard-surface, wheelchair-accessible trail to a bird blind as part of the delta's facelift. This hike follows this new trail and some of the delta's old roads to provide you with a good half-day jaunt.

From beside the privy, head out northeast on the Confluence Trail, a multiuse path also open to bikes, horses, and wheelchairs. Your canine companion should be on-leash on this trail. The way skirts a field edge of invasive blackberry backed by rows of oak and cottonwood. Views are good across the pasture to Mount Hood and Larch Mountain. Scores of primitive, often muddy and brushy trails radiate in every direction from this and the other official trails within the delta. Explore at will.

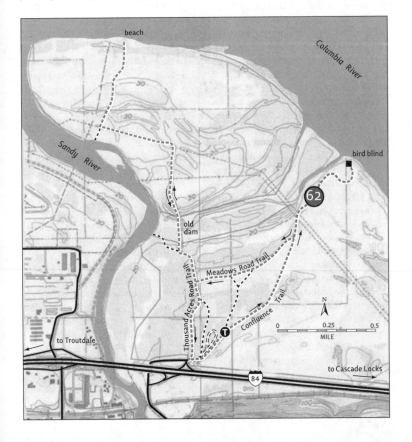

At 0.7 mile, just before crossing under a set of transmission wires, reach a junction with the Meadows Road Trail—you'll continue that way after proceeding right on the Confluence Trail to visit the bird blind. Enter a restoration area, rolling over old dunes, and then walk along an old channel of the Sandy River to reach the bird blind. It depicts the 134 species of plants and animals documented by Lewis and Clark and was designed by Maya Lin, who created the Vietnam War Memorial in Washington DC.

Scan the surroundings for some of those species, and then retrace your steps 0.6 mile to the Meadows Road Trail. Follow this path 0.6 mile, avoiding secondary trails and reaching the Thousand Acres Road Trail. If you've had enough, turn left and follow this old road 0.5 mile back to the parking lot for a 3-mile hike. Otherwise, turn right, following this old road up and over an old dike. Soon afterward, bear right at a junction and cross the old Sandy River Delta Dam, which was built in 1931 and cut off the upper channel of the river. Now mostly buried in accumulated matter and creating a slough where the river once ran, the dam will eventually be removed by the Forest Service.

Beyond the old dam, the road-trail continues, entering a large meadow. After passing under transmission wires, the road turns left, reaching a junction at about 0.4 mile after the powerlines. The primitive trail left leads to the Sandy River. Follow the main trail right for 0.4 mile to a nice sandy beach on the Columbia River, directly across from Washougal's Steamboat Landing Park (Hike 11). Explore the shoreline, take a break, or begin your return, following the same way back 1.6 miles to the Meadows Road Trail junction and then continuing straight another 0.5 mile back to the parking lot.

63 Rooster Rock State Park

RATING/ DIFFICULTY	LOOP	ELEV GAIN/ HIGH POINT	SEASON
**/2	3.3 miles	300 feet/ 190 feet	Year-round

Map: Green Trails Columbia River Gorge–West No. 428S; **Contact:** Oregon State Parks, (541) 567-5032, www.oregon.gov /OPRD/PARKS; **Notes:** $5 day-use fee or $30 annual pass. Dogs permitted on-leash; **GPS:** N 45 32.844 W 122 13.762

 Known for its three miles of gorgeous sandy beaches on the Columbia River, Rooster Rock State Park's quiet trails will delight hikers. Lewis and Clark camped here in 1805, and early settlers named the park's prominent and phallic rock after a different name for a male chicken. It was later changed to "Rooster" to be less offensive. Hikers offended by human flesh may want to steer clear of the park's eastern beach—it's one of Oregon's two officially sanctioned clothing-optional beaches, so you'll need to be bare aware while exploring it.

GETTING THERE

From Portland, follow I-84 east and take exit 25. After 0.5 mile pass the park entrance booth and turn right, proceeding 0.4 mile to farthest-west parking lot. The trail begins to the right of the restroom at the southeast corner of the parking lot (elev. 75 ft). Privy available.

ON THE TRAIL

Several trails take off from the field behind the restroom. The one you want is the wide one farthest south, next to the Frisbee golf course. Quickly enter forest and stay on the

Looking east toward Angels Rest

main path, avoiding side trails to Frisbee golf stations for the first 0.25 mile. The trail takes to the spine of a small rolling ridge, traveling through a lush, attractive forest of oak and maple. Mosses drape the hardwoods, while ferns line the way. Winter's lack of cover allows for window views out across the Columbia to Cape Horn.

While the trail makes no significant elevation gain, its constant dipping and climbing along the ridge crest means that significant elevation is accumulated on this hike. Trail runners may find this loop quite enjoyable. At about 0.4 mile you'll pass a small side trail, providing a shortcut. Continue straight on a roller coaster course through hip-high horsetails. At about 0.9 mile, catch glimpses through the trees of Sand Island, with its beautiful dunes.

At about 1.3 miles the trail loops back at a nice opening in the forest at the edge of a grassy slope (elev. 150 ft). Sit down on this sunny slope and enjoy the view east of the Columbia River, Angel's Rest, Beacon Rock, and Hamilton Mountain. If lured by the river, feel free to run down the slope toward it—otherwise, continue down the trail, now westward. More ups and downs and some attractive contorted hardwoods await you.

At 2.2 miles reach the highest point along the way (elev. 190 ft). At about 2.5 miles return to the Frisbee golf course, with shortcuts back to the trailhead. The main trail continues straight, dropping off the ridge to a meadow by the highway, with good views up to Crown Point. The trail concludes at 3 miles at the Group "A" Picnic Area (elev. 40 ft).

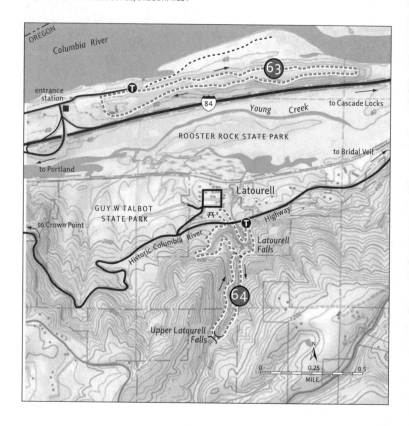

From here follow a paved path to the large parking lot and then walk east 0.3 mile to retrieve your vehicle.

EXTENDING YOUR TRIP

Consider a side trip to Rooster Rock's "Columbia River buffs." The park's beaches are absolutely stunning. Follow a trail from the left of the restroom down a staircase to the floodplain. From here a series of trails diverge. The Buffalo, Otter, and Dragonfly trails branch left to the river. Continue on the Forest Bluff Trail

for about 0.8 mile to a river channel. In summer it's possible to wade across the channel to the spectacular dunes on Sand Island. To minimize exposure to the fully exposed, opt for cold windy days in winter.

64 Latourell Falls

RATING/ DIFFICULTY	LOOP	ELEV GAIN/ HIGH POINT	SEASON
****/2	2.3 miles	540 feet/ 600 feet	Year-round

Map: Green Trails Columbia River Gorge–West No. 428S; **Contact:** Oregon State Parks, (541) 567-5032, www.oregon.gov/OPRD/PARKS; **Notes:** Dogs permitted on-leash; **GPS:** N 45 32.323 W 122 13.062

Following the lead of other early area homesteaders and civic leaders, in 1929 Guy and Geraldine Talbot donated the land surrounding a pair of gorgeous waterfalls to the Oregon State Parks system. Today, Talbot State Park's Latourell Falls ranks as one of the most popular hiking destinations in the Columbia River Gorge. Being close to Portland certainly helps Latourell's visitor numbers—notwithstanding, these falls, especially the lower one plunging 249 feet from basalt cliffs, are among the most beautiful in the state.

GETTING THERE

From Portland, follow I-84 east to exit 28 and proceed 0.4 mile to a junction with the Historic Columbia River Highway. Turn right (west) and continue 2.6 miles to the trailhead (elev. 190 ft). Privy available.

ON THE TRAIL

Follow a paved path 300 feet to a wonderful viewpoint of the breathtaking lower falls. By far the majority of Latourell's spectators only lumber this far. So carry on, continuing left and leaving the pavement to wind upward to different perspectives of the lower falls, including a behind the scenes look at the plummeting cascade. From a bluff above, enjoy views too out to Mounts Pleasant and Zion in Washington.

Walk along Latourell Creek through patches of big firs and moss-draped maples and at about 0.4 mile come to an unmarked

Lower Latourell Falls plunges into a basin of columnar basalt.

junction (elev. 370 ft). The right-hand trail crosses the creek, offering a shortcut to this loop. In winter, however, it may be difficult to cross the swollen waterway.

The loop continues left, working its way into a tight, lush, dank ravine. Cross numerous side creeks (bridged) and attractive cedar groves along the way. At 0.9 mile come to a spray-blasted bridge (elev. 600 ft) over Latourell Creek just beneath the 120-foot horsetail-like upper falls. Savor the mist in warm weather, retreat otherwise. The curious may want to get a closer look of the basalt grotto behind the falls.

The trail continues, now looping back to follow Latourell Creek on its west bank. Traversing steep slopes high above the tumbling waterway, gradually descend and reach the unmarked shortcut trail (elev. 450 ft) at 1.4 miles. Veer left, climbing to the rim (elev. 550 ft) of the lower falls basin. A spur leads right to a viewpoint above the falls. Exercise caution—a hiker tragically perished here several years ago, falling from the steep walls flanking the falls.

After passing a much safer viewpoint, the trail makes a wide swing west before switchbacking east at an oddly shaped and much-admired tree. Gradually losing elevation, the trail reaches the Historic Columbia River Highway. Carefully cross the road here to the park's picnic grounds (elev. 160 ft) and follow a paved trail beside Latourell Creek underneath one of the historic highway's remaining concrete arched bridges. Arrive at the base of the lower falls, one of the most glorious places in the Gorge. Stand mesmerized for as long as you'd like, staring at streams of silver water plummeting over an amphitheater of columnar basalt. Then content, cross the creek and climb back to the trailhead.

65 Bridal Veil Falls

RATING/ DIFFICULTY	ROUND-TRIP	ELEV GAIN/ HIGH POINT	SEASON
**/1	1.2 miles	175 feet/ 190 feet	Year-round

Map: Green Trails Columbia River Gorge–West No. 428S; **Contact:** Oregon State Parks, (541) 567-5032, www.oregon.gov/OPRD/PARKS; **Notes:** Dogs permitted on-leash; **GPS:** N 45 33. 209 W 122 10.967

A hidden, often overlooked waterfall, Bridal Veil Falls is the perfect destination for young hikers and, of course, cataract connoisseurs. The trail is short, making it the

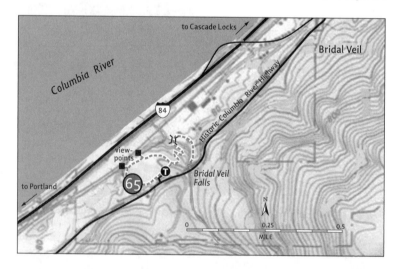

ideal add-on to your day after doing one of the many longer nearby hikes. And while the falls is the prime attraction here in this small state park, be sure not to skip a trip out to the interpretive loop trail perched on the bluff for good views and, in late spring, flowering camas.

GETTING THERE

From Portland, follow I-84 east to exit 28 and proceed 0.4 mile to a junction with the Historic Columbia River Highway. Turn right (west) and continue 0.7 mile to Bridal Veil Falls State Park and the trailhead (elev. 190 ft). Privy and water available.

ON THE TRAIL

Two trails begin near the restrooms. For the falls, head right on a paved path that soon yields to a gravel surface. Making one sweeping switchback, the trail descends into a deep, dank ravine and reaches a bridge over Bridal Veil Creek. The falls is still hidden here but quite audible. Downstream you'll notice remains of what obviously was some sort of industrial operation at some time. In the 1880s a lumber mill was constructed here, sprouting a company town. The mill's wood flume was destroyed by fire in 1937, and milling operations continued on the site until 1960. In 1990, the Trust for Public Land acquired much of the former townsite, demolished the remaining buildings, and transferred the property to the U.S. Forest Service. While I lament the removal of the historical buildings, I welcome the removal of invasive species that have carpeted much of the state park. Volunteers continue to eradicate the vegetative plague.

Cross the bridge and climb a stairway to a platform to catch a look at the bridal veil. The gorgeous two-tiered cascade plummets down a narrow chasm. After fawning

Bridal Veil Falls lies in a hidden chasm.

over its beauty, retrace your steps back to the trailhead and take the mossy paved path that diverts left from the restrooms. Follow this delightful interpretive loop trail for 0.5 mile along the rim of a basalt bluff, taking in good views of Sand Island and Cape Horn across the river. In springtime enjoy flowering camas, as this bluff supports one of Oregon's largest remaining camas fields in the western half of the Columbia Gorge. Look, too, for other beautiful blossoms, notably checker lily, Oregon iris, and cliff penstemon.

EXTENDING YOUR TRIP

Consider a visit to nearby Shepperds Dells Falls. The short path to this impressive multitiered waterfall can be reached by following the Historic Columbia River Highway west for 0.7 mile.

BEFRIENDING THE GORGE

The Friends of the Columbia Gorge was organized in 1980, under the leadership of Nancy Russell, to permanently protect the Gorge's natural values. Including such prominent politicians as former Oregon governors Tom McCall and Bob Straub and former Washington governor Dan Evans, the group set out to develop federal legislation to permanently protect the Gorge; create widespread public support for Gorge protection; and challenge inappropriate development proposals in the Gorge.

From 1981 to 1986, the Friends worked tirelessly to build political support for the creation of the Columbia River Gorge National Scenic Area. They worked closely with Senators Hatfield, Packwood, Evans, and Gorton, and Representatives AuCoin, Wyden, Weaver, and Bonker. They were met with much opposition by economic and resource development interests within the Gorge.

However, the Columbia River Gorge National Scenic Area Act was finally passed by both the U.S. Senate and House in October 1986, and the bill was signed by President Reagan on November 17, 1986, just hours before it would have died from a pocket veto. It's interesting to note that this preservation effort was bipartisan, with powerful Republican support. All four senators sponsoring this bill were Republicans, and Nancy Russell herself was a lifelong Republican.

Since the passage of the legislation, the Forest Service has purchased more than 38,000 acres along the Columbia for resource protection and enhancement. Russell herself personally bought thirty parcels, donating the land to the Friends and protecting it from development. Friends of the Columbia Gorge, which numbers more than five thousand members (including this author), continues to advocate for and act as a watchdog for this great American landscape. I encourage you to join them—good land stewardship is the responsibility of folks of all political persuasions, and we have a long history in this country to back that claim.

Nancy Russell passed away in 2008 at the age of seventy-six after a four-year battle with Lou Gehrig's disease. But the Great Guardian of the Gorge's spirit and inspiration lives on!

66 Angels Rest

RATING/ DIFFICULTY	ROUND-TRIP	ELEV GAIN/ HIGH POINT	SEASON
*****/3	4.6 miles	1475 feet/ 1600 feet	Year-round

Map: Green Trails Columbia River Gorge–West No. 428S; **Contact:** Columbia River Gorge National Scenic Area, (541) 308-1700, www.fs.fed.us/r6/columbia; **Notes:** Dogs permitted on-leash; **GPS:** N 45 33.627 W 122 10.363

If a celestial being were to pick a perch, this precipitous point high above the Columbia would be the perfect place. Heavenly views await all who make the trek to this weathered and fractured outcropping at the western gate of the Columbia Gorge. But be forewarned—just like the gates of heaven, this post is coveted by scads of folks. At this very popular trail within the scenic area, you won't want for company.

But it's also one of the most stunning hikes within the Gorge—one that no hiker should miss.

GETTING THERE

From Portland, follow I-84 east to exit 28 and proceed 0.4 mile to a junction with the Historic Columbia River Highway where trailhead parking (elev. 125 ft) is located immediately to your right. (From Hood River, take exit 35 off of I-84 and follow the Historic Columbia River Highway 7.2 miles west.) Overflow parking lies just to the west, on the south side of the highway.

ON THE TRAIL

Carefully cross the old highway and begin on what can be described as a highway of a trail. Wide and well-beaten, the Angels Rest Trail starts by slowly winding across a forested slope. Gradually gaining elevation, the trail cuts across a fernified basalt slope, with views out to Cape Horn, before cresting a bench (elev. 400 ft) above 150-foot Coopey Falls. Catch glimpses of the cataract

and carry on, coming to a bridged crossing of Coopey Creek (elev. 475 ft) just above a small cascade at 0.6 mile.

Now traversing a slope in a ravine above the crashing creek, steadily climb. At about 1.2 miles the forest cover thins as you enter a rather large burn zone from 1991. While the area continues to be recolonized by a wide array of flora, thank the fire for providing some nice views—and flowers! This is one of the breeziest spots in the Gorge (isn't it all windy?), so exercise caution during windy periods—the snags are prone to losing limbs and being blown over.

Continue climbing, switchbacking over ledge and broken rock, views growing with each step. At 2.2 miles reach an unmarked but obvious junction (elev. 1600 ft). Head left 0.1 mile to Angels Rest, a small plateau of fractured rock hovering above the Columbia River. The views are simply sublime. Though you'll see a slight resemblance to the Palisades along the Hudson River, it's no New Jersey you're looking out over. Gaze north across the Columbia to Cape Horn,

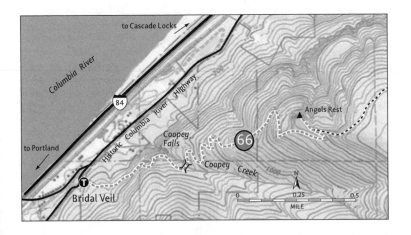

A pair of hikers roam along Angels Rest.

Silver Star, and Table Mountain, and west over Sand Island out to Crown Point. Keep children close by—it's a hell of a drop from this heavenly spot.

EXTENDING YOUR TRIP

Devils Rest (Hike 67) can also be accessed from this trail. Continue on the main trail another 0.2 mile to a junction. Head right, coming to a junction with the Foxglove Trail in 0.5 mile, and continue straight for 0.5 mile to Devils Rest (elev. 2450 ft). Make a loop by returning left on the Foxglove Trail, coming to the Angels Rest Trail (elev. 1850 ft) in 0.5 mile. Turn left (west) and return to Angels Rest in 1.2 miles. En route pass a lovely picnicking spot by a cascading creek in a nice grove of cedars.

67 Devils Rest

RATING/ DIFFICULTY	LOOP	ELEV GAIN/ HIGH POINT	SEASON
***/3	8.3 miles	2470 feet/ 2450 feet	Year-round

Map: Green Trails Columbia River Gorge–West No. 428S; **Contact:** Columbia River Gorge National Scenic Area, (541) 308-1700, www.fs.fed.us/r6/columbia; **Notes:** Dogs permitted on-leash; **GPS:** N 45 34.519 W 122 07.684

Nearly 1000 feet higher than nearby Angels Rest (Hike 66), Devils Rest may be closer to heaven but the wooded summit forecloses heavenly views. Don't be discouraged, though—good does triumph over evil here.

The path to the devil's lair is lined with rewards, from spectacular waterfalls to lush primeval forest, a rejuvenating spring and a pleasantly scenic viewpoint too. It's a devilishly delightful loop on an overcast day, so who needs spectacular views?

GETTING THERE

From Portland, follow I-84 east to exit 28 and proceed 0.4 mile, bearing left (east) onto the Historic Columbia River Highway. Continue for 2.5 miles to the Wahkeena Falls trailhead (elev. 80 ft). (From Hood River, take exit 35 off of I-84 and follow the Historic Columbia River Highway 4.7 miles west to the trailhead.)

ON THE TRAIL

This lollipop loop starts on the paved and popular Wahkeena Falls Trail. In 0.2 mile come to the breathtaking cataract that crashes down a basalt chute. Triple-tiered, the 242-foot falls will bring tears (actually mist) to your eyes from its intense spray. Cross the creek beneath the falls on a handsome stone bridge nearly a century old. Timber baron and philanthropist Simon Benson—a Norwegian immigrant born Simon Iversen—donated the land surrounding both Wahkeena and Multnomah Falls to the state.

Continue following the paved path on a switchbacking course, steadily gaining elevation. At 0.5 mile pass the junction with the closed Perdition Trail (elev. 325 ft). A victim of forest fire, subsequent erosion eternally damned Perdition to the land of lost trails. Staying on the paved path, weave up a gap between steep basalt walls.

At just shy of 1 mile the pavement ends (elev. 625 ft). A short spur leads right to Lemmons Viewpoint, named after a firefighter who lost his life fighting a fire in 1983. The

view is good across the river of Beacon Rock and Hamilton Mountain. Continue on good dirt tread, passing an abandoned (and potentially dangerous) trail that drops to the right, to the top of Wahkeena Falls.

Now paralleling Wahkeena Creek, the trail crosses it twice as it works its way up a tight slot. At 1.4 miles cross a side creek (elev. 920 ft) beneath 20-foot Fairy Falls, and 0.1 mile beyond come to a junction (elev. 1000 ft). You'll be returning on the right, so veer left on the Vista Point Trail, rock hopping across a small creek and then gently rounding a ridge with good but limited views. Pass a spur that leads to a vista, and at

Wahkeena Spring

2.4 miles, in a grove of big firs, come to the Wahkeena Trail (elev. 1530 ft; different from the Wahkeena Falls Trail).

Turn left and then immediately right onto the Devils Rest Trail. Any crowds you've contended with so far likely will get left behind here. On good tread, steadily climb steep slopes that are covered in ferns, dotted with mossy rocks, and shaded by big old conifers. At 3.1 miles ignore a side trail (elev. 1975 ft) on the left that leads to a Forest Service road, continuing right instead, now along the rim of a ridge. At 3.5 miles, ignore another spur left and come to a nice viewpoint out to Silver Star and company.

Beyond, the trail continues through a gorgeous grove of ancient hemlock, crosses a small creek, and at 3.9 miles comes to a nicer viewpoint (elev. 2250 ft). Climb a bit more,

reaching a junction with the Foxglove Trail at 4 miles, just below the wooded 2450-foot summit of Devils Rest. Bag the summit, and then return via the Foxglove Trail, steadily losing elevation.

In 0.5 mile bear right, continuing on the Foxglove Trail, which now follows an old road. The trail left leads to Angels Rest (Hike 66). In another 0.5 mile (5 miles from your start), reach the Angels Rest Trail (elev. 1850 ft). Head right (east), crossing a small creek before beginning to descend. Pass through an old burn zone that grants limited views through the trees. At about 6.2 miles come to a small spring (elev. 1200 ft) and begin a gradual ascent. Soon after, in a mossy maple grove, reach the robustly gushing Wahkeena Spring (elev. 1300 ft) that feeds the showy falls far below.

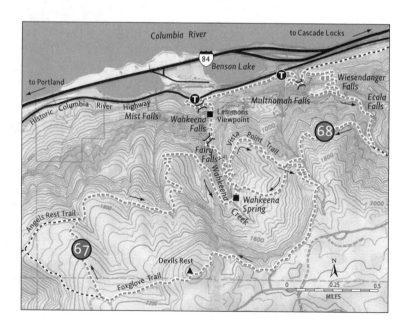

A few hundred feet farther (6.6 miles from your start), come to a junction with the Wahkeena Falls Trail. Veer left, rapidly losing elevation and coming to the familiar Vista Point Trail in 0.2 mile. Then continue left, retracing previously hiked ground for 1.5 miles and returning to your vehicle.

68 Multnomah Falls–Wahkeena Falls

RATING/ DIFFICULTY	LOOP	ELEV GAIN/ HIGH POINT	SEASON
****/3	5.4 miles	1550 feet/ 1525 feet	Year-round

Map: Green Trails Columbia River Gorge–West No. 428S; **Contact:** Columbia River Gorge National Scenic Area, (541) 308-1700, www .fs.fed.us/r6/columbia; **Notes:** Dogs permitted on-leash; **GPS:** N 45 34.656 W 122 07.034

Enjoy a spectacular loop to two of the Gorge's most gorgeous waterfalls, plus a couple of not too shabby ones too. Multnomah is Oregon's highest and most visited waterfall and the Columbia Gorge's quintessential cataract. And Wahkeena is no mere cascade—its name derives from a Native American word meaning "most beautiful," and it certainly is. This is the ultimate loop for waterfall lovers and, not surprisingly, hordes of hikers barrel up and down these trails. Get an early start, or save it for a rainy day.

GETTING THERE

From Portland, follow I-84 east and take exit 31. Park and walk through the highway underpass to the trailhead (elev. 50 ft). Alternatively, also from Portland, follow I-84 east and take exit 28, drive 0.4 mile and bear

Multnomah Falls' upper tier

left (east) onto the Historic Columbia River Highway. Continue for 3 miles to the trailhead. (From Hood River, take exit 35 off of I-84 and follow the Historic Columbia River Highway 4.2 miles west to the trailhead.)

ON THE TRAIL

Before proceeding to the falls, you'll need to pass by the beautiful Multnomah Falls Lodge, a National Historic Landmark built in 1925. The Forest Service maintains a visitors center there, and you can always catch breakfast beforehand or dinner afterward to enhance your hike.

Weaving in and out of camera-schlepping tourists, follow paved trail first to the base of the 620-foot two-tiered Multnomah Falls. Highest in the state and one of the highest in the nation, Multnomah Falls is a breathtaking sight—especially during winter's incessant rains. More than 75 inches of annual precipitation help fan the falls.

At 0.25 mile, cross Multnomah Creek between the two tiers on the elegant and heavily photographed Benson Bridge. Built in 1915 by entrepreneur and philanthropist Simon Benson, he also bequeathed to the state both Multnomah and Wahkeena Falls and hundreds of surrounding acres. Pause, gaze, gape, and contemplate, and then carry on, following a paved path that makes eleven switchbacks (They're signed).

At the second one, pass a junction with the Gorge Trail (elev. 280 ft). At switchback no. 9, crest a ridge (elev. 785 ft). Then slightly descend to the pavement's end and a junction (elev. 740 ft) at 1.1 miles. By all means take the 0.1-mile spur trail right, dropping to the top of the falls (elev. 660 ft). It's a spiraling and exhilarating view down to the lodge and river and one that may leave you feeling slightly dizzy. Thank heavens for the guardrail!

Return to the main trail, heading right. Immediately cross Multnomah Creek on a little bridge and come to the abandoned Perdition Trail. Closed in 1991 after fire scorched more than 1600 surrounding acres, the way is no longer safe for passage.

Your route hugs Multnomah Creek in a cool, moist gorge on blasted ledges and beneath basalt walls. Pass small Dutchman Falls and soon afterward come to the impressive 50-foot Wiesendanger (also known as Upper Multnomah) Falls, named for a former Forest Service ranger.

The trail then switchbacks above the falls and comes to yet another impressive cascade, 55-foot Ecola Falls (elev. 1050 ft). Also known as Hidden Falls, Ecola is a rather odd name for this cascade, considering it's the Chinook word for whale. Keep children and dogs close—the trail here teeters right above the crest of the plummeting water, sans guardrail.

Continue following the creek upward to a junction with the Wahkeena Trail (elev. 1200 ft; different from the Wahkeena Falls Trail) at 1.8 miles. Straight ahead leads to Larch Mountain and Franklin Ridge (Hikes 69 and 71). Turn right instead and climb steadily on good trail, traversing steep slopes cloaked in uniform forest. Pass some viewpoints out to the river and the Washington side of the Gorge.

Shortly after passing a crashing creek, reach the Devils Rest Trail (elev. 1525 ft) at 2.7 miles. Continue straight, passing the Vista Point Trail (or take it for a slightly longer return), descending in mature timber to a junction near Wahkeena Spring (elev. 1300 ft) at 3.1 miles. Turn right and rapidly descend. In 0.3 mile, turn left at the Vista Point Trail junction (elev. 1000 ft), coming to 20-foot Fairy Falls soon afterward.

Continue on a steep descent, crossing Wahkeena Creek twice before coming to a lookout and the beginning of paved trail. Lured by yet one more showy waterfall, carry on, reaching the spectacular 242-foot Wahkeena Falls at 4.5 miles. Cross beneath the falls on an impressive old stone bridge, and in 0.2 mile reach the Wahkeena Falls trailhead.

Then, locate the connector trail back to the Multnomah Falls trailhead and follow it 0.5 mile back to your vehicle. Have you ever seen so much falling water this side of Iguacu?

69 Larch Mountain

RATING/ DIFFICULTY	ROUND-TRIP	ELEV GAIN/ HIGH POINT	SEASON
****/4	14.4 miles	4000 feet/ 4055 feet	May–Nov

Map: Green Trails Columbia River Gorge–West No. 428S; **Contact:** Columbia River Gorge National Scenic Area, (541) 308-1700, www.fs.fed.us/r6/columbia; **Notes:** Dogs permitted on-leash; **GPS:** N 45 34.656 W 122 07.034

You can drive to this summit, but why? You'd miss a half-dozen waterfalls and some of the finest old-growth forest in the Gorge—plus the workout of your life! Follow a historical trail to the top of this ancient volcano, and gaze out at five active volcanoes from its open summit. The distance is long and the elevation grand, but most of the grade is moderate, following alongside tumbling creeks nearly the entire way. Just don't expect a golden forest streaking the mountain come fall—there are no larches.

GETTING THERE

From Portland, follow I-84 east and take exit 31. Park and walk through the highway underpass to the trailhead (elev. 50 ft). Alternatively, also from Portland, follow I-84 east and take exit 28, drive 0.4 mile and bear left (east) onto the Historic Columbia River Highway. Continue for 3 miles to the trailhead. (From Hood River, take exit 35 off of I-84 and follow the Historic Columbia River Highway 4.2 miles west to the trailhead.)

ON THE TRAIL

Constructed in 1915 by the Progressive Business Men's Club (which included some of Portland's most prominent citizens), a

Looking east across Hatfield Wilderness

fledgling U.S. Forest Service, timber baron and philanthropist Simon Benson, and the Trails Club of Oregon (which was officially formed on Larch Mountain), this trail's history is as varied and fascinating as the terrain it traverses.

Start at the Multnomah Falls Lodge, following the paved path past Oregon's most prominent waterfall and maneuvering between hordes of hikers. At 1.1 miles pass a spur that leads to the upper viewpoint of Multnomah Falls, and leave the majority of the masses behind.

Cross Multnomah Creek, following it upstream past Dutchman, Wiesendanger, and

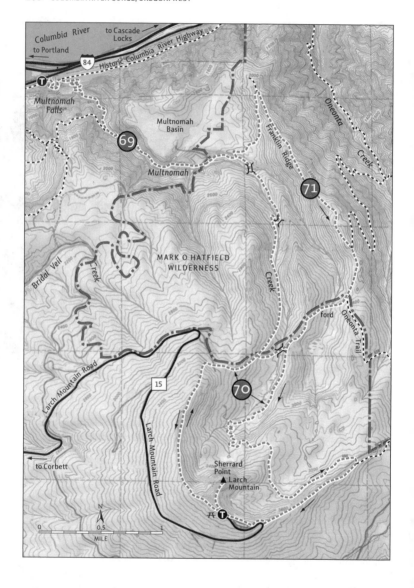

Ecola Falls, coming to the junction with the Wahkeena Trail at 1.8 miles (elev. 1200 ft; different from the Wahkeena Falls Trail). Continue left along Multnomah Creek into a lush and damp rainforest-like valley. Cross the creek on a high bridge and rock hop across several side creeks. At 2.7 miles the trail (elev. 1600 ft) splits into two routes—high- and low-water routes. The high route is slightly longer and involves some climbing. If winter rains have flooded the low route, you'll be heading up!

At 3 miles come to the closed Multnomah Basin Road (elev. 1650 ft). This old dirt road winds east 1 mile to the basin (more a flat) and to the Trails Club of Oregon's Nesika Lodge (open to members and their guests only). Continue south on the trail, soon entering land that was a 2009 addition to the Mark O. Hatfield Wilderness (see "Untrammeled Columbia River Gorge" in this section). Some of the finest old growth remaining in the Columbia Gorge can be found on the lower slopes of Larch Mountain and along nearby Franklin Ridge and Bells Creek. These areas' inclusion as wilderness assures their permanent protection.

At 3.3 miles the Franklin Ridge Trail (Hike 71) veers left. Continue right, through groves of ancient hemlock and fir—but no larch. Early lumberman erroneously referred to noble fir as larch (which grows on the drier eastern slopes of the Cascades), and a number of Larch Mountains popped up in western Washington and Oregon. Soon cross the West Fork Multnomah Creek using a log bridge, and at 3.9 miles cross the East Fork. Multnomah Creek is spring fed like many of the creeks in the Columbia River Gorge.

Climbing at a moderate grade, the trail veers away from the creek and traverses a large scree slope. At 5 miles, leave wilderness and come to the Multnomah Creek Trail (elev. 2950 ft). The Larch Mountain Trail continues right, steadily ascending a ridge rife with rhododendron. At 5.4 miles, intersect an old road (elev. 3300 ft) that provides hikers and mountain bikers a shortcut from the Larch Mountain Road.

Continue ascending through thick woods, reaching picnic tables and (gasp) a road (elev. 3850 ft) at 6.9 miles. Built in the 1930s as a Depression-works project, the paved Larch Mountain Road allows folks to enjoy the views you are about to receive without putting in the work! Try to make this hike in late spring after snow melt and before the road opens (which varies year to year) to enjoy summit solitude.

Locate the 0.3-mile paved Sherrard Point Trail (named for the forest supervisor at the time of the road's construction) and follow it to the fenced-in rocky and open 4055-foot summit. Wow! From this ancient shield volcano (the caldera is right below you), gaze out at five of the Northwest's most prominent active volcanoes: Hood, Jefferson, Adams, Saint Helens, and Rainier. Gaze out over the Gorge too. And if it's early summer, don't forget to cast your eyes downward to the showy rock gardens adorning the summit.

EXTENDING YOUR TRIP

If you have the energy, consider a loop around the summit crater. See Hike 70 for details.

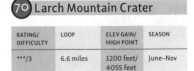

70 Larch Mountain Crater

RATING/ DIFFICULTY	LOOP	ELEV GAIN/ HIGH POINT	SEASON
***/3	6.6 miles	1200 feet/ 4055 feet	June–Nov

Map: Green Trails Columbia River Gorge–West No. 428S; **Contact:** Columbia River Gorge National Scenic Area, (541) 308-1700, www.fs.fed.us/r6/columbia; **Notes:** NW

Rock gardens adorn Larch's crater.

Forest Pass required. Dogs permitted on-leash. Road gated at milepost 10 Nov–May (sometimes longer, depending on snow cover); **GPS:** N 45 31.781 W 122 05.301

If Larch's summit is too much to tackle from Multnomah Falls, or you just don't want to weave through a flood of waterfall admirers getting to it, but you still want to get a little hiking in on this Columbia Gorge landmark, consider starting from the top of this ancient volcano. Take in the views and then head out on a surprisingly quiet loop through some of the finest remaining forests in the region.

GETTING THERE

From Portland, take I-84 east to exit 22 (Corbett) and follow the Corbett Hill Road south for 1.4 miles to the Historic Columbia River Highway. Turn left, proceeding west for 2 miles. Bear right onto paved Larch Mountain Road (which eventually becomes Forest Road 15), and follow it for 14.8 miles to its end at a summit picnic area (elev. 3850 ft). Privy available.

ON THE TRAIL

First things first. Before beginning the loop, make a beeline on the 0.3-mile paved Sherrard Point Trail to Larch's fenced-in rocky and open 4055-foot summit. From this ancient shield volcano, gaze out at five prominent, still active volcanoes: Hood, Jefferson, Adams, Saint Helens, and Rainier. And admire all the less prominent peaks in full view that span the horizon and hug the Columbia River Gorge. Then look below at Larch's broad caldera. You'll be making a loop around this heavily forested crater. Don't worry about views—you can always return to Sherrard Point upon completing your loop.

Locate the Larch Mountain Trail back at the picnic area and take it. Through scrappy forest the way descends—gently at first, then more rapidly. At 1.5 miles come to an old road (elev. 3300 ft), which leads 0.2 mile west to the Larch Mountain Road, an alternative approach to this loop (3.2 miles west from the summit, with limited parking).

Continue descending, now in attractive old-growth forest. Rhododendrons decorate the understory with plenty of pink and purple blossoms in May and June. At 1.9 miles come to a junction with the Multnomah Creek Trail (elev. 2950 ft). Bear right on it and at 2.2 miles, just after crossing Multnomah Creek

THIS SALAMANDER ROCKS!

While it's more common to see lizards (reptiles) scurrying across rocky areas in the Gorge than amphibians, keep your eyes out for the Larch Mountain salamander. This amphibian, endemic to and threatened in Oregon and Washington, lives in isolated patches of talus habitat, preferring scree, gravelly soils, and other areas of accumulated rock. A small striped salamander that was originally believed to be a subspecies of Van Dyke's salamander, the Larch Mountain salamander is a unique species and one of the ecological gems of the Columbia River Gorge.

on a bridge, come to another junction (elev. 2850 ft).

The Multnomah Spur Trail leads left 0.8 mile to the Oneonta Trail, offering a slightly longer loop option. Head right, into the crater, skirting a big swamp of pungent skunk cabbage and walking through impressive groves of giant firs and cedars. The way is pretty level for a while, allowing you to concentrate on the surrounding spectacular old-growth forest.

Eventually start climbing on an old logging railroad bed. No longer in old growth (the railroad served its purpose), begin a long traverse in second growth, with occasional views east breaking the monotony. Cross the headwaters of Oneonta Creek and reach the Oneonta Trail (elev. 3450 ft) at 4.7 miles.

Turn right on good tread hiking along a gentle ridge, reaching the Larch Mountain Road (elev. 3750 ft) at 5.6 miles. Follow the road to the right for 0.4 mile back to the summit parking lot to complete your loop.

EXTENDING YOUR TRIP

From the Multnomah Creek crossing, follow the Multnomah Spur Trail to the Oneonta Trail for a slightly longer loop (by about 1 mile)—but you'll miss the gorgeous old-growth forest in the crater.

71 Franklin Ridge

RATING/ DIFFICULTY	ROUND-TRIP	ELEV GAIN/ HIGH POINT	SEASON
***/4	12.2 miles	3025 feet/ 2925 feet	Apr–Nov

Map: Green Trails Columbia River Gorge–West No. 428S; **Contact:** Columbia River Gorge National Scenic Area, (541) 308-1700, www .fs.fed.us/r6/columbia; **Notes:** Dogs permitted on-leash; **GPS:** N 45 34.656 W 122 07.034

Wedged between the Multnomah Creek and Oneonta Creek valleys, two of the Gorge's most popular hiking destinations, Franklin Ridge is one of its least visited. Cloaked with some of the region's finest stands of old growth, views are limited, but solitude and tranquility aren't. Franklin is an ideal destination for a misty day or can be an alternative approach to Larch Mountain (Hike 70).

GETTING THERE

From Portland, follow I-84 east and take exit 31. Park and walk through the highway underpass to the trailhead (elev. 50 ft). Alternatively, also from Portland, follow I-84 east and take exit 28, drive 0.4 mile and bear left (east) onto the Historic Columbia River Highway. Continue for 3 miles to the trailhead.

Majestic old-growth forest along Franklin Ridge

(From Hood River, take exit 35 off of I-84 and follow the Historic Columbia River Highway 4.2 miles west to the trailhead.)

ON THE TRAIL

This hike starts at Multnomah Falls, following the Larch Mountain Trail (Hike 69). Minnie Franklin, whom Franklin Ridge is named for, was instrumental in creating this trail in 1915. After passing Multnomah, Dutchman, Wiesendanger, and Ecola Falls, come to a junction with the Wahkeena Trail at 1.8 miles (elev. 1200 ft; different from the Wahkeena Falls Trail). Continue left on the Larch Mountain Trail, following alongside cascading Multnomah Creek and reaching the closed-to-traffic Multnomah Basin Road (elev. 1650 ft) at 3 miles. Resume hiking south on the trail, entering the Mark O. Hatfield Wilderness and coming to the Franklin Ridge Trail (elev. 1800 ft) at 3.3 miles.

Any trailside company you've had thus far will probably fall away as you take to Franklin's lightly treaded tread. As you gently climb out of the dank Multnomah Creek valley, notice the forest transition to a drier, more open understory. And notice, too, a more peaceful environment, with soothing birdsong replacing an incessant river roar.

At 4 miles crest the ridge (elev. 2150 ft). Ignore a side trail that leads left to a private lodge and carry on southward, climbing higher along the thickly forested ridge. A few gaps in the forest provide window views north to the Columbia River, south to Larch Mountain, and east to Yeon Mountain.

The way steepens and the forest grows older. Now high on the divide between Oneonta and Multnomah Creeks, wind beneath gorgeous ancient Doug-firs and hemlocks. Come late spring, Pacific rhododendrons add pink bouquets to the primeval scene. At 5.5 miles come to a junction (elev. 2800 ft) with the Oneonta Trail. Left heads to Triple Falls (Hike 72). Proceed right instead, along the ridge, dropping 50 feet and then regaining it to reach the Multnomah Spur Trail at 6.1 miles.

Now outside of wilderness but deep within ancient forest, veer right on the Multnomah Spur, gently descending and coming to a potentially difficult crossing of the East Fork Multnomah Creek (elev. 2700 ft). The trail then begins to climb again, bear grass and rhodies lining the way. After reaching a small divide (elev. 2925 ft), descend once again, reaching a junction (elev. 2850 ft) at 6.9 miles. The way left leads to Larch Mountain (Hikes 69 and 70). Head right on the Multnomah Creek Way Trail, crossing said creek on a bridge and reaching the Larch Mountain Trail (elev. 2950 ft) after 0.3 mile.

Return to your vehicle, heading right on the Larch Mountain Trail and passing the Franklin Ridge Trail junction in 1.7 miles. From there its 3.3 more miles back to the trailhead.

EXTENDING YOUR TRIP
Strong hikers can combine Larch Mountain with this hike to make a big loop that follows the Multnomah Creek Trail to the summit and returns via the Larch Mountain Trail. See Hikes 69 and 70 for trail descriptions. Another long loop can be made by returning from Franklin Ridge via the Oneonta Trail and then taking the Gorge Trail back to Multnomah Falls.

72 Oneonta Gorge

RATING/ DIFFICULTY	ROUND-TRIP	ELEV GAIN/ HIGH POINT	SEASON
*****/2	2.7 miles	385 feet/ 375 feet	Year-round

Map: Green Trails Columbia River Gorge–West No. 428S; **Contact:** Columbia River Gorge National Scenic Area, (541) 308-1700, www.fs.fed.us/r6/columbia; **Notes:** Dogs permitted on-leash; **GPS:** N 45 35.450 W 122 04.108

A Columbia Gorge classic— a tight slot canyon, three spectacular waterfalls, including one you hike behind, and the option to see three more falls bundled as one. Plus, you get a few Columbia River views, a few big old trees, and an old restored tunnel to walk through. Kids will love this hike, but keep 'em close around the many drops-offs along the way.

GETTING THERE
From Portland or Hood River, follow I-84 to exit 35 and take the Historic Columbia River Highway west for 1.5 miles to the Horsetail Falls trailhead (elev. 40 ft). (Alternatively, from Portland, take exit 28 off of I-84 and follow the Historic Columbia River Highway 5.5 miles east to the trailhead.)

ON THE TRAIL
Just lacing up in the parking lot will grant you stunning scenery. Appropriately named Horsetail Falls plummets 176 feet right next to the trailhead. After shuttering away, head left on a wide and well-trodden trail, making a couple of switchbacks and coming to a junction with the Gorge Trail (elev. 200 ft) after 0.2 mile. Left leads to Ainsworth State Park (an alternative start if you're camping in the

Trail darts behind Ponytail Falls.

park). Continue right, up two more switchbacks, passing the Rock of Ages Trail, and at 0.4 mile duck into the cool amphitheater cradling Upper Horsetail Falls (elev. 300 ft), more widely referred to as Ponytail Falls.

The 80-foot cascade is yet another stunning Columbia Gorge waterfall. But kids (and maybe you too) will probably move this one to the top of your favorites once discovering that the trail skirts behind the falls, traveling beneath an overhanging basalt ledge. Stand behind the streaming water and feel the pulse of the waterfall!

The way then wraps around steep basalt walls, traversing a bench where two unmarked side trails lead right to excellent viewpoints over the Columbia out to Washington landmarks. Be extremely careful here (a memorial

attests), especially watching children, as the edge is abrupt and the drop precipitous.

Follow the main trail over rocky tread beneath more basalt cliffs that drip with runoff and dazzle with maidenhair ferns, larkspur, and other botanical beauties. After climbing to about 375 feet, begin dropping to reach a metal bridge (elev. 275 ft) that spans the whirling waters of Oneonta Creek. Gaze left, upstream to Upper Oneonta Falls plunging into an emerald punchbowl. Then look downstream toward Lower Oneonta Falls, which is hidden below within a 20-foot-wide, 200-foot-deep slot canyon. Forty-niner Carleton Emmons Watkins named the falls for his hometown in upstate New York—*Oneonta* is an Iroquois word meaning "place of open rocks." In this case, a name for narrow and mossy rocks would be more apropos.

After staring at the mesmerizing waters, steeply climb and reach a junction (elev. 325 ft) with the Oneonta Trail at 1.3 miles. For an excellent side trip, consider hiking left 0.9 mile to thrice delightful Triple Falls (see Hike 74). To close the loop head right instead, passing

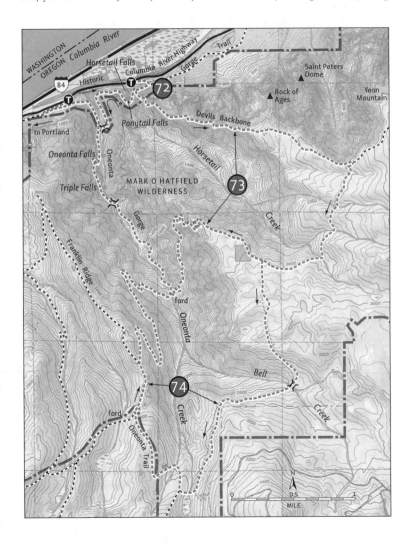

(or taking if you prefer) a short side loop to a viewpoint and coming to a junction (elev. 150 ft) at 1.9 miles with the Gorge Trail (which leads 2 miles west to Multnomah Falls). Continue right, and after 0.3 mile reach the Historic Columbia River Highway.

Walk to the right along the highway, passing through the Oneonta Tunnel, which served motorists from 1914 until 1948, when the highway bypassed it. Now beautifully renovated, it was reopened for pedestrians and bicycles in 2009. Next, pass the mouth of the Oneonta Gorge. An Oregon version of a Utah slot canyon, the basalt gorge is about a half-mile long, 200 feet deep, and only 15 to 20 feet wide. Horsetail Falls comes back into view shortly afterward, indicating the completion of your loop.

EXTENDING YOUR TRIP
In late summer and periods of low rainfall, intrepid hikers may want to explore the Oneonta Gorge. Don sports sandals or old running shoes and walk along gravel banks and through the cool refreshing waters of the creek for just over 0.5 mile to the foot of Oneonta Falls. Prepare to get wet and be careful not to disturb the plant life growing along the canyon walls. If you're claustrophobic, it's best to just admire the canyon from its mouth.

73 Rock of Ages Ridge

RATING/ DIFFICULTY	ROUND-TRIP	ELEV GAIN/ HIGH POINT	SEASON
***/5	10.9 miles	3300 feet/ 3000 feet	Apr–Nov

Map: Green Trails Columbia River Gorge–West No. 428S; **Contact:** Columbia River Gorge National Scenic Area, (541) 308-1700, www.fs.fed.us/r6/columbia; **Notes:** Unmaintained, extremely steep trail for experienced, strong hikers only. Not recommended for children or dogs; **GPS:** N 45 35.450 W 122 04.108

An unmaintained trail up an excruciatingly steep ridge, Rock of Ages is one of the most challenging and exhilarating hikes in the Gorge. The trail gains over 2000 feet in less than 2 miles, requiring strong quads, steady feet, and occasionally a good grip. The features here sound like they're straight out of a Dan Brown novel—you'll scramble along a ridge high above Saint Peters Dome before gingerly ascending the Devils Backbone. While your heart pounds, enjoy the views of the Columbia usually reserved for swifts.

GETTING THERE
From Portland or Hood River, follow I-84 to exit 35 and take the Historic Columbia River Highway west for 1.5 miles to the Horsetail Falls trailhead (elev. 40 ft). (Alternatively, from Portland, take exit 28 off of I-84 and follow the Historic Columbia River Highway 5.5 miles east to the trailhead.)

ON THE TRAIL
Rock of Ages is one of several beyond-steep user-built trails in the Gorge that border on scrambling (others include Munra Point and Ruckel Ridge). This means you'll use your hands in spots. And while only slightly exposed (at the Devils Backbone), the trail can be dangerous in wet, icy, and bad weather. Precipitous cliffs and ledges lie just to the east of the trail, making it imperative to stay on course. And finally, the route should not be descended—which creates another problem. The recommended return is via the Horsetail Creek Trail, requiring a ford of Oneonta Creek

that ranges from tricky to near impossible. Play it safe by doing this hike during dry spells and the warmer months.

Start on the Horsetail Falls Trail, hiking 0.4 mile to where the trail wraps around a ridge just before entering the basin (elev. 300 ft) that houses Upper Horsetail (Ponytail) Falls. Look left for a rough path ascending at an insanely steep grade. A "Trail Not Maintained" sign on a Douglas-fir will confirm you're on the correct path.

The route toils over rocks and roots, dipping around big trees along the way. Trekking poles and lug soles come in handy—especially on the slippery muddy sections. About 0.3 mile up the trail, bear left. About another 0.3 mile beyond, the way splits—either way will work, for they soon

meet up. Just beyond that, at around 800 feet elevation, the trail splits again. The way you want heads right, skirting ledges and sheer cliffs. The way left leads to those cliffs! Venture a short way left if you care (being extremely careful), for good views east over the Columbia and to a natural arch.

After skirting below ledges, the way brutally climbs again to reach a gap (be careful) on the ridge, providing glimpses of Saint Peters Dome, a rock pillar that looks like it belongs in Utah's Zion National Park. Then head straight up a thickly forested abrupt hillside, emerging at 1.2 miles on a grass and flower-covered gnarled narrow rock outcropping known as the Devils Backbone (elev. 1300 ft). Carefully work your way up the left side of this exposed

A pair of hikers on the Devils Backbone

ledge for excellent views of the Columbia River, Archer Mountain, and more! Take a break and let your heart rate subside. The worst is over—the trail becomes considerably easier to negotiate the higher you plug along. This is the climax too for views—so savor them.

The trail returns to forest, makes one more steep assault up the ridge, and then becomes increasingly gentle in its grade as it weaves through forest bearing signs of a long-ago fire. At 3.3 miles reach the Horsetail Creek Trail (elev. 3000 ft). Left heads to Yeon Mountain and Nesmith Point (Hike 75). You'll want to veer right, traveling a lightly hiked trail through gorgeous old growth along the rim of the basin draining into Horsetail Creek.

At 3.8 miles rock hop across the East Fork Horsetail Creek (elev. 2.875 ft). Climb 50 feet or so, and then descend to cross the Middle Fork Horsetail Creek (elev. 2760 ft) and shortly afterward the West Fork (elev. 2700 ft) crossing, both of which may require getting your shoes wet.

The trail then climbs to 2900 feet, coming to a junction shortly afterward with the Bell Creek Trail at 5.1 miles (Hike 74). Continue right and begin rapidly descending, at times steeply, reaching Oneonta Creek (elev. 1450 ft) at 7.4 miles. In late summer it's possible to rock hop across it—at other times the cold, fast-moving creek may be waist deep. Once across, reach the junction with the Oneonta Trail after a short climb and proceed to the right for 2.2 miles downriver to a junction with the Horsetail Falls Trail (elev. 325 ft). Turn right, returning to your vehicle in 1.3 miles.

EXTENDING YOUR TRIP

Return via Bell Creek instead, avoiding the Oneonta Creek ford and adding 4.6 miles

to your loop. Or, if transportation can be arranged, follow the Horsetail Creek Trail left from Rock of Ages for 2 miles to Nesmith Point (Hike 75), passing excellent viewpoints from Yeon Mountain along the way.

74 Bell Creek

RATING/ DIFFICULTY	LOOP	ELEV GAIN/ HIGH POINT	SEASON
****/4	15.3 miles	3400 feet/ 2975 feet	Apr–Nov

Map: Green Trails Columbia River Gorge–West No. 428S; **Contact:** Columbia River Gorge National Scenic Area, (541) 308-1700, www.fs.fed.us/r6/columbia; **Notes:** Requires potentially difficult ford of Oneonta Creek; **GPS:** N 45 35.323 W 122 04.696

Perhaps the loneliest trail on the Oregon side of the Columbia River Gorge National Scenic Area, Bell Creek is an excellent choice for quiet contemplation and for admiring a forest several centuries old. Some of the biggest and oldest trees, including massive western redcedars, grace this gentle path. How they survived the ax is nothing short of remarkable—and now protected within the Mark O. Hatfield Wilderness, they're free to continue their life cycles the way nature intended.

GETTING THERE

From Portland or Hood River, follow I-84 to exit 35 and take the Historic Columbia River Highway west for 1.9 miles to the Oneonta trailhead (elev. 40 ft). (Alternatively, from Portland, take exit 28 off of I-84 and follow the Historic Columbia River Highway 5.1 miles east to the trailhead.)

ON THE TRAIL

The Bell Creek Trail makes a gentle loop around its namesake's watershed. Most of the way is along a high forested bench between Larch and Palmer Mountains. The trail is easy, inviting you to dawdle and gawk at the finest old-growth forest within the national scenic area. What makes this hike difficult is the distance to reach it via other trails and a potentially difficult ford of Oneonta Creek that may be dangerous in high water.

Starting on the Oneonta Trail, steadily ascend. Bear left at the first junction, with the Gorge Trail at 0.3 mile, and right at the second, with the Horsetail Falls Trail (elev. 325 ft) at 0.9 mile. Now following along and above tumbling Oneonta Creek, the trail switchbacks and catwalks (keep children close and dogs leashed), climbing to 700 feet before reaching a fine overlook of triple treat Triple Falls (elev. 600 ft) at 1.8 miles.

Continue upstream, crossing Oneonta Creek on a beautiful bridge constructed in 2009 after floods claimed its predecessor. Then wind through a mossy, dank, near-rainforest valley alongside tumbling Oneonta Creek and over its cascading tributaries.

Cross Oneonta once again on a sturdy bridge, coming to a junction (elev. 1475 ft) shortly afterward, 3.1 miles from the trailhead. You'll be returning from the right. Head left on the Horsetail Creek Trail, dropping a little to Oneonta Creek. Scout around the boulders and rapids for a safe place to ford, usually fairly straightforward by midsummer. Once across, pick up light tread and steeply climb out of the valley, transitioning to drier forest.

The way can be rough with some slumping and brush, but it improves. Relentless switchbacks help you negotiate the steep

Bell Creek cuts through ancient forest.

hillside. At about 4.7 miles, pause at a small viewpoint (elev. 2400 ft) out to Franklin Ridge. The grade eases, and finally, at 5.3 miles, come to the Bell Creek Trail (elev. 2875 ft).

On light but discernible tread that occasionally doubles as a streambed, head right on a much-welcomed, near-level course. Far from the roar of Oneonta Creek, it's the chatter of nutcrackers, woodpeckers, chickadees, and chickarees now breaking the forest's silence. This uniform forest is interrupted with fire-scarred snags. Be patient—the old stuff is coming.

At 6 miles skirt a cedar swamp. Ascend a broad rise (elev. 2975 ft), and then begin descending alongside a chattering creek into primeval forest. Through a valley of coniferous giants—hemlocks, cedars, and Doug-firs—your jaw remains dropped and your neck crimped from constantly staring upward. On rockier and eroded tread, traverse a wet flat, coming to pretty Bell Creek (elev. 2725 ft) at about 6.9 miles.

Cross it on a large log bridge, and then travel across a few brushy sections before reentering magnificent ancient forest. The tread once again improves as you slowly ascend a ridge (elev. 2900 ft) adorned in old-growth majesty. Cross several creeks and a branch of Oneonta Creek flowing out of a large wetland.

At 8.6 miles intersect the Oneonta Trail (elev. 2850 ft). Left, heads to Larch Mountain (Hikes 69 and 70). You'll want to head right, soon crossing an Oneonta Creek that's much gentler than its lower self, before steeply climbing a ridge festooned with rhododendrons (elev. 2950 ft). Descend to a huckleberry flat (elev. 2.725 ft), passing the Multnomah Spur Trail (Hike 71) at 9.4 miles.

Then climb 75 feet or so before dropping 50 feet and then once again climbing. At 10 miles bear right at the Franklin Ridge Trail junction, cresting said ridge (elev. 2825 ft) shortly afterward. Then through an open forest of big Doug-firs, begin a long and

UNTRAMMELED COLUMBIA RIVER GORGE

While much of the Columbia River Gorge region lies within national forest, that doesn't necessarily mean it's fully protected. National forests are managed for "multiple use." While some uses—like hiking—are fairly compatible with land preservation, other uses—such as mining, logging, and off-road vehicle use—are not.

Recognizing that parts of our natural heritage should be altered as little as possible, with bipartisan support Congress passed the Wilderness Act in 1964 (passage in the House was by an overwhelming 373-1 vote). One of the strongest and most important pieces of environmental legislation in our nation's history, the Wilderness Act afforded some of our most precious wild landscapes a reprieve from exploitation, development, and harmful activities such as motorized recreation. Even bicycles are banned from federal wilderness areas. Wilderness is "an area where the earth and community of life are untrammeled by man," states the legislation. "Where man himself is a visitor who does not remain."

While the Columbia River Gorge had no shortage of qualifying lands for inclusion in the wilderness system back in 1964, no areas were designated. By 1984, however, the Trapper Creek Wilderness and the Columbia Wilderness (later renamed Mark O. Hatfield) were established. And in 2009, the Hatfield Wilderness was greatly expanded when President Obama signed his first piece of wilderness legislation in the form of an Omnibus Lands Bill.

Current wilderness acreage in the Columbia Gorge region is as follows:

> Trapper Creek Wilderness, 6050 acres
>
> Mark O. Hatfield Wilderness, 64,960 acres

While the expansion of the Hatfield Wilderness was a major environmental achievement, the Trapper Creek Wilderness remains small and should be expanded to include the adjacent 4540-acre roadless Bourbon Tract, with its extensive and impressive old-growth forests.

Silver Star across the Columbia from Nesmith Point

gentle descent on good tread. Switchbacks help ease pressure on the knees, and several viewpoints of the valley below break the monotony. At 12.2 miles return to the familiar Horsetail Creek Trail junction (elev. 1475 ft), from where it's 3.1 miles back to your vehicle.

75 Nesmith Point

RATING/ DIFFICULTY	ROUND-TRIP	ELEV GAIN/ HIGH POINT	SEASON
****/5	10 miles	3750 feet/ 3872 feet	Apr–Nov

Map: Green Trails Columbia River Gorge–West No. 428S; **Contact:** Columbia River Gorge National Scenic Area, (541) 308-1700, www.fs.fed.us/r6/columbia; **GPS:** N 45 36.742 W 122 00.279

One of the most prominent features on the Oregon side of the Gorge, hulking Nesmith Point hovers almost directly over the Columbia River. A lung buster of a climb, the hike to Nesmith provides great physical conditioning with a healthy helping of views along the way. Once the site of a long-gone fire lookout, only the privy remains—barely.

GETTING THERE
From Portland, follow I-84 east and take exit 35. Turn left toward Dobson, and then immediately turn right onto Frontage Road. Continue for 2.1 miles to the trailhead (elev. 120 ft). (From Hood River, follow I-84 west and take exit 37, continuing on Warrendale Road for 0.5 mile. Turn left and drive under

the freeway to a junction with Frontage Road. Turn left and continue for 0.4 mile to the trailhead.)

ON THE TRAIL

Named for a hardy Oregon Trail pioneer who hailed from New Hampshire (like this author—the New Hampshire part, not the hardy pioneer part), James W. Nesmith made quite a life for himself in his new home as a judge, provisional legislator, congressman, and senator. But he never climbed this peak, leaving that achievement for you.

From the trailhead shared with the popular Elowah Falls Trail (Hike 76), pass a leaky wooden water tank and soon come to a junction. Bear right on the Gorge Trail. Steadily climb through second-growth forest, coming to a washed-out junction (elev. 650 ft) at about 0.9 mile where you enter the Mark O. Hatfield Wilderness, this section having been added in 2009. The Gorge Trail—obliterated here—continues west beyond the creek washout to Dobson and Ainsworth State Park.

You, however, are heading left across a scree slope and then steeply up a draw to a small ridge. The way then enters another draw, passing some big hemlocks before steeply switchbacking to a small basin. Continue up a gully, catching your breath while taking in views out to Mount Saint Helens, Table Mountain, Hamilton Mountain, and the Soda Lake Peaks. The uphill grind is relentless, making the distance feel far greater. At about 2.7 miles enter a superb grove of giant cedars (elev. 2600 ft). It's then one last push out of the steep basin.

Now on a much saner approach, the trail winds through fire-succession forest on a broad ridge. At 3.9 miles stop at a spring (elev. 3200 ft) if you'd like to replenish fluids lost.

Then continue climbing, occasionally catching glimpses of Tanner Butte through the trees. Clumps of rhododendrons add cheerful bouquets along the way in May and June.

At 4.7 miles intersect an old abandoned road (elev. 3750 ft) that comes up from the Bull Run watershed (closed to public access). Head right, following the old road to Nesmith's 3872-foot summit. While the summit is primarily forested, there are some excellent views to the northwest of Washington's Archer Mountain, Silver Star, and Larch Mountain and west to Portland and some Columbia River islands. Past the old tower foundation slabs and the dilapidated privy (a can on its last stand), a path leads a few hundred feet down to a cliff edge (be careful) to good views north. Rest up and prepare your knees for the jarring descent.

EXTENDING YOUR TRIP

The best views on Nesmith are actually along the Horsetail Creek Trail west of the summit. To reach them, leave the summit and continue down the road 0.3 mile past the Nesmith Point trail junction. Then turn right, following trail for 0.7 mile to the viewpoint (elev. 3500 ft), which shows off Mount Saint Helens, Mount Adams, and Nesmith's sheer rocky face.

76 Elowah and Upper McCord Creek Falls

RATING/ DIFFICULTY	ROUND-TRIP	ELEV GAIN/ HIGH POINT	SEASON
***/2	3.4 miles	660 feet/ 620 feet	Year-round

Map: Green Trails Columbia River Gorge–West No. 428S; **Contact:** Columbia River Gorge National Scenic Area, (541) 308-1700, www.fs.fed.us/r6/columbia, and Oregon State Parks, (800) 551-6949, www.oregon

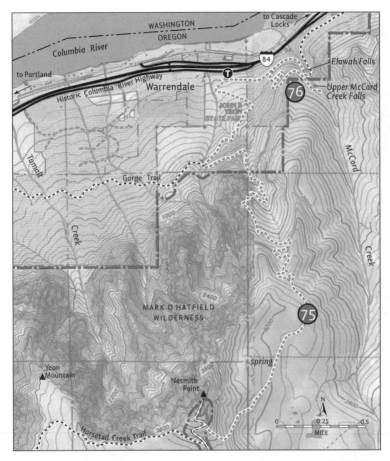

.gov/OPRD/PARKS; **Notes:** Dogs permitted on-leash; **GPS:** N 45 36.742 W 122 00.261

Hike to a pair of spectacular waterfalls, one in a deep hidden amphitheater canyon, the other one high above it. Plummeting well over 200 feet over layered basalt walls, Elowah Falls is one of the Columbia Gorge's greatest water shows. Upper McCord Creek Falls, while not as dramatic, requires a jaw-slacking approach along a catwalk blasted into sheer ledge—quite a spectacle in its own right.

GETTING THERE

From Portland, follow I-84 east and take exit 35. Turn left toward Dobson, and then immediately turn right onto Frontage Road.

Elowah Falls plunges into a lush verdant ravine.

Continue for 2.1 miles to the trailhead (elev. 120 ft). (From Hood River, follow I-84 west and take exit 37, continuing on Warrendale Road for 0.5 mile. Turn left and drive under the freeway to a junction with Frontage Road. Turn left and continue for 0.4 mile to the trailhead.)

ON THE TRAIL

Before beginning, read the interpretive sign about John B. Yeon, for whom this state park is named. Born Jean Baptiste Yeon in eastern Canada, Yeon became a timber magnate and prominent citizen of Portland. He financed what at one time was Oregon's tallest building and was a major financial backer of the Columbia River Highway.

Pass a leaky wooden water tank and soon come to a junction with the Gorge Trail. The way right leads to Nesmith Point (Hike 75) and requires a fair amount of vigor and determination. Veer left and, after steadily climbing 0.4 mile through uniform second-growth forest, reach a second junction (elev. 360 ft). It's your choice which waterfall you'd like to visit first.

Head right for Upper McCord Creek Falls, switchbacking over mossy scree and passing a couple of old rusty water-diversion pipes. Emerge beneath a steep wall of basalt cliffs. Then traverse it thanks to some past blasting that blazed the trail right into the basalt. Peer straight down upon Elowah Falls, which disappears into a deep, dark ravine. Take in some views, too, along the way, out across the Columbia to Hamilton Mountain. Guardrails help ease any anxiety you may experience along this catwalk above the cataracts. The way reenters forest to terminate above lovely Upper McCord Creek Falls (elev. 620 ft). Take time to admire the twin falls and then retrace your steps 0.8 mile back to the second junction.

Now continue right, dropping steeply into the dark and damp amphitheater basin that swallows up Elowah Falls. At 0.5 mile from the second junction, stand at the misty base (elev. 200 ft) of the 289-foot waterfall. One of the tallest and most stunning waterfalls within the Gorge, this natural masterpiece invites you to sit and stare.

EXTENDING YOUR TRIP

Turn this hike into an all-day affair by crossing McCord Creek at the base of Elowah Falls and hiking east on the Gorge Trail. After passing a picnic area, the trail gently descends and continues on a fairly gentle grade for 3 miles to Tanner Creek, where you can continue farther to Wahclella Falls

(Hike 77). The way stays pretty close to the freeway, however, so peace and quiet are not the order of the day.

77 Wahclella Falls

RATING/ DIFFICULTY	ROUND-TRIP	ELEV GAIN/ HIGH POINT	SEASON
****/2	1.8 miles	350 feet/ 350 feet	Year-round

Map: Green Trails Columbia River Gorge–West No. 428S; **Contact:** Columbia River Gorge National Scenic Area; (541) 308-1700, www.fs.fed.us/r6/columbia; **Notes:** NW Forest Pass required. Dogs permitted on-leash; **GPS:** N 45 37.805 W 121 57.243

A two-tiered four-star cascade set in a deep basin littered with mossy boulders, Wahclella is one of the prettiest waterfalls in the Gorge. Follow a lollipop loop to the base of the horsetail lower falls, soaking up spray while snapping photos. Then soak your feet in a nearby pool while watching flittering dippers comb the rapids for appetizing insect larvae.

GETTING THERE
From Portland or Hood River, follow I-84 to exit 40 (Bonneville Dam), turning south and bearing right to reach the trailhead (elev. 50 ft).

ON THE TRAIL
One of the Gorge's more popular destinations, up until the 1980s the trail to Wahclella Falls was a rough affair. And the falls itself has had a wavering history of nomenclature. Originally known as Tanner Creek Falls, then renamed Wahclella by the Mazamas for an old Native American village, then once again referred to as Tanner Creek Falls—Wahclella is once again in vogue!

Start by following an old road along Tanner Creek that's lined with showy maples and shadowed by the steep walls of Munra Point. At 0.2 mile the road ends at a small dam and intake pipe for the nearby fish hatchery. Now on trail, immediately come to a bridge directly beneath a fanning cascade from a tumbling tributary.

The canyon tightens as you hike deeper into it. While kids will enjoy this hike, keep them close by, as the way climbs high above the river at several points. Steps aid travel along the rocky way. At 0.7 mile the trail splits (elev. 300 ft). Head left, crossing a gully and

Wahclella Falls thunders through a tight chasm.

climbing higher to about 350 feet before descending to spray-blasted cedars at the base of the falls (elev. 300 ft). The lower falls drops 60 feet, fanning out of a tight slot across basalt ledge. The upper falls is harder to see as it careens down the west side of the narrow chasm above the lower falls.

Cross Tanner Creek on a nice bridge below the splash pool and travel beneath an overhanging ledge. When sunlight penetrates the canyon floor, nice wading can be found here among mossy boulders. The way then travels beneath stark canyon walls across a floor littered with massive boulders,

remnants from a 1973 landslide. Cross Tanner Creek once again, this time on a high bridge (elev. 250 ft), and then ascend via a few switchbacks to close the loop. Head left and return to the trailhead.

EXTENDING YOUR TRIP

From near the trailhead follow the Gorge Trail east for 2.2 miles to the Wauna Viewpoint Trail (Hike 80) or west for 3 partly paved miles, passing the Munra Point Trail (a difficult and potentially dangerous unmaintained path for experienced scramblers only), to Elowah Falls (Hike 76).

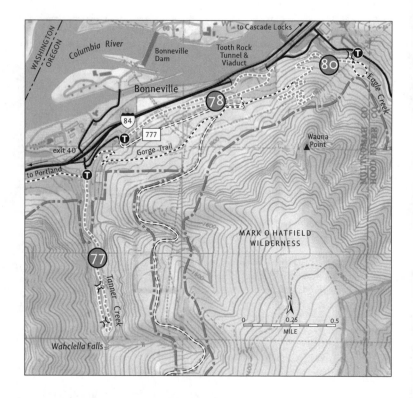

Remnants of the Historic Columbia River Highway

78 Tooth Rock

RATING/ DIFFICULTY	ROUND-TRIP	ELEV GAIN/ HIGH POINT	SEASON
**/1	2.1 miles	315 feet/ 450 feet	Year-round

Map: Green Trails Columbia River Gorge–West No. 428S; **Contact:** Columbia River Gorge National Scenic Area, (541) 308-1700, www .fs.fed.us/r6/columbia; **Notes:** Partially wheelchair accessible. Dogs permitted on-leash; **GPS:** N 45 38.074 W 121 56.888

A short history lesson on transportation through the Gorge is what you'll get on this short and easy hike. Walk along one of the more interesting and scenic sections of the Historic Columbia River Highway Trail to a restored viaduct that wraps around Tooth Rock, a basalt bluff that impeded travel. Then return via an old wagon road that also brushes against Tooth Rock.

GETTING THERE

From Portland or Hood River, follow I-84 to exit 40 (Bonneville Dam). Turn south and then immediately turn left (east), continuing 0.4 mile to the large Tooth Rock parking area (elev. 160 ft).

ON THE TRAIL

From the trailhead, I-84 spreads out before you, cars and trucks whizzing by at 60-plus miles per hour. But the first vehicles through the Gorge couldn't have flown by if they wanted to. The original Columbia River Highway, masterpiece of landscape architect and engineer Samuel C. Lancaster, was meant to be driven slowly. Constructed from 1913 until 1922, it was the first planned scenic highway in the country. But by the late 1930s it was no longer adequate for transportation needs. It was replaced by a new highway, and much of it was later obliterated with the construction of the interstate.

In 1996 the Oregon Department of Transportation restored this section of the old highway as a paved trail for hiking and biking. It's a pleasant walk except for the freeway noise. Head east and reach a junction in 0.2 mile (elev. 225 ft). You'll be returning on the right, so continue left, soon coming to the viaduct.

The freeway tunnels below, through Tooth Rock. Your route wraps around the Tooth, providing good dam (Bonneville dam that is) views and nice ones of Table Mountain too. Admire the arched rubble guardrails. A small pullout, dubbed the Eagle's Nest by Lancaster, was intended for extended viewing but proved a boon to insurance underwriters due to the number of rear-enders.

Continue along the viaduct, crossing over the freeway and coming to a staircase at 1 mile, which was built in 1996 to reconnect levels of the old highway. Don't take the stairs. Instead, locate an unmarked trail (elev. 200 ft) on the right just before them. After an initial steep start, this trail follows an 1850s portage road around Tooth Rock from the south.

Steadily climb along the narrow forested track, and after 0.5 mile come to a junction (elev. 450 ft). The steep, short trail to the left connects to the now closed Forest Road 777 (Hike 79) and the Gorge Trail and makes for an alternative approach to the Wauna Viewpoint (Hike 80). The old portage road now slowly descends, returning to the paved

highway path, from where it's 0.2 mile west back to the parking lot.

EXTENDING YOUR TRIP

Extend your loop by taking the connector trail 0.1 mile to the Gorge Trail. Then follow that trail west 1.9 miles and return east 0.4 mile on the paved road to the trailhead.

79 Dublin Lake

RATING/ DIFFICULTY	ROUND-TRIP	ELEV GAIN/ HIGH POINT	SEASON
**/5	13 miles	3990 feet/ 3850 feet	May–Nov

Map: Green Trails Columbia River Gorge–West No. 428S; **Contact:** Columbia River Gorge National Scenic Area, (541) 308-1700, www.fs.fed.us/r6/columbia; **GPS:** N 45 38.061 W 121 56.894

This long forested hike, up a closed road and steep trail to a small so-so lake, has no wow factor—except as in, "Wow that wasn't an easy journey!" Then why go? You'll get a good workout, certainly, and pretty old-growth forest along the ridge. It's also an excellent choice for a rainy or cloudy day. You'll probably have plenty of solitude here, which is a real commodity in this part of the Gorge. And you'll get to watch frolicking newts and fishing osprey too.

GETTING THERE

From Portland or Hood River, follow I-84 to exit 40 (Bonneville Dam). Turn south and then immediately turn left (east), continuing 0.4 mile to the large Tooth Rock parking area (elev. 160 ft).

ON THE TRAIL

Walk back 0.1 mile on the road you drove in on to reach a gated dirt road (Forest Road 777)

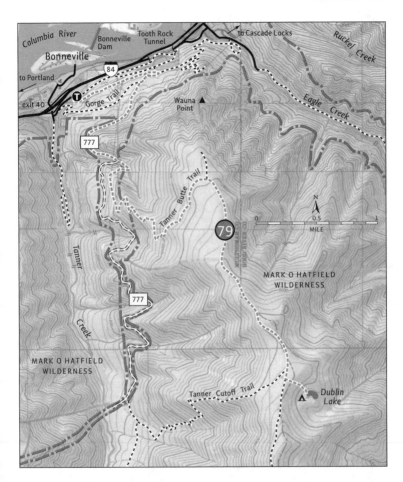

near a water tower. Head up this road, and in 0.1 mile an unmarked trail takes off right to join the Gorge Trail. You can head that way and turn left, returning to the road for a slightly longer but nicer route, or continue on the more direct way up the road. Consider mountain biking the road section of this hike, allowing for a fast and enjoyable finish to this long trip.

Pass a powerline swath and a view down to the river before coming to a junction (elev. 525 ft) with an unmarked trail at 1 mile. That trail leads to Tooth Rock and the Gorge Trail east to Wauna Viewpoint. Stay on the road instead, and after another 0.2 mile bear left at a junction with the Gorge Trail, this time that heads west to Tanner Creek.

Serene Dublin Lake is home to osprey.

The road crosses another set of power-lines and steadily climbs, traversing nice stands of old growth. At 2.4 miles, in a shady gulch harboring a couple of small cascades, come to the Tanner Butte Trail (elev. 1150 ft). Take it, immediately entering the Mark O. Hatfield Wilderness. Clamber around those cascades and a few more, possibly getting your feet wet in the process. On good tread and a decent grade, the way then ascends. Plenty of elevation needs to be subdued!

Once again cross a powerline swath—this one granting good views west to Munra Point. Then it's up, up, and away across a uniform forest of Doug-fir with an under-story of vine maple. After passing a few window views to the south, enter an older, more impressive forest of Doug-fir. Soon

after, passing a small creek and spring, come to an unmarked junction (elev. 2750 ft) at 4.8 miles. The unmaintained trail left drops 600 feet in 0.7 mile to Wauna Point, a precipitous viewpoint dangling over Eagle Creek. The trail grows progressively dangerous as it descends and should only be attempted by hikers comfortable with scrambling and unbothered by dizzying heights.

The way to Dublin Lake continues safely right, now on a less trodden path and at a gentler grade along a ridge shrouded in old-growth giants. Pass the old Hatfield Wilderness boundary (the area was greatly expanded in 2009), and at 6 miles reach the Tanner Cutoff Trail (elev. 3800 ft). Continue straight for another 0.1 mile, turning left on the Dublin Lake Trail (elev. 3850 ft). Rapidly and steeply descend into a hidden forested basin, reaching the little lake (elev. 3550 ft) after 0.4 mile.

Like most of the lakes within the western reaches of the Hatfield Wilderness, Dublin is small and not very impressive. Still, though, it attracts a fair share of backpackers, and the resident newts and ospreys find the lake much to their liking. Rest up for the long haul back.

EXTENDING YOUR TRIP

Tanner Butte, while a great destination, lies 4 miles away, putting it out of day-hiking distance. For a loop trip you can follow the Tanner Cutoff Trail for 2.8 very steep, unmaintained, hard to follow, at times brushy miles to the little-used Tanner Creek Trail. Then turn right and walk 0.2 mile to FR 777, from where it's 5.8 miles and a climb of 450 feet back to your vehicle.

80 Wauna Viewpoint

RATING/ DIFFICULTY	ROUND-TRIP	ELEV GAIN/ HIGH POINT	SEASON
***/3	3.8 miles	1000 feet/ 1100 feet	Year-round

Map: Green Trails Bonneville Dam, OR No. 429; **Contact:** Columbia River Gorge National Scenic Area, (541) 308-1700, www.fs.fed.us/r6/columbia; **Notes:** NW Forest Pass required. Dogs permitted on-leash; **GPS:** N 45 38.405 W 121 55.427

If you wanna hike to a decent viewpoint over the Columbia River Gorge but don't wanna sacrifice your knees nor exhaust your daily sweat quotient, then you'll definitely wanna check out the Wauna Viewpoint. From this perch 1000 feet above Eagle Creek, enjoy an eagle's-eye view right down to the creek, Table Mountain, the Bridge of the Gods, and the Bonneville Dam.

GETTING THERE

From Portland, follow I-84 east to exit 41 (Eagle Creek, Fish Hatchery). (From Hood River, leave I-84 at exit 40, get back on the freeway, and drive 1 mile east to exit 41.) Turn right. At 0.1 mile bear right at a parking area and reach another parking area in 0.2 mile (elev. 100 ft). Privy available.

ON THE TRAIL

The trail starts from the west side of the parking area on a big wooden suspension bridge over Eagle Creek. In winter watch for spawning salmon—and smell them too, their rotting carcasses lining the creekbed (keep dogs away from the dying fish, as they contain a bacteria toxic to your pooch). And any time of year look for dippers flitting on rocks, diving for larvae or flying close to the surface of the rippling creek.

Once across the bridge, bear right on the Gorge Trail, or take a short side trip on the Shady Glen Trail to the left. This short path meanders along Eagle Creek before looping back to the Gorge Trail in 0.2 mile. The Gorge Trail gently climbs out of the valley, passing ancient trees, a couple of good viewpoints, and a couple of old and weathered stone trail markers.

The tread is wide and the grade is gentle. After 1 mile come to a junction (elev. 600 ft). The Gorge Trail continues right, crossing mossy scree slopes with good views before dropping a little to reach the old Tanner Creek Road (Forest Road 777) (elev. 540 ft) in 0.3 mile, an alternative approach. Head left on the Wauna Viewpoint Trail, gently climbing another 400 feet to

Table and Greenleaf Mountains rise above the Bonneville Dam.

the trail's end (elev. 1100 ft) at a powerline swath in 0.9 mile. Don't let the accompanying electrical lines discourage you. The views are excellent.

Stare straight down at the Columbia River, Wauna as it was called by the area's First Peoples. Look up at the Benson Plateau, tracing rugged Ruckel Ridge that leads up to it. Look west to Munra Point and Cape Horn; east to Augspurger, Grassy Top, and Mount Adams. Then look north, straight across to Table and Greenleaf Mountains, and witness the aftermath of the great landslide that blocked the Columbia (see "The Gods Must Be Angry" in the Western Washington section). The river bends here, around the slumped earth that came crashing off of

those peaks. Pretty impressive—it was one earth-shattering event.

For a better view, consider Wauna Point. But don't even think about hiking to it from here or you may very well come crashing down off a mountain too.

81 Eagle Creek

RATING/ DIFFICULTY	ROUND-TRIP	ELEV GAIN/ HIGH POINT	SEASON
*****/3	12 miles	1100 feet/ 1200 feet	Mar–Dec

Map: Green Trails Bonneville Dam, OR No. 429; **Contact:** Columbia River Gorge National Scenic Area, (541) 308-1700, www .fs.fed.us/r6/columbia; **Notes:** NW Forest

Pass required. Dogs permitted on-leash. Steep drop-offs—keep children near; **GPS:** N 45 38.298 W 121 55.215

🛡️🏠 *One of the most spectacular trails in America, the route along Eagle Creek winds through a deep emerald chasm on tread that's as much an engineering feat—blasted into ledges and tunneling behind a waterfall—as it is a scenic splendor. You'll encounter a half dozen waterfalls, old-growth forest, and towering canyon walls. Not surprisingly, Eagle Creek is also one of the most popular trails in the Gorge, so prepare for company. And while dogs are permitted, they're discouraged—the trail has steep drop-offs and rough tread. Children will love this hike, but close supervision is advised.*

GETTING THERE

From Portland, follow I-84 east to exit 41 (Eagle Creek, Fish Hatchery). (From Hood River, leave I-84 at exit 40, get back on the freeway, and drive 1 mile east to exit 41.) Turn right, and after 0.1 mile bear right, continuing for 0.4 mile to the trailhead (elev. 125 ft). Privy available. If the lot is full, park back at the picnic area near the hatchery.

ON THE TRAIL

For nearly a century, folks of all walks of life have been enjoying this hike. The trail was constructed in 1915 in tandem with the Columbia River Highway. And the nearby campground was opened in 1916, the first U.S. Forest Service campground in the country. The recommended hike here is to Tunnel

Maidenhair ferns adorn Tunnel Falls' tunnel.

Falls, but any distance along this trail to any of the falls will suffice and satisfy.

Through a canyon draped in greenery, the well-trodden trail takes off along the creek, here its temperament well contained. Gradually the way leaves the creek to climb ledges nearly 100 feet above it. Grab onto cable handrails if you're not feeling so surefooted. At about 1.5 miles come to the first of two overlooks (elev. 400 ft) of Metlako Falls, named for the Native word for the goddess of salmon. The anadromous fish definitely needs a higher power to negotiate this 100-plus-foot plunge, one of the tallest of Eagle Creek's copious cascades.

Next, hop across Sorenson Creek, which cascades into Eagle Creek but whose waterfall is not visible from the trail. At 1.7 miles reach a spur that drops about 100 feet to the base of one of the Pacific Northwest's most photographed cascades—the quintessential waterfall of Eagle Creek, 35-foot Punch Bowl Falls. If it looks familiar, check your old calendars.

At 1.9 miles pass an overlook of Punch Bowl Falls and enjoy a different perspective of its carved-out aquatic amphitheater plunge pool. Then continue upstream, crossing Tish Creek on a high bridge and then Fern Creek on an even higher bridge. The surrounding valley walls grow tighter, the scenery more dramatic. The trail is blasted into ledges and there is considerable exposure. Keep children and dogs close.

At about 3.1 miles stand mesmerized by the slender 90-foot Loowit Falls that tumbles into a roiling, thundering Eagle Creek. Then clutch your heart—and the railings—and mosey across High Bridge, a solid steel structure spanning a fern-lined mossy tight chasm 120 feet above Eagle Creek.

The terrain now becomes a little less intimidating but nevertheless remains spectacular. Oaks and moss cling to basalt walls, and tributary creeks cascade into the canyon. At 3.5 miles come to thundering Skoonichuk Falls (elev. 600 ft), and shortly afterward reach Tenas Camp, one of several designated (and crowded) camping spots within the canyon.

At 4 miles cross Eagle Creek on 4½ Mile Bridge (the trail used to start at the car campground, hence the mileage difference), returning to the east side of the canyon and closer to water level once again. The big trees begin to intersperse with younger growth and old burnt snags—evidence of a large fire that swept through in 1902.

After passing the Wy'East Camp, enter the Mark O. Hatfield Wilderness (elev. 900 ft) at about 4.9 miles. At 5.2 miles come to the junction with the Eagle-Benson Trail, a very steep, difficult, and lightly maintained trail that climbs nearly 3000 feet in 3 miles. Continue upstream instead for the crème de la crème of Eagle Creek's waterfalls, following rocky trail that's at times blasted through ledges. Pass Blue Grouse Camp and reach Tunnel Falls (elev. 1200 ft) at 6 miles.

Here, Eagle Creek's East Fork plummets 160 feet over sheer basalt walls cloaked with maidenhair ferns into a verdant pool. Impressive, yes, but even more so is the trail that tunnels behind it. The early trail builders blasted a tunnel behind the falls and a catwalk into the surrounding ledge. Wet and potentially treacherous, it's also an exhilarating trek through the tunnel and across the waterfall basin. Take your time and savor this Northwest classic!

EXTENDING YOUR TRIP

If you have more energy, hike another 0.25 mile to the appropriately named 200-foot

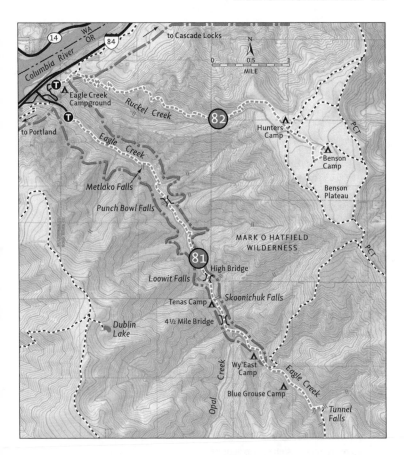

Twister Falls (a.k.a. Eagle Creek Falls). But be careful—the trail travels along an exposed ledge 200 feet above the creek. Overnighters have lots of terrain to explore beyond. Classic loops include Tanner Butte and Benson Plateau. If you can arrange a car shuttle, embark on a one-way 13.5-mile downhill hike from Wahtum Lake (Hike 91).

82 Benson Plateau via Ruckel Creek

RATING/ DIFFICULTY	ROUND-TRIP	ELEV GAIN/ HIGH POINT	SEASON
***/5	11.2 miles	3900 feet/ 4000 feet	Late May– Nov

Map: Green Trails Columbia River Gorge–West No. 428S; **Contact:** Columbia River Gorge National Scenic Area, (541) 308-1700, www.fs.fed.us/r6/columbia; **Notes:** NW Forest Pass required; **GPS:** N 45 38.459 W 121 55.587

🔥 ⚙️ 🏠 *A bulky, imposing, and nearly level peak in the heart of the Columbia River Gorge, the Benson Plateau is the closest thing in western Oregon to a bona fide mesa. While views are slim from the thickly forested summit of this flat-topped peak, there are some decent vistas along the way. Find flowers, too, and Native American vision quest pits. And a whole lot of elevation gain makes this hike among the Gorge's most challenging.*

GETTING THERE

From Portland, follow I-84 east to exit 41 (Eagle Creek, Fish Hatchery). (From Hood River, leave I-84 at exit 40, get back on the freeway, and drive 1 mile east to exit 41.) Turn right and reach the parking area in 0.1 mile (elev. 100 ft). Attractive stone privy available.

ON THE TRAIL

From the parking area, follow the road left toward the Eagle Creek Campground. After a few hundred feet depart the road and head left on the Gorge Trail. Climb a bluff above the freeway, skirting the campground, and then drop beneath a canopy of big trees to reach a paved path at 0.4 mile. Turn right on the paved path, now part of the Gorge Trail, following the route of the Historic Columbia River Highway. At 0.7 mile reach tumbling Ruckel Creek and cross it on one of the last remaining old highway bridges. Timber baron and hotel builder Simon Benson was one of the financial backers of the highway. Benson Plateau is named for him.

Beside the pretty waterway, the Ruckel Creek Trail takes off right. But within min-

utes the trail departs its namesake. You won't see the cascading creek again until approaching Benson's summit. Steeply climbing, cross a powerline swath with a good view to Hamilton Mountain, and enter the Mark O. Hatfield Wilderness. The trail gets steeper as it winds its way to and through a mossy talus slope (elev. 700 ft). Scan the talus for depressions. Like on several other ridges and peaks throughout the Gorge, pits were constructed and used by Native peoples for vision quests. They're more than a millennium old. Respect them by not disturbing them.

Your quest now is about to get more difficult. Aggressively climbing a fluted ridge, the trail climbs insanely. Pass several good viewpoints before emerging at an excellent clifftop vista at about 2.5 miles (elev. 1900 ft). It's a long drop, so be extremely careful as you enjoy an eagle's-eye perspective of the Bonneville Dam, the Bridge of the Gods, Wauna Lake, and Table and Greenleaf Mountains.

Beyond the vertigo-inducing viewpoint, the grade thankfully eases. Clusters of oaks and flowered slopes help soothe the way. The trail soon traverses grassy slopes bursting with wildflowers. Enjoy nice views, too, down into the Eagle Creek valley. After passing a spring decorated by showy monkey flowers, the trail once again ratchets upward. And as you approach Ruckel Creek, the trail enters cool old growth and begins yet another brutal ascent.

A climbing reprieve is finally granted upon cresting the plateau at about 4.6 miles. Here, just beyond the former wilderness boundary (before 2009 legislation greatly expanded the Hatfield Wilderness), reach a junction at about 3750 feet elevation with the abandoned Rudolph Spur Trail on the left and the unmaintained Ruckel Ridge Trail on the right (more on that later). Ruckel Creek is easily accessed by following this latter path a short distance.

To explore Benson Plateau, continue straight up the Ruckel Creek Trail. Beyond this point you can easily roam for miles on the plateau's several trails. Elevation gain is minimal. Delight in attractive forest, pocket meadows, and acres of showy bear grass. Just don't anticipate any good views.

At about 5.1 miles, at Hunters Camp, intersect the Benson Way Trail (elev. 3900 ft). Left heads 1.4 miles north to the Pacific Crest Trail. Right travels south 1.8 miles to the PCT. Using the PCT, you can make a 5.5-mile loop along the plateau's rim. Otherwise, continue straight and soon come to the Benson-Ruckel Trail, which heads 0.9 mile northeast to intersect with the PCT, another loop option. The Ruckel Creek Trail continues right, fording Ruckel Creek before climbing a little to arrive at yet another junction at 5.5 miles. The 0.5-mile Benson Spur Trail leads right here, passing some small wetland pools before reaching the Benson Way Trail, offering yet another loop option.

The Ruckel Creek Trail continues left to Benson Camp (elev. 4000 ft), perched alongside the creek and some small meadows, making it a good lunch and turnaround spot. Or you can continue another 0.5 mile to the PCT and craft a loop option.

EXTENDING YOUR TRIP

From the Ruckel Creek Trail's terminus, follow the PCT south for 1.3 miles to Camp Smoky in a small gap (elev. 3850 ft). Continue south along the PCT for about a mile to an open knoll for some nice views. Or, from Camp Smoky, head to the right, down the rough and steep and occasionally maintained Eagle-Benson Trail for 3-plus

Grassy bench offers respite from incessant climbing.

rough miles (passing through a 1990s burn) to the Eagle Creek Trail. Follow Eagle Creek back to your vehicle for a challenging 16-mile loop.

From the Eagle Creek Campground you can follow the Buck Point Trail for 0.5 mile to a viewpoint. Beyond, a rocky and at times potentially dangerous unmaintained trail travels for more than 4 miles along Ruckel Ridge to connect with the Ruckel Creek Trail. Views are outstanding along this route, but it can't be recommended to most hikers because of its exposure, steepness, and rugged nature.

83 Dry Creek Falls

RATING/ DIFFICULTY	ROUND-TRIP	ELEV GAIN/ HIGH POINT	SEASON
***/3	5.2 miles	750 feet/ 875 feet	Year-round

Map: Green Trails Columbia River Gorge–West No. 428S; **Contact:** Columbia River Gorge National Scenic Area, (541) 308-1700, www.fs.fed.us/r6/columbia; **Notes:** NW Forest Pass required; **GPS:** N 45 39.745 W 121 53.791

There is no shortage of fine waterfalls within the Columbia River Gorge National Scenic Area. Nor is there any shortage of waterfall admirers scouring the trails on any given day. However, at Dry Creek Falls there's a good chance that you'll get to stand in awe without your fellow Columbia Gorge travelers. One of the best kept secrets in the Gorge, the hike to Dry Creek Falls holds hidden delights on this quiet stretch of the Pacific Crest Trail.

Dry these falls are not.

GETTING THERE

From Portland, follow I-84 east to exit 44 at Cascade Locks. Proceed for 0.3 mile and then bear right onto the access road for the Bridge of the Gods to Stevenson. (From Hood River, follow I-84 to exit 44 at Cascade Locks, and proceed about 1.5 miles on Wa Na Pa Street through town, turning left onto the bridge access road.) In 0.2 mile reach the trailhead on your right (before the toll booth; elev. 175 ft). Privy available.

ON THE TRAIL

From the trailhead in Toll House Park, carefully cross the bridge access road and follow the Pacific Crest Trail south. Cross under I-84 and bear right onto a gravel road. After a

short distance come to a junction (0.25 mile from the trailhead). The east-west Cross-Gorge Trail No. 400 departs the road to the right, here as a narrow dirt track. The PCT bids the road adieu and veers left.

On smooth tread and climbing gently, the national scenic trail (see "Mexico to Canada" in the Western Washington section) meanders through an attractive forest of Doug-fir and vine maple. In autumn the maples streak the understory gold, nicely complementing the emerald canopy. At 1.1 miles cross a powerline swath and, shortly afterward, pass beneath a mossy basalt knob, a signature formation in the Columbia Gorge.

The trail continues its moderate ascent, traversing forested hillsides. At about 1.8

miles it makes a slight descent. Cascading water soon replaces the distant lull of traffic and trains. At 2.3 miles reach a junction with an old woods road at Dry Creek (elev. 725 ft). Turn right on the old woods road, reaching Dry Creek Falls (elev. 875 ft) in 0.3 mile after a short and brisk climb. Plummeting 50 feet into an old catch basin beneath mossy basalt walls, the falls is quite impressive and, as you can see, lonely too. And you've probably also realized by this time that Dry Creek is a bit of a misnomer.

EXTENDING YOUR TRIP

Continue following the PCT south for another pretty waterfall, some interesting landforms, and some nice views. In 1 mile cross a basalt talus slope that grants good views of Stevenson across the Columbia. In 2 miles after cresting a ridge spur (elev.

975 ft), reach a pair of basalt pinnacles (elev. 835 ft) that peek through the thick forest. In another 0.25 mile find a cataract plummeting down a tight chasm. Continue farther still, traversing a long talus slope with excellent views of the Columbia River and Washington peaks and ridges. At 2.7 miles the PCT reaches the Herman Bridge Trail (elev. 1000 ft). This is a logical spot to call it quits. If you're interested in what lies beyond, consult Hike 84.

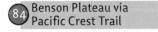

84 Benson Plateau via Pacific Crest Trail

RATING/ DIFFICULTY	ROUND-TRIP	ELEV GAIN/ HIGH POINT	SEASON
****/5	16 miles	3980 feet/ 4170 feet	Late May– Nov

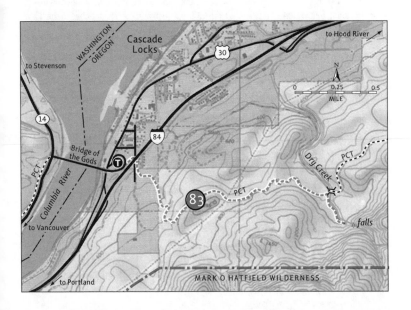

Map: Green Trails Columbia River Gorge–West No. 428S; **Contact:** Columbia River Gorge National Scenic Area, (541) 308-1700, www.fs.fed.us/r6/columbia; **Notes:** NW Forest Pass required; **GPS:** N 45 40.969 W 121 50.540

A geographical oddity, this nearly flat, broad hulking summit is the remnant of an ancient giant lava flow. The agents of erosion have done a wonderful job over the millennia carving out its steep fluted ridges and making it appear like a giant citadel seated at the center of the Gorge. Getting to Benson's expansive flat top requires a bit of storming the castle. Several trails lead to this fortress—all of them steep. The Pacific Crest offers the easiest route—but also the longest.

GETTING THERE

From Portland, follow I-84 east to exit 44 for Cascade Locks. Proceed 1.8 miles through town on the main drag (Wa Na Pa Street) to a stop sign. Go straight, underneath I-84, and then bear left onto Frontage Road for 1.6 miles to the Herman Creek Campground entrance. (From Hood River, leave I-84 at exit 47 and follow the Frontage Road for 0.7 mile to the campground entrance.) In 0.2 mile bear right, coming to the trailhead (elev. 250 ft) shortly afterward. Privy available.

ON THE TRAIL

Follow the well-traveled Herman Creek Trail for 0.7 mile, crossing a powerline service road before reaching a junction (elev. 650 ft). Bear right onto the Herman Creek Bridge Trail and traverse a small talus slope with views up to citadel Benson before descending to the sturdy steel bridge over cascading Herman Creek (elev. 500 ft).

Resume climbing, soon coming to another talus slope with impressive views up the steep basalt parapets of the plateau. At 1.9 miles enter the Mark O. Hatfield Wilderness and come to the Pacific Crest Trail (elev. 1000 ft). Right leads to Dry Falls and Cascade Locks (Hike 83). You're heading left and up to the heavens. In typical PCT fashion, the trail climbs at a moderate pace, making long switchbacks to tackle the 3000 vertical feet that must be subdued.

Cross talus slopes with good views out to the Columbia and Stevenson. At 2.7 miles pass a dry campsite and good viewpoint (elev. 1460 ft) before beginning a long journey across timbered slopes. Some impressive trees cling to Benson's steep ridges. At about 5 miles crest an open ridge and pause to take in excellent views of the Herman Creek valley, Nick Eaton Ridge, the Columbia River, and more. Enjoy the flowers too, which add colored touches to the brown rocky slope.

The way continues ever upward, across slopes of bear grass with their resplendent blossoms in early summer. At 5.5 miles, in a grove of big hemlocks, come to Teakettle Springs (elev. 3475 ft), the only water source beyond Herman Creek.

At 6 miles the relentless climb ceases as you crest Benson's long northeastern arm of a ridge (elev. 3775 ft). Give your quads a break with a slight descent before reaching a junction with the Benson Way Trail (elev. 3790 ft) at 6.5 miles. After hiking a great distance and much elevation, you are now left standing in a grove of big hemlocks, though some views are available from this forested mesa. Continue south on the PCT for another 0.25 mile of climbing and then enjoy near-flat wandering through colonnades of silver fir and waves of bear grass.

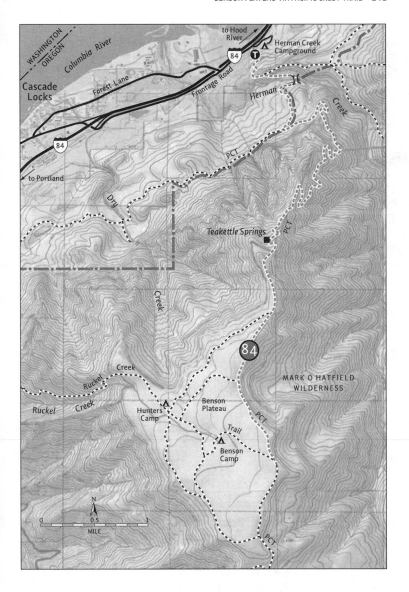

At 7.1 miles pass the lightly used Benson-Ruckel Trail (elev. 3980 ft). Continue another 0.7 mile to the Ruckel Creek Trail junction (elev. 4120 ft)—just beyond, some rimtop views to the east can be had. Tough hike but to an interesting formation, even without far-reaching knockout views.

EXTENDING YOUR TRIP

If you have more energy, enjoy relatively level wandering on Benson's summit. Hike down the Ruckel Creek Trail 0.7 mile to Benson Camp (elev. 4000 ft), situated alongside the creek in pocket meadows. Or continue 0.9 mile on the PCT, cresting Benson's 4200-foot high point, and then return to the PCT via the 3.2-mile Benson Way Trail for a trip around the plateau rim. En route pass an excellent viewpoint west over Eagle Creek. In early season expect wet feet crossing Ruckel Creek.

Openings along the way provide views and flower gardens.

Opposite: Looking east from Wygant Trail to Mitchell Point

columbia river gorge,
oregon: east

Plentiful sunshine, steep gorge walls, and bluffs that come alive with brilliant wildflower blossoms in the spring—this is what you can expect while hiking in the eastern reaches of Oregon's Columbia River Gorge. Challenge yourself on some of the Gorge's toughest trails and highest peaks, or leisurely meander on nature walks along flower-studded slopes. Hike back into time, exploring historical trails, roads, and travel routes, or venture high above the Gorge into the Mark O. Hatfield Wilderness to alpine lakes and summits providing spectacular views. Summer can be hot. Fall is lovely. Spring is best. Cascade Locks, Hood River, and The Dalles all provide excellent visitor services—and be sure to visit the superb Columbia Gorge Discovery Center in The Dalles. You'll find nice car camping at Herman Creek and Wyeth, administered by the U.S. Forest Service, and at Viento and Deschutes River state-run parks.

85 Herman Creek Ancient Cedars

RATING/ DIFFICULTY	ROUND-TRIP	ELEV GAIN/ HIGH POINT	SEASON
****/4	15 miles	2600 feet/ 2800 feet	Late Apr– Nov

Map: Green Trails Columbia River Gorge–West No. 428S; **Contact:** Columbia River Gorge National Scenic Area, (541) 308-1700, www.fs.fed.us/r6/columbia; **Notes:** NW Forest Pass required; **GPS:** N 45 40.969 W 121 50.540

With one of the finest remaining stands of old-growth red cedars in the Columbia Gorge, this long but fairly moderate hike is ideal for overcast days or for when you want to escape the crowds of neighboring trails. Forested for nearly the entire way, the trail also wanders through ancient giant noble firs, hemlocks, and Douglas-firs. And there are a couple of waterfalls along the way too, but Herman Creek itself remains pretty evasive even though the trail is named for it.

GETTING THERE

From Portland, follow I-84 east to exit 44 for Cascade Locks. Proceed 1.8 miles through town on the main drag (Wa Na Pa Street) to a stop sign. Go straight, underneath I-84, and then bear left onto Frontage Road for 1.6 miles to the Herman Creek Campground entrance. (From Hood River, leave I-84 at exit 47 and follow the Frontage Road for 0.7 mile to the campground entrance.) In 0.2 mile bear right, coming to the trailhead (elev. 250 ft) shortly afterward. Privy available.

ON THE TRAIL

Providing access for several other trails, the Herman Creek Trail starts off wide and well trodden. Pass a powerline service road before reaching a junction (elev. 650 ft) with the Herman Creek Bridge Trail at 0.7 mile. Herman Creek crashes below—about the only evidence for some time that the creek is near.

Continue left and soon come to an old road. Bear right and, after a short climb, enjoy fairly level walking to Herman Camp at a three-way junction (elev. 1000 ft) at 1.4 miles. The Gorton Creek Trail to Nick Eaton Ridge (Hike 86) and the Gorge Trail to the Wyeth Campground veer left. You want to continue right on an old road, coming to a junction with the Nick Eaton Trail in another 0.1 mile.

Continue right, now on real trail, slightly descending and eventually leaving uniform second growth for older and bigger trees. Pass a tall slender waterfall, an oak-topped bluff providing valley views, and the old

Mark O. Hatfield Wilderness boundary (changed in 2009 to now encompass most of the Gorge Face north of the Gorton Creek Trail) before reaching Camp Creek, which may dampen your boots.

The way continues deeper upvalley—peaceful, and quite a contrast from noisy and busy Eagle Creek. At 3.9 miles reach a junction (elev. 1500 ft) with the extremely steep and lightly maintained Casey Creek Trail that heads left to Nick Eaton Ridge. An unmarked side spur here drops to the right, losing 400 feet in 0.3 mile to meet the confluence of Herman Creek and its East Fork.

Continue straight, through big firs. Cross Casey Creek, heading farther upvalley across more creeks, through old-growth and fire-succession forests, and across a big scree slope before reaching pretty Slide Creek Falls. After two potentially tricky creek crossings—at Mullinix and Whiskey—the way ascends more steadily into a lush, more primeval setting. Giant hemlocks, noble firs, and Doug-firs line the way. And the East Fork Herman Creek now runs close to the trail.

At 7.2 miles come to a junction with the Herman Creek Cutoff Trail (elev. 2800 ft), which leads up toward Green Point Mountain. You can roam the ancient cedar swamp, straight ahead, for 0.3 mile. Campsites dot the magnificent grove—one of the finest old-growth cedar stands in the entire Gorge. Find a spot to sit and savor this forest, which was old even when our nation was young.

EXTENDING YOUR TRIP

Strong hikers may want to continue 1.9 miles up the Herman Creek Trail, crossing the East Fork and passing more camps to reach the Mud Lake Trail, although the lake is easier to reach from Wahtum Lake (Hike 91). Very strong hikers can make a loop by taking the

Author takes notes in the ancient cedar grove.

Herman Creek Cutoff Trail to Nick Eaton Ridge. This option adds more than 2000 vertical feet and 4.5 miles to the round-trip.

86 Nick Eaton Ridge

RATING/ DIFFICULTY	LOOP	ELEV GAIN/ HIGH POINT	SEASON
★★★★/4	8.8 miles	2900 feet/ 2950 feet	Late Apr–Nov

Map: Green Trails Columbia River Gorge–West No. 428S; **Contact:** Columbia River Gorge National Scenic Area, (541) 308-1700, www .fs.fed.us/r6/columbia; **Notes:** NW Forest Pass required; **GPS:** N 45 40.969 W 121 50.540

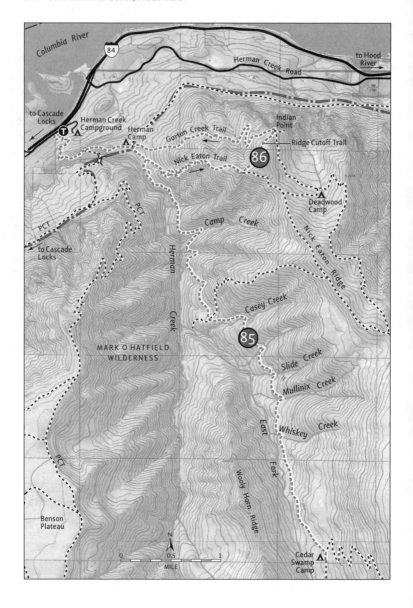

This nice loop follows good trails through beautiful old growth to a flower-studded hillside with excellent views up the Herman Creek valley and to the lofty peaks flanking its watershed. Then, if you're not prone to vertigo, venture down a rough and tumble (but generally good) path to Indian Point, a basalt thumb that precariously floats 2000 feet above the Columbia River. With clenched chest, breathe deep, and enjoy one of the most exhilarating views of the Gorge.

GETTING THERE

From Portland, follow I-84 east to exit 44 for Cascade Locks. Proceed 1.8 miles through town on the main drag (Wa Na Pa Street) to a stop sign. Go straight, underneath I-84, and then bear left onto Frontage Road for 1.6 miles to the Herman Creek Campground entrance. (From Hood River, leave I-84 at exit 47 and follow the Frontage Road for 0.7 mile to the campground entrance.) In 0.2 mile bear right, coming to the trailhead (elev. 250 ft) shortly afterward. Privy available.

ON THE TRAIL

The starting point for an array of adventures, Herman Creek is a major trail hub in the Gorge. Follow the wide and well-trodden Herman Creek Trail, passing a powerline service road before reaching a junction (elev. 550 ft) with the Herman Creek Bridge Trail at 0.7 mile. Continue left and soon come to an old road. Bear right, and at 1.4 miles come to Herman Camp at a three-way junction (elev. 1000 ft) at 1.4 miles.

The trail to your immediate left is the Gorge Trail, which travels more than 5 miles to the Wyeth Campground. The trail just to the right of it is the Gorton Creek Trail, your return route. Take the trail farthest right,

Indian Point hovers high above the Columbia River.

continuing for just over 0.1 mile to another junction. Now head left onto the Nick Eaton Trail, passing through a magnificent stand of old-growth firs now protected within the Mark O. Hatfield Wilderness. The route grows increasingly steep—the tread is generally good, but farther up the trail small, loose rocks act as ball bearings intent on messing up your balance. I find it easier to ascend this section than descend it, and the Gorton Creek Trail is much gentler on the knees coming down, hence the counterclockwise direction of this loop.

At 3 miles your toil is rewarded. The way breaks out of woods onto a steep grassy ledge—in early season decorated with showy flowers and year-round providing fabulous views. Pause to absorb the blossoms and marvel at the vista—west down the Columbia and up the steep slopes of Benson Plateau, and south into the wild Herman Creek valley with Woolly Horn Ridge (you have to love that name) sitting in the center.

At 3.6 miles come to a junction (elev. 2950 ft). The Nick Eaton Trail continues right, up its namesake, sprawling ridge, named for ole Nick who farmed the valley below in the early 1900s. The way is lonely and insanely steep. Forget about it! Go left instead, continuing 0.6 mile on good tread on the Ridge Cutoff Trail, dropping to meet up with the Gorton Creek Trail (elev. 2700 ft).

Before turning left to close the loop, a mandatory side trip is in order for hikers not too skittish about heights (best to leave children and dogs behind—with a trusted companion, of course). Turn right and almost immediately come to an unmarked trail heading left. Follow this path under a jumble of vine maples, dropping 200 feet in less than 0.2 mile to emerge at an extremely narrow ledge (use caution) that leads to Indian Point, a protruding basalt thumb hovering more than 2000 feet above the valley. Forget about scaling Indian Point lest you find yourself in Indian Heaven—instead, just gasp at its rugged beauty from a safe distance, along with taking in breathtaking views of the Columbia and points east—Augspurger, Dog, Wygant, Mitchell Point, Shellrock . . . and Adams floating above them!

Climb back up to the Gorton Creek Trail and head right for 2.8 miles on a knee-friendly descent, on excellent tread through beautiful old growth back to the Herman Camp junction. Continue right for 1.4 familiar miles back to the trailhead.

EXTENDING YOUR TRIP

The Gorton Creek Trail continues beyond Indian Point 0.8 mile to Deadwood Camp (elev. 2575 ft) in a beautiful forest of live wood. From there, loop back to Nick Eaton

Ridge via the 0.6-mile Deadwood Trail, or continue 3 lonely miles to the next junction. From there, turn right and return 2.8 miles to the Ridge Cutoff junction on the Nick Eaton Trail, cresting the 4000-plus-foot ridge and steeply dropping along the way.

87 North Lake

RATING/ DIFFICULTY	ROUND-TRIP	ELEV GAIN/ HIGH POINT	SEASON
***/5	13.6 miles	4000 feet/ 4000 feet	Late May–Nov

Map: Green Trails Columbia River Gorge–West No. 428S; **Contact:** Columbia River Gorge National Scenic Area, (541) 308-1700, www.fs.fed.us/r6/columbia; **Notes:** NW Forest Pass required; **GPS:** N 45 41.268 W 121 46.316

This fair-sized lake surrounded by old-growth forest is tucked in a cirque within reach of lofty and verdant Green Point Mountain. While you can reach the lake by a much shorter and easier route, starting from the Wyeth Campground avoids a long car approach over bumpy dirt roads, replaced instead by a long foot journey up the imposing Gorge Face via one of the loneliest trails in the national scenic area. After this great conditioner, your reward will be solitude and the satisfaction gained from tackling one of the Gorge's most challenging trails.

GETTING THERE

From Portland, follow I-84 east to exit 51. Turn right and then immediately turn right on Herman Creek Road. After 0.1 mile turn left into the lovely Wyeth Campground, continuing 0.2 mile to the trailhead (elev. 250 ft). Privy available.

ON THE TRAIL

Begin your journey from Wyeth, Oregon, a tiny outpost named after inventor and explorer Nathaniel Wyeth. Once a train stop, then a Civilian Conservation Corps camp, then a Civilian Public Service Camp for conscientious objectors during World War II—this spot has a lot of fascinating history, and you'll have plenty of time over plenty of miles to contemplate it.

First the bad news: the trail is actually longer than what most maps show. Why? Because parts have been rerouted into longer switchbacks, easing the grade. And that's the good news: the trail isn't as steep as it used to be! Walk about 0.1 mile along Gorton Creek on old road to a junction. The Gorge Trail leads to the right to Herman Creek. Head left instead, immediately climbing a knoll, dropping 50 feet (ignore path on the left coming in from the campground), and crossing a powerline swath.

At 0.4 mile rock hop across Harphan Creek, soon after entering the Gorge Face addition of the Mark O. Hatfield Wilderness. Now on good tread in beautiful open forest, steadily climb, the grade steepening from time to time. Ascending a ridge above Harphan Creek, switchback up steep slopes—up, up, up!

At about 3.7 miles cross a brushy talus slope. Then round an open bluff (elev. 2800 ft), taking a moment or two to catch your breath and views out to the Wind River valley across the Columbia. Continue higher, passing across another bluff, pretty in summer when it's decked out in blossoms.

Enter beautiful mature forest as you relentlessly toil, subduing vertical feet. Finally, when you feel you can't take any more climbing, the way eases. At 5.5 miles come to a junction with the Green Point

Ridge Trail (elev. 3900 ft). Stay left on a path lined with huckleberry bushes and boughs of bear grass, traversing gentle terrain beneath Green Point Ridge. Catch occasional glimpses east of towering Mount Defiance. After crossing a talus slope, descend into a beautiful grove of giant firs (elev. 3700 ft). Then climb again, crossing Lindsey Creek and soon after arriving at a junction (elev. 4000 ft) at 6.8 miles.

North Lake lies just ahead—follow the path right a few hundred feet to the lake's outlet on what appears to be an old earthen dam. The lake is shallow and surrounded by towering old conifers and steep brushy scree slopes. Not dramatic, but still a nice little

Bear grass along North Lake's shoreline

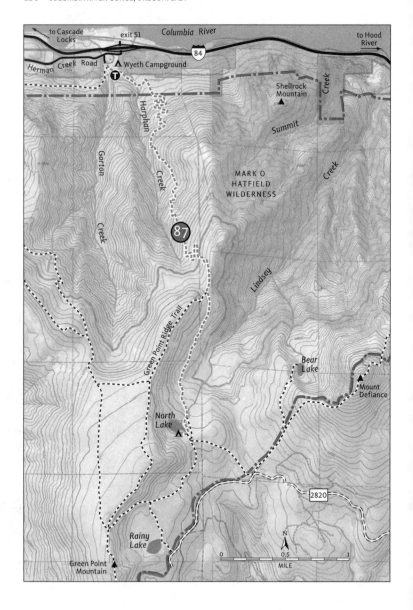

to Cascade Locks

exit 51

Columbia River

84

to Hood River

Herman Creek Road

△ Wyeth Campground

T

Harphan

Creek

Gorton

Creek

Shellrock Mountain ▲

Creek

Summit

MARK O HATFIELD WILDERNESS

87

Lindsey

Green Point Ridge Trail

Bear Lake

▲ Mount Defiance

North Lake
△

2820

Rainy Lake

N

Green Point Mountain ▲

0   0.5   1

MILE

spot—and often popular with backpackers coming in from the shortcut.

EXTENDING YOUR TRIP

Rainy Lake is much prettier and is worth the extra effort if you have the energy. Continue on the Wyeth Trail past North Lake for 0.2 mile (passing a trail leading right to campsites), coming to a junction. The Wyeth Trail continues left 0.8 mile to Forest Road 2820 (elev. 3800 ft). Turn right on the Rainy Lake Trail. After a couple of hundred feet, turn left (the trail right leads to camps on North Lake), descending to a creek crossing (elev. 3950 ft). The brushy and at times muddy trail then climbs, reaching a junction at 1 mile near a marshy opening (elev. 4150 ft). Turn left here, reaching Rainy Lake (elev. 4100 ft) beneath the cliffs of Green Point Mountain in 0.5 mile.

Super ambitious hikers can return via the Green Point Ridge Trail across terrain that sees very few human footprints. And excellent views can be had from Green Point's 4736-foot summit.

88 Mount Defiance

RATING/ DIFFICULTY	LOOP	ELEV GAIN/ HIGH POINT	SEASON
*****/5	12.9 miles	4890 feet/ 4960 feet	Late June–Nov

Map: Green Trails Columbia River Gorge–West No. 428S; **Contact:** Columbia River Gorge National Scenic Area, (541) 308-1700, www.fs.fed.us/r6/columbia; **GPS:** N 45 41.298 W 121 41.446

The Granddaddy Guardian of the Gorge, Mount Defiance rises nearly one vertical mile above the Columbia River, the highest peak in the Gorge.

Mount Hood from Mount Defiance summit talus slope

Many a hiker defies Defiance each year, accepting the challenge of 4800 vertical feet. The trails here are used by mountain climbers and trail runners to condition for even bigger peaks, but conquering this hulking landmark is no small feat in itself. A spectacular loop, complete with one of the Gorge's prettiest alpine lakes, rewards your effort with sweeping views.

GETTING THERE

From Portland, follow I-84 east to exit 55 and the Starvation Creek trailhead (elev. 150 ft). Privy available. (From Hood River, follow

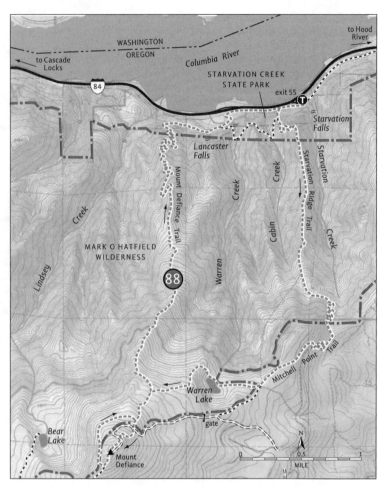

I-84 to exit 51 and then double back to exit 55, which is an eastbound exit only.)

ON THE TRAIL

Despite the fact that Defiance's summit is defiled with communication towers, the way up and the near-summit scree slopes pro-

vide gorgeous Gorge viewing. You can make a much easier and shorter approach from the north (see Hike 94), but bragging rights go only to those who tackle this mountain from the river. The loop described here uses the Starvation Ridge Trail, which adds some distance but is well worth it—it's advisable to ascend via that trail due to its insanely steep grades (yes, even steeper than the Mount Defiance Trail's worst sections).

Start by strolling on a paved path along the busy interstate, coming to the Starvation Cutoff in 0.2 mile. Take it, climbing steeply on rocky terrain to reach the Starvation Ridge Trail in 0.5 mile (elev. 600 ft). You can make an excellent short loop (or longer approach) by using the trail to the right, which drops to Cabin Creek (elev. 560 ft), climbs to airy ledges (elev. 800 ft), and connects to the Mount Defiance Trail in 1 mile. The trail is rife with poison oak and skirts steep drop-offs—not recommended for children and dogs.

Carry on left, traversing a grassy bluff beneath powerlines. Despite the high-tension lines above, the views from this flower-studded bluff are tremendous, especially of Dog Mountain. At 1.4 miles crest the narrow bluff (elev. 1200 ft) by a lone fir and head southward into forest, entering the Mark O. Hatfield Wilderness.

Now following a narrow ridge dividing the Cabin and Starvation creek drainages, sharply climb—it's insanely steep at times, with a few intermittent tiny teaser spots of level walking to ease the suffering. Trekking poles are a must—so is a heavily caffeinated breakfast beforehand.

At 3.2 miles cross a talus slope and transition into a forest of hemlock, soon leaving the wilderness area. At 3.7 miles, traverse a large talus slope (elev. 3250 ft) that grants a nice view north to Mount Adams. Soon afterward, at the edge of an old cut, the hike becomes pleasurable as the Starvation Ridge Trail transitions to the Mitchell Point Trail (which no longer heads to its namesake) on an easy grade along a broad ridge. Enjoy occasional views north to Saint Helens along the way.

At 4.8 miles reach a junction (elev. 3800 ft). The trail left leads 0.4 mile to the Mount Defiance summit service road (gated at the trailhead). Don't be surprised to encounter fresh-faced, sweat-free hikers here on their way to Warren Lake. Follow them back into the wilderness, reaching pretty Warren Lake (elev. 3720 ft) in 0.4 mile. Set in a bowl surrounded by shiny slabs of scree and lined with vine maples (pretty in autumn), Warren is one of the more picturesque alpine lakes in the Gorge.

Now clamber over rock toward Defiance's broad rounded summit. Views north to snowy Washington volcanoes and endless verdant ridges are excellent. Swaying bear grass lines the way as you enter scrappy lodgepole pine forest. At 5.9 miles reach the Mount Defiance Trail (elev. 4240 ft), where you turn left and head up. At 6.1 miles stay left at an unmarked junction—you'll be returning on the right. Continue through cool forest, crossing the summit road twice and arriving at the less-than-appealing 4960-foot summit at 6.6 miles.

But rejoice! You made it! Congratulate yourself and then leave the towered summit, following trail south across shiny scree speckled with purple penstemon to a junction (elev. 4800 ft) at 6.8 miles. The best views are here, and this is where you'll want to lunch, with Mount Hood staring right at you. Enjoy more excellent views to the lofty green peaks surrounding Wahtum Lake.

From the junction, head right. The trail left drops 1000 feet to a logging road—it's the easy noncongratulatory way up Mount Defiance (Hike 94). Now rounding beneath the summit, traverse several scree slopes, watching your footing and taking time out to gasp at the unfurling sprawling views east and south. At 7.5 miles, come to the Mount Defiance Trail (elev. 4500 ft).

Turn left and begin the long descent. Be sure to bear left at 7.7 miles. You don't want to head down Starvation Ridge! The grade isn't too bad at first but gets much steeper the farther along you go. At about 10 miles, in old-growth forest, the trail wastes little time losing elevation. Pass a couple of excellent viewpoints along the way. Then a series of steep switchbacks tests your knees for the final descent.

At 11.6 miles reach a powerline swath. The trail turns east here, passing beneath lovely (and perfect for head dunking) Lancaster Falls (elev. 350 ft) at 12 miles. Reach the Starvation Ridge Trail 0.1 mile beyond. Then continue straight, dropping into a cool ravine and crossing Warren Creek on a bridge below Hole-in-the-Wall Falls (created in 1938 by highway workers to divert water away from the old highway). Reach the trailhead at 12.9 miles—and soak your feet upon returning home!

EXTENDING YOUR TRIP

Be sure to check out Starvation Falls while in the area. It's a mere 0.1 mile away on paved path. For a return trip, walk the paved Historic Columbia River Highway Trail 1.3 miles to Viento State Park, where there's good car camping.

89 Wygant Peak

RATING/ DIFFICULTY	ROUND-TRIP	ELEV GAIN/ HIGH POINT	SEASON
***/4	9.2 miles	2075 feet/ 2200 feet	Late Mar– Nov

Map: Green Trails Columbia River Gorge–West No. 428S; **Contact:** Columbia River Gorge National Scenic Area, (541) 308-1700, www.fs.fed.us/r6/columbia; **GPS:** N 45 42.161 W 121 37.172

 Despite being located right off of busy I-84, the Wygant Trail is one of the quietest hikes in the Gorge. Granted, the summit is forested and reaching it requires steep climbing over a rapidly decaying trail. But the lower sections of this trail are in good shape, leading to excellent viewpoints of the river and surrounding prominent peaks. And there are flowers aplenty too—and poison oak, so cover up or save this one for October.

GETTING THERE

From Portland, follow I-84 east to exit 58 (Mitchell Point Overlook) and drive 0.2 mile to a large parking area (elev. 175 ft). Privy available. (If coming from the east, there is no access, so continue to exit 56 at Viento State Park and return east 2 miles to exit 58.)

ON THE TRAIL

Walk back on the road a short distance to a gated road and sign for the Wygant Trail. Follow the closed road 0.3 mile to an old foundation and real trail that veers right. After crossing Mitchell Creek in attractive woods, come to a surviving section of the old Columbia River Highway. Follow it west for about 0.4 mile, and then leave the old road for trail that leads left into a little ravine. Beside a small waterfall, steeply switchback out of the gully to a broad forested bench.

At 1.1 miles come to junction (elev. 300 ft) with the Chetwoot Trail. Built by volunteers in the 1970s, this nice loop into the Perham Creek canyon can no longer be recommended because it's missing a bridge and has a dangerous slid-out section. A resuscitation of this path would be welcomed. For now, just enjoy the attractive trailhead sign sporting a black bear, which is what *chetwoot* means in Chinook Jargon, a trade

Columbia River and causeway formed Drano Lake.

language derived from English, French, and Coast Salish.

Continue straight another 0.1 mile to a junction with a spur trail, which leads a short distance right along an oak bluff to a poor view of Dog Mountain. Skip it—there are better views ahead. Head left, dropping to Perham Creek (elev. 250 ft), where as of 2010 a twisted damaged bridge spanned the waterway. Use caution crossing. Then climb out of the ravine through oak forest to a powerline swath, soon afterward coming to an excellent viewpoint (elev. 400 ft), just off the trail, of Dog Mountain and Cook Hill across the Columbia and Mitchell Point to the east.

The trail continues, switchbacking across the swath and through oak groves, reaching another viewpoint (be careful) about 0.25 mile before intersecting with the upper terminus of the Chetwoot Trail (elev. 1000 ft) at about 2.8 miles. Head right, to stay on the Wygant Trail, using caution on slumping tread, and switchbacking through mature forest to a mossy knoll (elev. 1300 ft) at 3.4 miles. Enjoy excellent viewing here above the river and out to Mount Adams. This is the highlight of this hike. Consider whether you wish to continue to the summit on very poor tread that's brushy at times and hasn't seen a maintenance crew since probably the 1980s.

If your tenacity overcomes your common sense, plod on another 1.2 at times steep miles to the forested summit, located just within the newly expanded Mark O. Hatfield Wilderness. En route, where the tread disappears into a tangle of vine maple, head upslope to the right, reaching trail again above the mess. The 2200-foot summit is cloaked in Doug-fir. No views. However, if you're willing to crash a little brush, continue about 0.25 mile southwest, dropping about 200 feet to a sprawling meadow that affords excellent views west to Table, Defiance, Greenleaf, Wind, and other peaks. The meadow makes a good napping spot, too, after all that work!

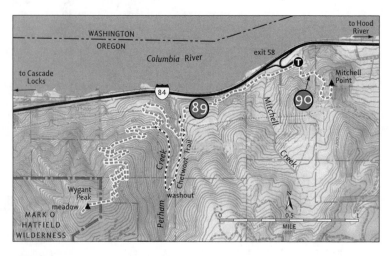

90 Mitchell Point

RATING/ DIFFICULTY	ROUND-TRIP	ELEV GAIN/ HIGH POINT	SEASON
***/3	2.2 miles	1000 feet/ 1178 feet	Year-round

Map: Green Trails Columbia River Gorge–West No. 428S; **Contact:** Columbia River Gorge National Scenic Area, (541) 308-1700, www.fs.fed.us/r6/columbia; **Notes:** Final stretch involves some exposure, not safe for children or dogs; **GPS:** N 45 42.174 W 121 37.109

A prominent rocky knoll along the Columbia River just west of Hood River, Mitchell Point was once the site of a beautiful five-window tunnel on the old Columbia River Highway, modeled after Switzerland's Axenstrasse. In 1966 this engineering marvel was destroyed to make way for I-84. Lament. Fortunately, the Mosier Twin Tunnels still stand, and Mitchell Point still provides breathtaking views. This hike is short but not easy, and some hikers may find the final few feet a tad exposed for comfort.

GETTING THERE
From Portland, follow I-84 east to exit 58 (Mitchell Point Overlook) and drive 0.2 mile to a large parking area (elev. 175 ft). Privy available. (If coming from the east, there is no access, so continue to exit 56 at Viento State Park and return east 2 miles to exit 58.)

ON THE TRAIL
Locate the paved path that angles from the privy to a picnic table, and immediately veer off of it left onto a wide gravel path. Pass an old foundation on your right as you head left into the woods and climb! As the way starts to switchback, ignore a path veering right toward a water intake. The way grows steeper and rockier in places.

At about 0.4 mile, ignore a side trail heading left. Soon afterward, it's slow going as you switchback up a scree slope. Reenter forest, and then at 0.9 mile come to a saddle in a powerline swath. Turn left and head up the spine of Mitchell Point—first through oaks (and poison oak, be aware) and then onto open rocky ledge. In spring and early summer, an assortment of flowers paints the stark rocky ridge and sheer cliffs.

The ridgeline grows narrower as you approach the 1178-foot summit. Chances are that the winds will be whipping along it too. The views are both breathtaking and dizzying! Stare down at the highway and across the river to Drano Lake, site of the last log flume in America. Then cast your eyes west to Mount Defiance, Wygant Peak, and Dog Mountain; and east to the town of White Salmon cradled below Hospital Hill.

Get the trekking poles ready for the steep descent!

91 Wahtum Lake and Chinidere Mountain

RATING/ DIFFICULTY	ROUND-TRIP	ELEV GAIN/ HIGH POINT	SEASON
****/3	4.2 miles	1075 feet/ 4673 feet	June–Nov

Map: Green Trails Columbia River Gorge–West No. 428S; **Contact:** Mount Hood National Forest, Hood River Ranger Station, (541) 352-6002, www.fs.fed.us/r6/mthood; **Notes:** NW Forest Pass required; **GPS:** N 45 34.635 W 121 47.566

  Enjoy some of the finest views and one of the largest lakes within the 64,960-acre Mark O. Hatfield Wilderness, all for only a minimum amount of expended sweat! Walk among old-growth giants flanking rippling Wahtum Lake, and then climb to the windblown open summit of Chinidere Mountain, where five volcanoes and practically every prominent peak lining the Gorge vies to get in your face.

GETTING THERE

From Portland, follow I-84 east to Hood River at exit 62. Turn right onto US 30 (Cascade Avenue) and drive 1.3 miles. Then turn right onto 13th Street (County Road 281), which is signed for the airport and as a scenic route. Continue south on CR 281, which eventually becomes Tucker Road, making several sharp left and right turns. At 5.1 miles bear right onto Dee Highway (after crossing the bridge over Hood River), which is still CR

Looking east from Mitchell Point

Chinidere Mountain across Wahtum Lake

281 (signed for Dee-Parker). Continue for 6.2 miles, bearing right (near milepost 11) to another bridge crossing Hood River (signed for Dee-Lost Lake), and then bear left onto Lost Lake Road (signed for Wahtum Lake). After 4.9 miles bear right onto paved but narrow Forest Road 13. After 4.5 miles bear right onto FR 1310. Follow this paved road 6 miles to the trailhead at a small car campground (elev. 3950 ft). Privy available.

ON THE TRAIL

On the west end of the campground, locate the Wahtum Express Trail and immediately enter the wilderness area, rapidly descend-ing to the lake via more than 250 steps. If your knees are fretting, opt for the slightly longer horse route instead.

At 0.2 mile the horse and express routes reunite (at the Pony Express junction?). Just a little farther is the Pacific Crest Trail (elev. 3750 ft). You'll be returning on the right, so head left along Wahtum's old-growth-graced shores. Pause occasionally to soak feet or soak in views. At 0.5 mile reach a junction with the Eagle Creek Trail near an inviting and well-used backcountry camping area.

Turn right and continue another 0.1 mile to a junction. Left heads more than 13 glorious miles down the Eagle Creek valley. Head right on the Chinidere Cutoff, crossing the lake's outlet on a log jam and catching a good view of the lake. The word *wahtum* is Native American in origin, meaning "lake," and therefore Wahtum Lake is a bit redundant—but it's never tiresome to visit.

Pass some more campsites and then begin a steep climb through silver firs and showy bear grass reaching the PCT (elev. 4200 ft) at 1.5 miles. Turn left and after a hop, skip, and jump (or a leisurely walk if you prefer) reach a junction with the Chinidere Mountain Trail.

Take this short and sweet, steep little trail for 0.4 mile to the heavens, passing a ledge halfway that grants views south and west and reaching the juniper-clutching, flowers-swaying, covered-in-shale, windblown and wide-open 4673-foot summit with views in every direction. Five volcanoes—count 'em: Jefferson, Hood, Adams, Saint Helens, and Rainier! Marvel at Indian Mountain to the south, Tanner Butte in the west, Defiance in the east, and rocky Tomlike Mountain and mesalike Benson Plateau to the north. Named after a Wasco chief, this former lookout site ranks chief among Columbia Gorge viewpoints.

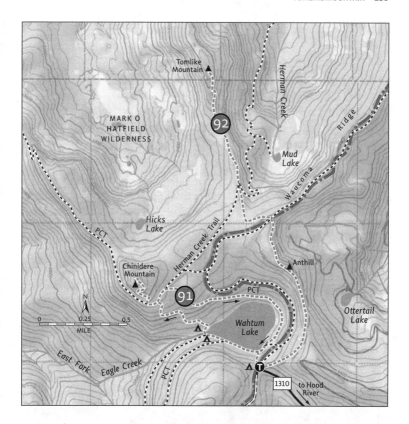

Once you've had your share of alpine rhapsody, retrace your steps to the PCT. Turn left and follow it back 1.7 miles, bearing right at the Herman Creek Trail junction and gently rounding the lake basin to descend back to the Wahtum Express. It's 0.2 mile up those 250-plus steps back to your vehicle.

EXTENDING YOUR TRIP

Hike too short? Follow the Herman Creek Trail 0.8 mile to the Anthill Trail and combine this hike with Tomlike Mountain (Hike 92).

92 Tomlike Mountain

RATING/ DIFFICULTY	ROUND-TRIP	ELEV GAIN/ HIGH POINT	SEASON
*****/3	6 miles	1300 feet/ 4555 feet	June–Nov

Map: Green Trails Columbia River Gorge–West No. 428S; **Contact:** Mount Hood National Forest, Hood River Ranger Station, (541) 352-6002, www.fs.fed.us/r6/mthood; **Notes:** NW Forest Pass required; **GPS:** N 45 34.654 W 121 47.551

Mount Hood and Tomlike Mountain's open rocky ridgeline

At this rocky, windswept high point of the Woolly Horn Ridge, only an Anthill stands between the trailhead and Tomlike's much-to-like, flower-adorned, view-bursting summit. And the Anthill, actually a moundlike ridge hovering above the shimmering waters of Wahtum Lake, is decked out in swaying bear grass—not in crawling insects. This hike starts high and stays high, with a few ups and downs along the way—but your mood will always be up!

GETTING THERE

From Portland, follow I-84 east to Hood River at exit 62. Turn right onto US 30 (Cascade Avenue) and drive 1.3 miles. Then turn right onto 13th Street (County Road 281), which is signed for the airport and as a scenic route. Continue south on CR 281, which eventually becomes Tucker Road, making several sharp left and right turns. At 5.1 miles bear right onto Dee Highway (after crossing the bridge over Hood River), which is still CR 281 (signed for Dee-Parker). Continue for 6.2 miles, bearing right (near milepost 11) to another bridge crossing Hood River (signed for Dee–Lost Lake), and then bear left onto Lost Lake Road (signed for Wahtum Lake). After 4.9 miles bear right onto paved but narrow Forest Road 13. After 4.5 miles bear right onto FR 1310. Follow this paved road 6 miles to the trailhead at a small car campground (elev. 3950 ft). Privy available.

ON THE TRAIL

Locate the Anthill Trail that takes off from behind the privy. This nice trail, often overlooked by the crowds that flock to Wahtum Lake, gradually ascends the spine of a ridge that divides the Eagle Creek and Hood River watersheds. En route there are excellent views of Wahtum, Chinidere Mountain, Mount Hood, and even Mount Jefferson.

At about 1.1 mile crest the Anthill's high point (elev. 4475 ft), and then gradually descend through huckleberry patches to reach an old road—now the Wahtum–Rainy Lake Trail—at 1.5 miles. Continue straight, soon entering the Mark O. Hatfield Wilderness and coming to the Herman Creek Trail (elev. 4150 ft) at 2 miles.

Turn right, and after a few strides look for an unmarked trail taking off left, just before the main trail bends right and descends.

Time for fun. While the way to Tomlike's summit is more a bootpath than bona fide trail, it's a pretty straightforward route along the ridge crest, albeit at times a little brushy.

After climbing 50 feet or so, the way drops into a small saddle (elev. 4140 ft) and continues on ledges lined with stunted junipers. Hikers who hail from the Northeast will feel right at home on this peak, as it looks like it could be right out of New Hampshire's rocky White Mountains.

At 2.6 miles veer to the left and follow cairns up and over a rocky knoll. At 2.8 miles emerge from a lodgepole pine grove, with the summit block now in full view. Carefully work your way up shale and scree, reaching the 4555-foot summit at 3 miles.

Hold on to your hat, for if the strong winds don't knock it off, the horizon-spanning views will! From Washington's Larch Mountain to Oregon's Larch Mountain, Silver Star, Rainier, Saint Helens, Adams, Dog, Tanner Butte, the fluted flattop Benson Plateau, and glistening Mount Hood rising above them all. And wildflowers and bear grass too, swaying in the strong breezes.

Tomlike was Chief Chinidere's son, and naming this beautiful mountain and the adjacent peak just to the south after these two members of the Wasco Tribe is a deep honor. And you'll probably be honoring the beauty of the Columbia Gorge country from atop this peak.

EXTENDING YOUR TRIP

Despite the less-than-enticing name, little Mud Lake twinkling below is actually quite lovely. Follow the Herman Creek Trail 0.8 mile and then take a spur trail 0.3 mile to the lake (elev. 3600 ft). Dippers, newts, and osprey will keep you company.

93 Indian Mountain

RATING/ DIFFICULTY	ROUND-TRIP	ELEV GAIN/ HIGH POINT	SEASON
****/4	9.4 miles	1440 feet/ 4892 feet	June–Nov

Map: Green Trails Columbia River Gorge–West No. 428S; **Contact:** Mount Hood National Forest, Hood River Ranger Station, (541) 352-6002, www.fs.fed.us/r6/mthood; **Notes:** NW Forest Pass required; **GPS:** N 45 34.635 W 121 47.566

Some of the finest views in the entire Gorge can be had from this little-known peak not far from busy Wahtum Lake. From its windswept rocky and juniper-hugging north ridge, enjoy unsurpassed views of the Eagle Creek watershed and its lofty Columbia Gorge guardian peaks. From Indian's open summit stare right into the glistening ice adorning Oregon's majestic number one peak, Mount Hood.

Indian Mountain provides excellent close-up views of Mount Hood.

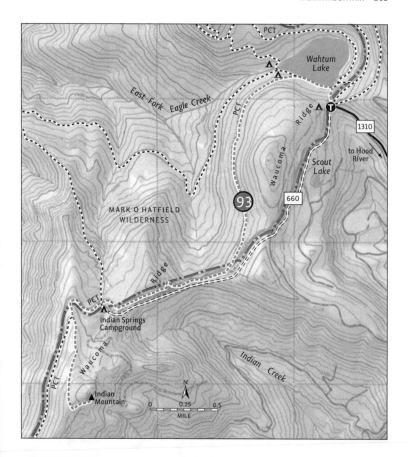

GETTING THERE

From Portland, follow I-84 east to Hood River at exit 62. Turn right onto US 30 (Cascade Avenue) and drive 1.3 miles. Then turn right onto 13th Street (County Road 281), which is signed for the airport and as a scenic route. Continue south on CR 281, which eventually becomes Tucker Road, making several sharp left and right turns. At 5.1 miles bear right onto Dee Highway (after crossing the bridge over Hood River), which is still CR 281 (signed for Dee-Parker). Continue for 6.2 miles, bearing right (near milepost 11) to another bridge crossing Hood River (signed for Dee-Lost Lake), and then bear left onto Lost Lake Road (signed for Wahtum Lake). After 4.9 miles bear right onto paved but narrow Forest Road 13. After 4.5 miles bear right onto FR 1310. Follow this paved road 6 miles to the trailhead at a small car campground (elev. 3950 ft). Privy available.

ON THE TRAIL

While it's possible to drive all the way to Indian Springs, knocking off several miles from this hike, why would you do that? The road is narrow and rough, while the trail is smooth, offering pure hiking delight. And isn't that what you're here for—some wonderful hiking?

From the Wahtum Campground, take the Wahtum Express Trail and immediately enter the Mark O. Hatfield Wilderness, rapidly descending to Wahtum Lake via more than 250 steps. At 0.3 mile reach the Pacific Crest Trail (elev. 3750 ft). Turn left and head toward Mexico, traveling along Wahtum Lake's forested shoreline.

At 0.5 mile reach a junction with the Eagle Creek Trail near a popular backcountry camping area. Continue left on the PCT, traveling through beautiful groves of old-growth forest that are occasionally interrupted with a teaser view out to distant landmarks. The way rounds a knoll and gently ascends along Waucoma Ridge. At 2.3 miles the trail leaves the wilderness, now paralleling an old Forest Service road. After briefly brushing the road, the trail crosses a scree slope, providing excellent views of Mount Hood. After cresting a knoll (elev. 4260 ft), the trail dips a little, crossing the road to arrive at the primitive Indian Springs Campground (elev. 4210 ft) at 3.4 miles. Here a trail takes off right, passing the springs and descending toward Eagle Creek.

Continue left on the PCT, soon emerging on an open ridge adorned in showy bear grass, ground-hugging junipers, and blueberry bushes. The view north will leave your mouth agape. From Tanner Butte to Table Mountain, Benson Plateau to Mount Adams, it's one of the finest alpine views in the region.

At 3.7 miles reach a junction with the Indian Mountain Trail (elev. 4340 ft). Turn left and follow this rocky former road past another old road and weather tower, then continuing up Indian's open north ridge. Pass through groves of wind-stunted trees before reaching a stand of mature timber just beneath the summit. At 4.7 miles reach the 4892-foot summit, a former fire lookout site with smoking-hot views! Gaze at the horizon from the Columbia Hills to Badger Mountain, Mount Saint Helens to Mount Jefferson, and of course Mount Hood, right in your face—practically close enough to feel the cool breezes blowing off its glaciers.

EXTENDING YOUR TRIP

The PCT stays high on Waucoma Ridge for several miles south of Indian Mountain. Feel free to roam along it.

94 Bear Lake

RATING/ DIFFICULTY	ROUND-TRIP	ELEV GAIN/ HIGH POINT	SEASON
***/2	2.4 miles	475 feet/ 4100 feet	Mid-June– Nov

Map: Green Trails Columbia River Gorge– West No. 428S; **Contact:** Mount Hood National Forest, Hood River Ranger Station, (541) 352-6002, www.fs.fed.us/r6/mthood; **GPS:** N 45 38.176 W 121 44.556

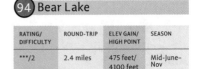 *Set in a remote basin beneath the talus-sloped summit of Mount Defiance, the highest summit in the Gorge, Bear Lake is one of the prettiest alpine lakes in the Mark O. Hatfield Wilderness. This is an easy hike ideal for children and solitude seekers short on time or energy—bring along a book or a fishing rod to while away the afternoon. And if you suddenly feel the urge to burn some more*

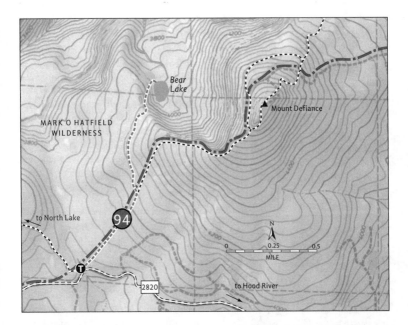

calories, nearby Mount Defiance's 4960-foot summit can be climbed on a much shorter and easier path than the steep approach from the Columbia River.

GETTING THERE

From Portland, follow I-84 east to Hood River at exit 62. Turn right onto US 30 (Cascade Avenue) and drive 1.3 miles. Then turn right onto 13th Street (County Road 281), which is signed for the airport and as a scenic route. Continue south on CR 281, which eventually becomes Tucker Road, making several sharp left and right turns. At 5.1 miles bear right onto Dee Highway (after crossing the bridge over Hood River), which is still CR 281 (signed for Dee-Parker). Continue for 6.2 miles, bearing right (near milepost 11) to another bridge crossing Hood River (signed

for Dee-Lost Lake), and then bear right onto Punch Bowl Road. After 1.4 miles (ignore the left after a bridge), continue straight on gravel Forest Road 2820 toward Rainy Lake. Follow this bumpy road for 10 miles to the trailhead (elev. 3825 ft) on the right. It's marked with a small sign—park on the left.

ON THE TRAIL

Immediately come to a junction by a kiosk with a nice map. Left leads 1 easy mile to North Lake and 1.5 additional fairly easy miles to Rainy Lake (see Hike 87). These are nice destinations if you're looking to do a little lake bagging while in the area. For Bear Lake, bear right!

On a gentle grade through a nice forest of mountain hemlock and understory of huckleberries, a favorite with the bears, reach

Placid Bear Lake reflects talus slopes on Mount Defiance.

a junction (elev. 4050 ft) in 0.5 mile. Bear left and immediately enter the Mark O. Hatfield Wilderness, setting out on a fairly easy ramble. After gently climbing to about 4100 feet and crossing a small scree slope, begin descending.

At 1.2 miles come to Bear Lake (elev. 3900 ft), denned down beneath the rocky upper slopes of Mount Defiance. Cradled in a quiet bowl and surrounded by old forest and shiny talus slopes, Bear is one of my favorite alpine lakes in the Hatfield Wilderness. Remove your shoes, find a good sitting log, soak your feet, and enjoy this nice little backcountry lake.

EXTENDING YOUR TRIP

After staring at Mount Defiance's summit you might suddenly have an urge to tackle it. Retrace your steps to the last junction and head left for 0.7 mile on a moderate grade through a mostly shaded route, reaching a junction (elev. 4800 ft) in a view-filled talus slope. The 4960-foot towered summit lies 0.2 mile to the right, but the best views of Mount Hood and everything else are from the talus slope you're standing on—the ones just to the left, on the trail that skirts beneath the mountain's summit, are mighty fine too.

95 Mosier Twin Tunnels

RATING/ DIFFICULTY	ROUND-TRIP	ELEV GAIN/ HIGH POINT	SEASON
***/2	9.4 miles	730 feet/ 540 feet	Year-round

Map: Green Trails Columbia River Gorge–East No. 432S; **Contact:** Oregon State Parks, (800) 551-6949, www.oregon.gov/OPRD/PARKS; **Notes:** $5 day-use fee or $30 annual pass. Wheelchair accessible. Dogs permitted on-leash. Paved trail is popular with cyclists; **GPS:** N 45 42.205 W 121 29.240

An absolutely beautiful section of the old Columbia River Highway has been reincarnated as the Historic Columbia River Highway Trail. This easy paved path delivers sweeping views, gorgeous wildflowers, a fascinating historical perspective—and the opportunity to stroll high above the river through two surviving tunnels of the old roadway. The trail is popular with families, runners, and bicyclists of all ages—but it makes for a perfectly wonderful hike as well.

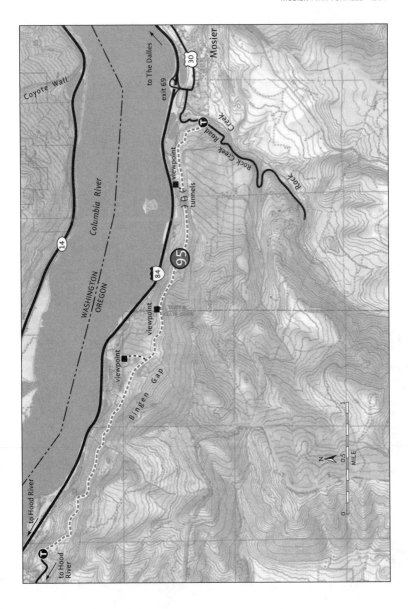

GETTING THERE

From Portland, follow I-84 east to Hood River at exit 64 and turn right onto State Route 35. Travel 0.4 mile to a stop sign and turn left (east) onto the Historic Columbia River Highway. Continue for 1.1 mile to the Senator Mark O. Hatfield West Trailhead (elev. 350 ft). Privy available. To reach the east trailhead, follow I-84 to Mosier at exit 69 and continue 0.2 mile. Turn left onto Rock Creek Road and follow it for 0.7 mile to the parking area just past the trailhead. Privy available.

ON THE TRAIL

Like the sprawling federal wilderness area to the west, this state park trailhead carries

Elegant stone guards accent the scenery.

the name Hatfield. Oregon's longest-serving U.S. senator (for thirty years) and two-term popular governor before that, this progressive Republican and evangelical Christian was a champion of civil rights, human rights, education, and environmental causes, leaving an amazing legacy to his native state, including the Columbia River Gorge National Scenic Area. Perhaps only fellow progressive Republican Tom McCall (whose name also graces many a state landmark) left a larger legacy as an Oregon political figure.

Currently one of three sections of the old Columbia River Highway reborn as the Historic Columbia River Highway Trail, this 4.7-mile stretch is the most interesting and scenic. This description starts from the west trailhead and involves traveling out and back. If you're intent on just seeing the tunnels, start from the east trailhead.

Starting on a basalt bench 300 feet above the river, follow the old highway east, transitioning from a wet fir and maple forest clime to a semiarid one punctuated with ponderosa pine. In spring and early summer, showy flowers—poppies, asters, lupine, scarlet gilia, desert parsley, and more—line the way, and lizards scurry back and forth across the warm asphalt.

Gently climb to an elevation of about 440 feet before gently descending 50 feet to a shaded picnic area and seasonal cascade at 1.3 miles. Commence with a long gradual climb, passing original concrete mileposts, handsome stone railings, and basalt pinnacles. At 2.4 miles, just after cresting a ridge (elev. 470 ft), a short side trail leads left to excellent views of the town of Bingen on the river and the rolling hills and synclines of the Catherine Creek country.

Still gently ascending, skirt beneath a big ledge and arrive at an excellent viewpoint (elev. 540 ft) of the Coyote Wall and Columbia

Clifftop views along Rowena Plateau

Hills at 2.9 miles. Now gradually descend, coming to a rather stark-looking concrete shed (elev. 340 ft) that covers the trail at 3.7 miles. The 700-foot-long shed was constructed to protect trail users from falling rock (notice the big dents in the pavement nearby) and connects to the much more elegantly designed Twin Tunnels, with their timber supports and windows. Built from 1919 to 1921 and closed and backfilled in the 1950s, the tunnels were reopened and rehabilitated in the late 1990s.

Continue to the tunnels, passing through the small one first and then immediately afterward the longer one (288 feet in length), with its two windows granting views out to the Columbia and surrounding rolling hills in Washington. After emerging from the tunnels, a short side trail (elev. 400 ft) leads left to a spectacular viewpoint east. The main paved trail descends across a heat-reflecting patch of basalt talus, terminating at 4.7 miles at the eastern trailhead (elev. 220 ft).

EXTENDING YOUR TRIP

You can hike two other sections of the Historic Columbia River Highway Trail: from Cascade Locks to Tooth Rock (see Hike 78) and a nice 1.3-mile section from Viento State Park to Starvation Falls (see Hike 88).

96 Rowena Plateau

RATING/ DIFFICULTY	ROUND-TRIP	ELEV GAIN/ HIGH POINT	SEASON
***/2	2.2 miles	260 feet/ 700 feet	Year-round

Map: Green Trails Columbia River Gorge–East No. 432S; **Contact:** Oregon Nature Conservancy, The Dalles Office, (541) 298-1802, www .nature.org/wherewework/northamerica /states/oregon, and Mayer State Park, www .oregon.gov/OPRD/PARKS; **Notes:** Dogs prohibited. Watch for rattlesnakes; **GPS:** N 45 40.980 W 121 18.132

🚶 ⚙ ⭐ *A beautiful heroine in Sir Walter Scott's 1819 novel Ivanhoe, the Rowena in Oregon is a beautiful crest renowned for its wildflowers. A land of swales, vernal pools, abrupt cliffs, and incredible biological diversity due to its location in the transition zone between the wet west and arid east, from February to June the Rowena Plateau radiates with flowering beauty. The trail is short and easy but you'll want to linger long. Just stick to the established paths so that this special preserve will continue to dazzle visitors and harbor a wide array of species.*

GETTING THERE

From Portland, follow I-84 east to Mosier at exit 69. Then continue east on US 30 (Historic Columbia River Highway) for 6.6 miles to the Rowena Crest Viewpoint. (From The Dalles, take exit 76 off of I-84 and follow US 30 west 2.8 miles to the viewpoint.) The trailhead (elev. 700 ft) is located on the left and has limited parking—additional parking is available on the viewpoint loop.

ON THE TRAIL

The Rowena Plateau is a mixture of state, federal, and private conservation lands. This hike traverses The Nature Conservancy's 271-acre Tom McCall Preserve. The Nature Conservancy is an international conservation group that has protected millions of acres of natural lands since its inception in the 1950s. Tom McCall, whom this preserve was named for, was a popular Republican governor of Oregon from 1967 to 1975 and was responsible for some of the state's landmark conservation acts, including growth management, the bottle bill, and public access to shorelines.

The wide trail takes off across the open plateau. Warning signs alert hikers to the eastern Gorge's trifecta of hazards: rattlers, poison oak, and ticks—with poison oak being the one you should be most concerned with.

Arrowleaf balsamroot adds its golden touch in the spring, but you'll probably notice that it isn't profuse here. For a long time this plateau was grazed by cattle who happen to have a penchant for this leafy member of the sunflower (*Asteraceae*) family. Volunteers have been busy restoring the plateau to its pregrazing glory. Nevertheless the plateau blossoms with shooting star, larkspur, desert star—the list goes on. The preserve is also home to Thompson's broadleaf lupine, Columbia desert parsley, Thompson's waterleaf, and Hood River milkvetch, all species endemic to the Gorge.

The trail gently descends along the sloping plateau, reaching a junction at 0.3 mile. The trail right loops around a small pond ringed with oak (both poison and Oregon white). You'll likely hear melodious blackbirds and crooning frogs. It also passes by a ledge side viewpoint above the Columbia River, directly across from the mouth of the Klickitat River. Now or on the return, definitely check this trail out.

The main path continues across the plateau, passing another small pond and several short spurs leading to cliffside belvederes. Look for deer and ground squirrels when not looking out at the river and surrounding golden hills. At 1.1 miles the trail comes to a halt at the western edge of the plateau (elev. 440 ft). Keep children close at hand. Look down. While much of Rowena's windswept plateau is bare of trees, oak groves flourish in the sheltered dales below the rim.

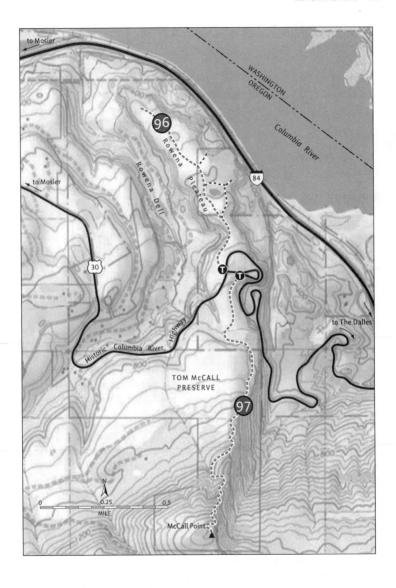

The floral show on McCall Point ranks among the Gorge's best.

97 Tom McCall Point

RATING/ DIFFICULTY	ROUND-TRIP	ELEV GAIN/ HIGH POINT	SEASON
****/3	3.2 miles	1000 feet/ 1722 feet	May–Oct

Map: Green Trails Columbia River Gorge–East No. 432S; **Contact:** Oregon Nature Conservancy, The Dalles Office, (541) 298-1802, www.nature.org/wherewework/northamerica/states/oregon, and Mayer State Park, www.oregon.gov/OPRD/PARKS; **Notes:** Dogs prohibited. Trail closed Nov 1–Apr 30 to limit tread damage; **GPS:** N 45 40.965 W 121 18.042

Climb to a rounded grassy summit on a peak honoring one of Oregon's conservation champions. The only thing better than the far-flung views from along this hike are the flowers. They carpet the peak's open slopes, accent its abrupt ridges, and decorate its oak and pine groves in a multitude of brilliant colors. A Nature Conservancy preserve, more than two hundred species of plants thrive here, including several endemic to the Columbia Gorge.

GETTING THERE

From Portland, follow I-84 east to Mosier at exit 69. Then continue east on US 30 (Historic Columbia River Highway) for 6.6 miles to the Rowena Crest Viewpoint. (From The Dalles, take exit 76 off of I-84 and follow US 30 west 2.8 miles to the viewpoint.) The trailhead (elev. 700 ft) is located on the left and has limited parking—additional parking is available on the viewpoint loop.

ON THE TRAIL

The well-maintained and trodden trail takes off south across a grassy tableland along the edge of basalt cliffs. While the Tom McCall Preserve is legendary among wildflower aficionados (May is prime), birders will also delight here. Look for canyon wrens and horned larks and western meadowlarks, Oregon's state bird.

At 0.3 mile come to an old road at the base of a talus slope that sports oaks and pines. Turn left to skirt the talus, and travel through big showy plumes of desert parsley. Look below at the snaking Historic Columbia River Highway, an engineering work of art. The trail emerges onto an upper plateau that explodes with blossoms in the spring. Lupine and balsamroot dominate, streaking the countryside in enough purple and gold to make a UW Husky fan blush—and a UO Duck unnerved!

The view only gets better as you continue up the at times steep trail. Look east to the Columbia Hills, west to Mount Defiance, king of the Gorge, north to the giant snow cone Adams, and south to snowy cloud-catcher Hood. The trail does a short stint along a steep ridgeline before weaving back across sun-kissed and wind-whipped grassy slopes. At around 1200 feet you'll pass through a patch of ponderosa pine. In May a handful of glacier lilies brighten the grove. Continue climbing, and continue awestruck at the amazing arrangement of wildflowers: grass widows, prairie stars, shooting stars, Indian paintbrush, Oregon sunshine—the list goes on!

At 1.6 miles and after a 1000 feet of climbing, crest the round grassy summit of McCall Point. Plop down (being careful not to harm the flowers) and soak up as much sun and scenic splendor as your little (and probably now stronger) heart desires.

EXTENDING YOUR TRIP

Don't be tempted to follow paths heading south from the summit, as they enter adjacent private land. Instead, add the Rowena Plateau (Hike 96) to your day if you're inclined to cover more ground.

98 Deschutes River

RATING/ DIFFICULTY	LOOP	ELEV GAIN/ HIGH POINT	SEASON
****/3	4.6 miles	650 feet/ 750 feet	Year-round

Map: Green Trails Columbia River Gorge–East No. 432S; **Contact:** Oregon State Parks, (800) 551-6949, www.oregon.gov/OPRD/PARKS; **Notes:** $5 day-use fee or $30 annual pass.

Dogs permitted on-leash. Watch for rattlesnakes; **GPS:** N 45 37.760 W 120 54.485

The Wild and Scenic Deschutes River is one of Oregon's grandest waterways and one of the Columbia's major tributaries. Here at its confluence with the Columbia, at the eastern gateway of the Gorge national scenic area, a delightful state park provides miles of family-friendly trails along the Deschutes, across sun-scorched desert steppe, and to a high bluff with grand views of the wide canyon cut by the powerful river.

Lupine colors the desert steppe in springtime.

GETTING THERE

From Portland, follow I-84 east to exit 97 (signed "Celilo Park"). Then follow State Route 206 (Biggs-Rufus Highway) east for 3 miles, crossing the Deschutes River and turning right into the Deschutes River State Recreation

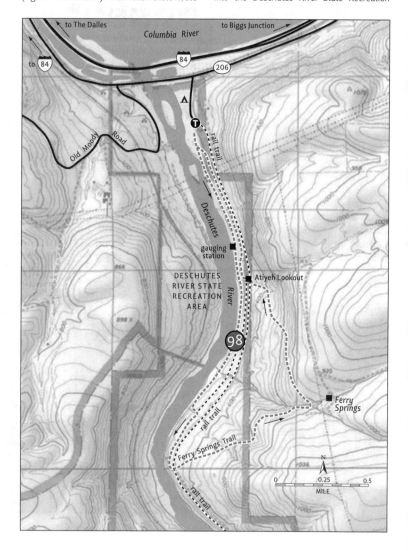

Area. (If coming from the east, take exit 104 at Biggs Junction off of I-84 and follow the Biggs-Rufus Highway west for 3.4 miles to the recreation area entrance.) Proceed 0.4 mile south through the park to trailhead parking (elev. 160 ft). Privy available.

ON THE TRAIL

Three trails parallel the river, while another takes off for the hills above it. This recommended loop combines three of them—the fourth, an old railbed, is better suited for mountain biking. Start by walking south about 0.2 mile across a grassy lawn to a junction. You'll be returning on the left, so bear right onto the Blackberry Trail (also known as the Atiyeh Deschutes River Trail).

Hug the river through a swath of riparian greenery—quite a contrast from the brown surrounding hills. Named by French Canadian fur traders as Rivière des Chutes (River of Waterfalls), the Deschutes is a popular whitewater run, with its many rapids, some of which you'll be walking by.

At 0.6 mile pass a gauging station and a connecting trail to the parallel Riverview Trail. Continue straight along the river, passing a cable crossing and a lone big rocky ledge before coming to a small creek crossing and boardwalk. At 1.2 miles pass a privy and nice sandy beach that tempts feet soaking—or if you're crazy enough to do this trail in the summer, perhaps a full-body submersion!

The trail continues to Moody Rapids and then makes a quick ascent to meet up with the Riverview Trail (elev. 270 ft) at about 1.5 miles. Head right, traversing a bluff to a spectacular overlook (elev. 340 ft) above a series of roiling rapids.

At 1.9 miles reach the rail trail. Walk a short distance on it to the right, to the Ferry Springs Trail. Then follow this trail north and up—across purple- (lupine) and gold- (balsamroot) streaked open slopes in spring, gray sun-scorched open slopes in summer, or barren and cold windblown open slopes in winter.

The way steadily climbs, views increasing with elevation gain. Gaze down upon the

TRAIL'S END—ALMOST!

The Columbia River Gorge has long been a busy transportation corridor, and for the thousands of emigrants that came west on the Oregon Trail during the 1840s and 1850s the Gorge was the last major hurdle before the promised land of the fertile Willamette Valley. After enduring many hardships along the 2000-mile trail, the settlers when they arrived at The Dalles had to float their possessions, livestock, and families on rafts down the treacherous rapids of the Columbia through the Gorge. Some emigrants lost everything at this point—some even lost their lives.

By 1846 some overland routes, such as the Barlow toll road through Lolo Pass, were developed, bypassing the Gorge and offering the pioneers an alternate route. But even these trails were treacherous and harrowing, and the tolls were often steep. Look out at modern I-84 now and try to imagine what travel was like through this beautiful but potentially dangerous landscape before Oregon became a state in 1859. No doubt the pioneers of yesterday would be a bit miffed that we come to the Gorge now to recreate and hike—they had done enough hiking on their trek across America!

river's frothy silver streak across a stark landscape—or peer north to the Columbia Hills marred by giant wind turbines. After reaching an elevation of 750 feet, the way descends into a lush draw, compliments of Ferry Springs.

Climb over a barbed-wire fence (don't worry, there are stairs), and begin a long descent on an old wagon road constructed in the 1860s to connect isolated eastern Oregon communities with The Dalles. At 3.7 miles once again reach the rail trail. Locate a spur that drops back to the Riverview Trail at the Victor G. Atiyeh Lookout. Governor of Oregon between 1979 and 1987, Atiyeh was responsible for helping to protect the lower 18 miles of the Deschutes River.

Turn right and walk through sage-covered terrain, passing the connector trail to the river and continuing straight on a rolling 0.7 mile back to the junction at the grassy lawn. Your vehicle is 0.2 mile away.

EXTENDING YOUR TRIP

Run, bike, or hike all or a part of the 16-mile rail trail. A primitive trail follows the river's west bank—access it from the Heritage Landing Boat Ramp. Consider spending a night at the park's shaded campground.

99 Columbia River Heritage Trail

RATING/ DIFFICULTY	ROUND-TRIP	ELEV GAIN/ HIGH POINT	SEASON
**/2	4 miles	25 feet/ 300 feet	Year-round

Maps: USGS Irrigon, USGS Patterson, trail map from website; **Contact:** Columbia River Heritage Trail, www.columbiarivertrail.org; **Notes:** Dogs permitted on-leash. Watch for rattlesnakes; **GPS:** N 45 54.042 W 119 29.534

There's no dramatic gorge here in the far-eastern reaches of the Columbia's Oregon-Washington border flow. Between the great bend at Wallula Gap and the canyon housing the John Day River, the Columbia languidly (thanks to dams) drifts through a monotonous landscape of sun-parched low-lying hills of sage, wheat, and grapevines. But this section of river is also ecologically important (and threatened), providing habitat for scores of species. Hikers need to get to know it, and thanks to this new trail they can now explore a much-overlooked region.

GETTING THERE

From Portland, follow I-84 east to exit 168. Turn left onto US 730 and proceed east 7.5 miles to the city of Irrigon, turning left onto 10th Street signed for the marina. (From the Tri-Cities, take exit 1 off of I-82, following US 730 west for 8.1 miles and turning right onto 10th Street.) Proceed for 0.2 mile to Irrigon Marina Park and the trailhead (elev. 275 ft). Privy available.

ON THE TRAIL

The Columbia River Heritage Trail was developed jointly as part of the Lewis and Clark Bicentennial Celebration by Morrow County, the National Park Service, the cities of Boardman and Irrigon, the U.S. Army Corp of Engineers, the U.S. Fish and Wildlife Service, the Oregon Department of Fish and Wildlife, the Confederated Tribes of the Umatilla Indian Reservation, and the Boeing Agri-Industrial Company. While currently touted as 12 miles long (with another 12 miles in the planning stage), much of the trail follows roads.

The 2.5-mile section east from the marina to the County Line Road, which travels mainly through the Irrigon Wildlife Refuge and passes

The Columbia River Heritage Trail traverses dry and open terrain along the river.

a Lewis and Clark campsite en route, is interesting but pretty rough in places. Your best introduction to this trail is the 2-mile section west from the marina to the fish hatchery.

From the boat launch, locate the trail heading west 0.1 mile across a lawn by a nice beach. After reaching a fence line, enter a more natural environment dominated by antelope bitterbrush and rabbitbrush. At 0.3 mile come to a fishing access road (heavily littered by unenlightened anglers), and walk it a short distance west. Now back on trail, traverse open, deserty terrain on both soft and hard sandy tread.

The trail continues across an undeveloped swath owned by the Army Corps of Engineers. Houses are set back on the left, while there is nothing but Columbia River on the right—and views, too, to the low-lying hills and buttes across the water in Washington.

At 0.7 mile pass the remains of an old estate and at 0.9 mile a boat navigation beacon. Look for deer in the tall grasses. Listen to raucous magpies. In spring, admire showy blossoms. Pass occasional pines and locust trees and at 1.3 miles pass an irrigation pump house. Walk west a short way on the access road and pick up trail again. Now higher on a bluff (elev. 300 ft), scan the river—with its muddy, slow-moving water it almost looks like the Mississippi. At 1.8 miles the trail passes closely to a set of newer homes.

Continue for another 0.2 mile to another trailhead (on 8th Road) and lands now managed by the Umatilla Fish Hatchery. This is a good point to turnaround.

EXTENDING YOUR TRIP

One of the nicest sections of the Columbia River Heritage Trail follows a long-abandoned section of the original Columbia River Highway across bird-bursting McCormack Slough in the nearby nearly 30,000-acre Umatilla National Wildlife Refuge. Access the trail from Parking Lot D off of the Auto Route Loop. The 0.5-mile trail is kid friendly and wheelchair accessible, but dogs are not permitted and it's closed from October 1 to February 1.

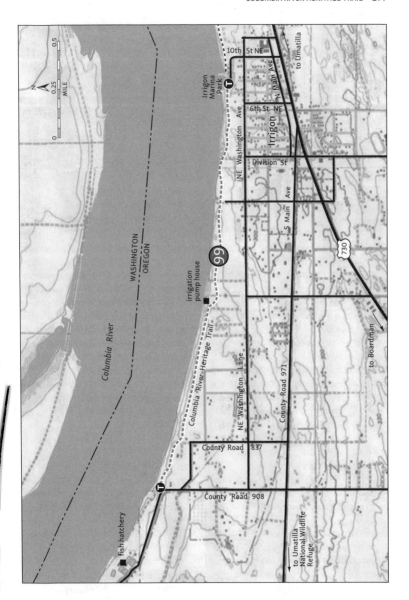

100 Hat Rock

RATING/ DIFFICULTY	LOOP	ELEV GAIN/ HIGH POINT	SEASON
**/1	0.75 mile	75 feet/ 400 feet	Year-round

Map: USGS Hat Rock; **Contact:** Oregon State Parks, (541) 567-5032, www.oregon.gov/OPRD/PARKS; **Notes:** Dogs permitted on-leash. Watch for rattlesnakes; **GPS:** N 45 54.926 W 119 10.208

 *One of Oregon's most distinctive geological landmarks, Hat Rock sits at the mouth of Wallula Gap, a mini yet impressive gorge at a massive bend in the Columbia. It is here that the river first forms the Washington–Oregon border in the east, and it is here that Lewis and Clark first entered what later became the state of Oregon. Enjoy this easy hike rife with natural and human history. And if Hat Rock isn't enough, cap this hike off with*

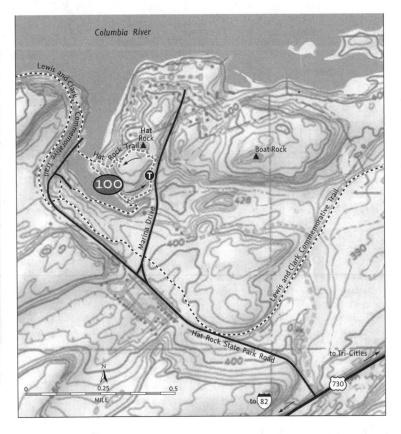

a trip down the adjacent Lewis and Clark Commemorative Trail.

GETTING THERE

From Portland, follow I-84 east for 179 miles, turning north onto I-82. Continue north for 6 miles to the exit signed for Umatilla and Mc-Nary. (If coming from Tri-Cities, Washington, follow I-82 south and take the first exit after crossing the Columbia River.) Head east on State Route 730 for 8.1 miles, turning left onto Hat Rock State Park Road. Continue for 0.8 mile. Bear right on Marina Drive, and after 0.3 mile reach the trailhead on the left (elev. 350 ft). Privy and water available in the park.

ON THE TRAIL

Though the basalt monolith that is Hat Rock stands pretty much the same as it did when the Corps of Discovery paddled by on October 19, 1805, the surroundings don't. Homes line the shoreline here. And the McNary Dam, built in 1953, has turned this part of the Columbia into a lake, inundating the original shoreline as well as numerous Native and early American sites and artifacts. Even the vegetation is different. Those black locust trees providing much-appreciated shade are transplants from the east.

But this area still possesses great beauty, albeit in a world of contrast between the past and present, natural and modified. Wind your way up the wide and well-manicured trail to the base (elev. 400 ft) of the hat-shaped landmark, a remnant of the massive lava flows that covered this region more than twelve million years ago. Subsequent ice age floods channeled and scoured the lava flows, leaving behind canyons and outcroppings like 70-foot-high Hat Rock. Good interpretive signs along the trail will give you a better appreciation for the area's natural and human history.

Continue along the trail, passing a nice view-

Hat Rock is a well-recognized landmark along the Columbia River.

point looking west to the Columbia River, and then begin a short descent, coming to a junction at a small pond (elev. 325 ft). Right heads across a dike to a boat launch, more parking, and access to the 7.6-mile Lewis and Clark Commemorative Trail. Head left and follow along the trout- and duck-filled waters of the small pond. At the far end of the pond the trail splits. Right leads around the pond to another parking area. Left leads back to your car.

EXTENDING YOUR TRIP

The 7.6-mile Lewis and Clark Commemorative Trail travels right through the park. The west section of this multiuse, nonmotorized rail trail that leads to McNary Beach Park will particularly delight day hikers. Enjoy good river and cliff views. Liberally apply sun screen before heading out.

Appendix I: Bonus Hikes

These twenty-five additional hikes and walks within and near the Columbia River Gorge are worth considering. Have fun exploring them.

1. **Whipple Creek:** Find 4.3 miles of trails in this 300-acre Clark County park, near the county fairgrounds south of Ridgefield, Washington. Heavy equestrian use.
2. **Salmon Creek:** Beautiful 3-mile paved trail in greenbelt along Salmon River between Hazel Dell and Felida, north of Vancouver, Washington.
3. **Frenchman's Bar:** Nice 2.5-mile paved trail along Columbia River to Vancouver Lake just west of Vancouver, Washington.
4. **Stairway:** Seldom-hiked, steep and rough 3.7-mile trail to ridge east of Silver Star, Washington's Silver Star Scenic Area. Experienced hikers only.
5. **Ridell Lake:** Quiet, oft-overlooked short nature trail to small pond beneath Beacon Rock, in Washington's Beacon Rock State Park, near Skamania.
6. **Doetsch Loop:** Very nice 1-mile paved trail (ADA) in the Beacon Rock State Park's Doetsch Day-Use Area, near Skamania, Washington.
7. **Zig Zag Lake:** Half-mile trail to small remote lake (accessed from FR 42, near Carson, Washington) between Trapper Creek Wilderness and Mowich Butte.
8. **Falls Creek Falls:** Nice 1.7-mile trail to pretty cascade just east of Trapper Creek Wilderness. Access from Wind River Road, near Carson, Washington.
9. **Three Corner Rock:** Easy 4.8-mile or challenging 18-mile hike to prominent landmark north of Table Mountain on the Pacific Crest Trail. Washington State DNR road access near Skamania, long and rough.
10. **Nestor Peak:** Round-trip 8 miles in heavily logged and roaded state forest to a 3088-foot former lookout site. Access is from SR 141, near White Salmon, Washington.
11. **Monte Cristo:** Round-trip 5 miles to 4000-foot peak and excellent views. Access is from Oklahoma Road north of Willard, Washington.
12. **Monte Carlo:** Round-trip 4 miles to 4100-foot peak and excellent views. Access is from Oklahoma Road north of Willard, Washington.
13. **Burdoin Mountain:** Miles of mainly mountain-bike trails on peak above White Salmon, Washington. The Forest Service is reviewing the area and working on a trail plan.
14. **Rowland Hill:** Nice couple-mile loop on old roads across meadows and open forest in Catherine Creek Area, near Lyle, Washington.
15. **Smith and Bybee Wetlands:** Paved ADA nature trail through 2000-acre wetland Metro Park within Portland city limits. Excellent bird-watching opportunities.
16. **Council Crest:** Hike to Portland's highest summit for stunning city and country views from Marquam Park, located just south of downtown.
17. **Mary S. Young State Park:** Several miles of quiet trails in small state park on the Willamette River in West Linn, south of Portland.
18. **Trout Lake:** Nice but busy park with nature trails in Troutdale, east of Portland.

19. **Munra Point:** Scramble path up prominent landmark near Eagle Creek, near Cascade Locks, Oregon. Experienced scramblers only.
20. **Tanner Creek–Moffett Creek:** Quiet, nearly abandoned trail along Tanner Creek, near Cascade Locks, Oregon. Solitude guaranteed.
21. **Ruckel Ridge:** Very difficult unofficial trail up Ruckel Ridge on Benson Plateau, near Cascade Locks, Oregon. Strong hikers only, with scrambling skills.
22. **Shellrock Mountain:** Round-trip 3 miles on user-built trail halfway up Shellrock Mountain, providing excellent views. Access is from I-84 near Cascade Locks, Oregon, milepost 53.
23. **Viento Lake and Starvation Creek Falls:** Small nature trail to Viento Lake in Viento State Park, near Hood River, Oregon, and nice 1.3-mile paved path from the park to Starvation Creek Falls.
24. **Hood River Mountain:** Short, easy loop hike up small mountain to big views on SDS Lumber Company land. Access is from Old Dalles Road from Hood River, Oregon.
25. **The Dalles Waterfront Trail:** Very nice paved riverfront trail, accessed from several points from downtown in The Dalles, Oregon.

Appendix II: Recommended Reading

Bishop Morris, Ellen. *Hiking Oregon's Geology*. 2nd ed. Seattle: The Mountaineers Books, 2004.

Cottrell Houle, Marcy. *One City's Wilderness: Portland's Forest Park*, 3rd ed. Corvallis, OR: Oregon State University Press, 2010.

Dietrich, William. *Northwest Passage: The Columbia River*. Seattle: University of Washington Press, 1996.

Egan, Timothy. *The Big Burn: Teddy Roosevelt and the Fire that Saved America*. New York: Houghton Mifflin Harcourt, 2009.

Jolley, Russ. *Wildflowers of the Columbia Gorge: A Comprehensive Field Guide*. Portland: Oregon Historical Society Press, 1988.

Manning, Harvey, Bob Spring, and Ira Spring. *Mountain Flowers of the Cascades and Olympics*. 2nd ed. Seattle: The Mountaineers Books, 2002.

Mueller, Marge, and Ted Mueller. *Exploring Washington's Wild Areas*. 2nd ed. Seattle: The Mountaineers Books, 2002.

———. *Washington State Parks: A Complete Recreation Guide*. 3rd ed. Seattle: The Mountaineers Books, 2004.

Renner, Jeff. *Lightning Strikes: Staying Safe Under Stormy Skies*. Seattle: The Mountaineers Books, 2002.

Stewart, Martyn, Stephen Whitney, and Elizabeth Briars Hart. *Birdsongs of the Pacific Northwest*. CD and field guide. Seattle: The Mountaineers Books, 2006.

Whitney, Stephen R., and Rob Sanderlin. *Field Guide to the Cascades and Olympics*. 2nd ed. Seattle: The Mountaineers Books, 2003.

Appendix III: Conservation and Trail Organizations

Cape Horn Conservancy
http://capehorntrail.org

Columbia Gorge Refuge Stewards
www.refugestewards.org

Columbia Land Trust
(360) 696-0131
www.columbialandtrust.org

Forest Park Conservancy
(503) 223-5449
www.forestparkconservancy.org

Friends of the Columbia Gorge
(503) 241-3762
www.gorgefriends.org

Friends of Powell Butte Nature Park
www.friendsofpowellbutte.org

Friends of the Ridgefield National
Wildlife Refuge
www.ridgefieldfriends.org

Friends of Tryon Creek
(503) 636-4398
www.tryonfriends.org

Klickitat Trail Conservancy
www.klickitat-trail.org

Mazamas
(503) 227-2345
www.mazamas.org

The Mountaineers
(206) 521-6001
www.mountaineers.org

The Nature Conservancy
Oregon Field Office
(503) 230-1221
www.nature.org

The Nature Conservancy
Washington Field Office
(206) 343-4344
www.nature.org

Pacific Crest Trail Association
(916) 285-1846
www.pcta.org

Spring Trust for Trails
springtrailtrust.org

Trails Club of Oregon
www.trailsclub.org

Trailkeepers of Oregon
www.trailkeepersoforegon.org

Washington Trails Association
(206) 625-1367
www.wta.org

Index

About the Author

Craig first saw the Columbia River in 1980 while on a cross-country bicycle trip from the East Coast. Nine years later, Washington State lured him from New Hampshire, where he had first fallen in love with the natural world. A former Boy Scout, backcountry ranger in the White Mountain National Forest, and ski bum in Vermont, Craig found his calling in the outdoors. He has traveled extensively, including working as a guide for several seasons in Europe's Pyrenees Mountains. From Alaska to Argentina, Sicily to South Korea, Craig has hit the trail seeking wild and spectacular landscapes. He ranks Washington State among the most beautiful places on the planet, and he has thoroughly hiked it—over 14,000 miles worth, from Cape Flattery in the northwest to Puffer Butte in the southeast, Cape Disappointment in the southwest to the Salmo-Priest Wilderness in the northeast. He has spent many a mile in Oregon too, from Cascade Head on the coast to Steens Mountain in the Great Basin.

An avid hiker, runner, kayaker, cyclist, and dedicated conservationist, Craig has written about these passions for over a dozen publications, including *Adventures NW*, *AMC Outdoors*, *Backpacker*, *CityDog*, *Northwest Runner*, *Outdoors NW*, and *Seattle Met*. He also writes regular content for HikeOfTheWeek.com, which he cofounded in 2005. Author of eight books, among them *Day Hiking: Olympic Peninsula* and *Backpacking Washington*, and coauthor of two others, Craig is currently working on *Day Hiking: Eastern Washington* (The Mountaineers Books) with Rich Landers of the *Spokane Spokesman Review*. Craig's *Columbia Highlands: Exploring Washington's Last Frontier* was recognized in 2010 by Washington Secretary of State Sam Reed and State Librarian Jan Walsh as a Washington Reads book for its contribution to the state's cultural heritage.

Taking notes on Oregon's Green Point Mountain

Craig holds several degrees: an AA in forestry from White Mountains Community College (in New Hampshire) and, from the University of Washington, a BA in history and a masters in education. He lives with his wife, Heather, and cats Giuseppe and Scruffy Gray in Skagit County, where he enjoys watching swans and snow geese fly overhead when he's not hiking. Visit him at http://CraigRomano.com and on Facebook at "Craig Romano Guidebook Author."